MARKET CITIES, PEOPLE CITIES

Market Cities, People Cities

The Shape of Our Urban Future

Michael Oluf Emerson *and* Kevin T. Smiley

NEW YORK UNIVERSITY PRESS

New York

NEW YORK UNIVERSITY PRESS
New York
www.nyupress.org

References to Internet websites (URLs) were accurate at the time of writing. Neither the author nor New York University Press is responsible for URLs that may have expired or changed since the manuscript was prepared.

Library of Congress Cataloging-in-Publication Data
Names: Emerson, Michael Oluf, author. | Smiley, Kevin T., author.
Title: Market cities, people cities : the shape of our urban future / Michael Oluf Emerson and Kevin T. Smiley.
Description: New York : New York University Press, [2018] | Includes bibliographical references and index.
Identifiers: LCCN 2017034138| ISBN 9781479856794 (cl : alk. paper) | ISBN 9781479800261 (pb : alk. paper)
Subjects: LCSH: City planning—Environmental aspects. | Urban economics—Environmental aspects. | Community development, Urban.
Classification: LCC HT166 .E474 2018 | DDC 307.1/216—dc23
LC record available at https://lccn.loc.gov/2017034138

New York University Press books are printed on acid-free paper, and their binding materials are chosen for strength and durability. We strive to use environmentally responsible suppliers and materials to the greatest extent possible in publishing our books.

Manufactured in the United States of America

10 9 8 7 6 5 4 3 2 1

Also available as an ebook

CONTENTS

Introduction

The Claim

Market City	People City
So Busy	An Equal Diddy
Business and Growth	Few Fret
Love them Both	Safety Net
Amidst the Jobs	Life Is Good
Faint Sobs	The Collective Could
How Do We Know	One Concern
We Asked	We Heard
They Told Us So	Will it Last or Will It Turn

History screams truth. The truth about cities is that they rise and fall—sometimes slowly, sometimes with head-spinning speed—because of their relationship to the times. What is an advantage in one era is of little use in the next. Cities must adapt—always and continually—or they wilt and drop, become shriveled and used up, at least until they find a way to adjust to the new times.

Rightly assessing the future is fundamental to the work of cities. Prepare correctly and prosper. Guess incorrectly, put the proverbial eggs in the wrong basket, or simply focus on the now, and join the junkyard of has-been cities.

We are in the midst of changes, of a new time. We will explore these changes—and make sense of them—by drawing on stories and data from dozens of cities across the world, and exploring in depth two cities, each going its own way, hedging its bet on a different future. Each is staking its claim to a different fundamental focus. This tale is told so that we can understand more broadly the choices cities face and the directions they may go, and so we can consider the possible outcomes.

Lots of urban prognosticators are currently busy prognosticating. They tell cities things like "you have to cater to the creative class," "you have to focus on bio-tech," "you have to go green," "you have to attract jobs," "you have to redesign your transportation system." The list goes on. In the end, cities must focus. They must create a *priorities rubric* through which they make their decisions from a myriad of possibilities and choices.

At its core, this book argues that cities now orient themselves in one of two main directions as they move forward. They either privilege the market or they privilege people. Put more directly, some cities exist first and foremost for the market, some first and foremost for people. The difference is profound, so profound that we must conceive of them as different entities: *Market Cities* or *People Cities*.

To be sure, both types of cities care about both the market and people. After all, both of these must be present to be a city. We have not seen a city yet that does not want a strong economy, and it is difficult to find a city that does not want a good life for its citizens. But cities ultimately privilege one over the other, often because they view their focus as the best way to achieve the other objective. That is, for Market Cities their reasoning is something like this: "Want a good quality of life and a vibrant community? Then you must work to have a strong economy, producing jobs, luring companies to your city, spurring lots of start-ups, and being business friendly." And for People Cities, their reasoning is something like this: "Want a strong economy and lots of good jobs? Then you must work to make your city a place where people want to live, a city that is friendly to their needs, that is lively, healthy, safe, sustainable, and most of all, livable."

These simple terms, we will argue, have far-reaching implications. People's lives in Market Cities and People Cities—the very experience and meaning of being human and living with others—are poles apart. From urban form to diversity to crime to transportation decisions to sustainability, the choices cities make to be Market Cities or People Cities reverberate across lives and across generations.

Market and People Cities in Action

Cities have choices, choices about what they exist for and about what they want to be. We will describe a coalescing of these choices such that we are witnessing fundamentally different types of cities emerging across the globalized, developed world. We will describe mind-boggling sprawl and purposeful density, social parity and racial inequality, public infrastructure and private largess, gleaming skyscrapers and humble shops, legions of bikes and armies of cars, crime and peace, and a can-do spirit and a must-do spirit. Contrasts abound.

But underpinning these contrasts are two essential similarities. The first is that cities across the world are subject to the same structural and institutional influences that paradoxically necessitate these immense contrasts. We live in a global age, one in which urban transformation is seen as a central component of any city agenda. Where that city agenda is directed is the primary subject of this book, and it is demonstrated through the contrasts, but that the contrasts are born out of the same globalized world is no small matter. The globalized world makes cities focus.

How cities respond in our interconnected globe has much to do with the second similarity: that residents of a city, whether political leaders, economic elites, homeowners, or the most marginalized citizens, rely on, respond to, and re-create the gravitational pull of cultural beliefs about what is possible and what should be prioritized in their city. This book centers on the idea that cities have their own cultural milieu, and what the most powerful resident and the everyday resident believe about their city is in large part thanks to this cultural milieu. This is not to say that residents within cities are homogeneous—we urbanists love cities because of their heterogeneity—but instead simply that that heterogeneity centers on fundamental ideas. And it's not to say that culture is the end-all factor in cities: indeed, history, politics, and economics all play crucial roles. We believe, though, that culture has long been neglected in the study of cities, and that how it interacts with those other important institutions over time can tell us a lot about how a city will respond in the global age. And taking a new look at how residents think is critical to that task. We detail more about our theoretical perspective in a separate article.[1]

It is the cultural, political, and economic responses to the global world that compose the thesis of this book. Nearly all cities in the Western and developed world have been around for at least a century, most much longer, and we think that the historical paths that cities have taken allow for many of the cities to easily answer the question: Why do we exist as a city?

Cities have *culturally imbued priorities rubrics through which policymakers and residents focus attention, take action, and orient their future.* Market Cities and People Cities are two ends of a spectrum of priorities rubrics, with many cities today clustered toward one end or the other. Few cities, though, epitomize each ideal type quite like Copenhagen and Houston.

Let's consider two quotations from city leaders. The first is from Tina Saaby, the head city architect of the city of Copenhagen:

> We seek to make a livable city. Our approach is that we consider urban life before urban space, and urban space before buildings. Urban life is for people. . . . Our goal is that in the next five years, 80% or more of Copenhageners will feel they belong to the city and it meets their needs. . . . We use a people strategy. Our task is to help people make things happen, be creative, be social in the city, and have good health. Instead of a list of "no's" we work with the residents to let them create the city they want.

The second quotation is from Angela Blanchard, the head of Neighborhood Centers, the largest local nonprofit in Houston:

> If you're poor, you want to be poor in Houston, because there's a ladder here. Our purpose is not to eliminate poverty. People do that on their own. What we're doing is to provide the rungs of the ladder. . . . The starting point for community change is looking at your city and the DNA of your city and understanding, what is that city really built around. What are the aspirations here? . . . Houston was built to work, and for work. The people that Neighborhood Centers works with came here to work. Everybody in Houston understands that.[2]

Houston, the city "built to work, and for work," is the quintessential Market City: it is geared to wealth accumulation, and holds individualism as a core value. Copenhagen, where "urban life is for people," is the quintessential People City: the city is collective-minded and focused on ensuring quality of life at a scale understandable to its citizens. The quotations from influential citizens epitomize the priorities rubric of each type of city.

Defining Market Cities and People Cities

Market Cities and People Cities are not just the sum of their priorities rubrics or cultural beliefs. Instead, they are played out actively in the diverse realms of the city. From crime to taxes to the environment and everywhere in between, being a Market City or a People City provides for different social outcomes. These social outcomes also operate in a feedback loop with the priorities rubric, and with each other. What we are arguing is simple: the many important institutions of urban life go together. With the co-varying character that is underwritten by city character, Market Cities and People Cities should exhibit similarities along a number of social indicators. Table I.1 shows many of these urban institutions, and how we expect they should vary for Market Cities and People Cities.

To unpack this further, consider directly how we believe these urban institutions go together. First, Market Cities have priorities rubrics that emphasize individualism, and the city overall is focused on making money, increasing regional wealth, and attracting businesses and jobs. Inequality is high in Market Cities, rewarding the economically privileged and providing less support for the poor. Market Cities have laissez-faire economic systems and governments, tend to have low taxes (except Market Cities with high governmental graft), and many city services are privatized. Governments are decentralized among municipalities, many of which spar with one another. Crime is a constant in Market Cities, in good part due to its other characteristics of individualism, segregated diversity, inequality, and emphasis on material acquisition.

Other things being equal, cars dominate in Market Cities, and transportation services are reactive to individual patterns of behavior and developers' desires. Market Cities have more environmental degradation and distribute it more unequally. Students in Market Cities attend public schools of high quality and low quality, private schools and charter schools (often operating under school choice policies), while higher education costs increasingly threaten equal access. Diversity is seen as a virtue in Market Cities because all people are welcomed to make a life, achieve something great, and add to the dynamism of the city, even while the diversity is residentially and socially segregated. Few provisions are made to alleviate any inequality across diverse intersections.

In some ways, People Cities operate similarly to Market Cities. They have priorities rubrics that are engaged in a back-and-forth with many facets of urban life, but the substance of their rubric and the facets of urban life could not be more different. People Cities are other-regarding and are focused on quality-of-life issues: these are the primary parts of the People Cities priorities rubric. Inequality is relatively low in People

Cities because social and economic parity is a core value—both between citizens and between neighborhoods—and protections are regulated to that effect. Government is strong in People Cities: much of the work of public space and public policy is carried out in city hall corridors and in concert with citizens. Governance is also centralized, and regional authorities have regulatory power. Crime is low in People Cities, as trust is high, there is less emphasis on material goods and winning, and the relative equality necessitates less taking from others.

TABLE I.1. Characteristics of Market Cities and People Cities

	People City	Market City
Land use	Dense, walkable, even in suburban areas. Residents often design spaces in concert with government.	Sprawl, low density for areas built after 1950s. Suburban growth is primary method of growth; land use policies lax.
Transportation	Multimodal. Public transit, walking, and bicycling encouraged; cars discouraged.	Car-centric. Transportation funds mostly for roads and street improvements.
Crime	Low crime, especially violent crimes.	High crime, especially violent crimes.
Environment	Low overall levels of environmental degradation, and less inequality among neighborhoods. Committed to climate change reform.	Higher overall levels of environmental degradation and greater inequality between neighborhoods. Limited commitment to climate change reforms.
Inequality	Low inequality. Strong social safety net and smaller gap between rich and poor.	High inequality. Inconsistent safety net, large gap between rich and poor.
Civic participation and trust	High levels of civic participation and trust of others.	Low levels of civic participation and trust of others.
Government	Strong, and regionally focused. City government is key convener on all city issues. Governments have clear responsibilities, and municipalities are not in competition.	Decentralized, with weak regional governance. Only sometimes convenes relevant stakeholders on key city issues. Municipalities are in competition for resources and people.
Racial diversity and immigration	Variation on racial and ethnic tolerance. Stress policies of inclusion. Immigration can be a threat to unity. Residential segregation is low, while social segregation can be high.	Encourages racial and ethnic diversity in the metropolitan area. Often open to immigration. Residential and social segregation between racial and ethnic groups is high.
Nonprofits and foundations	Most public work is done in government, but civil society outside of it keeps it accountable.	Strong. Many public services and issues are championed through this sector.
Health care	Strong, centralized health care institutions. Free or low cost.	Strong, privatized health care institutions. Cost varies, and access varies accordingly.
Taxes	High taxes.	Low taxes.
Parks and public spaces	Many public spaces. Are well maintained throughout the city.	Few public spaces, not well maintained, unequal.

Transportation options are diverse in People Cities, with many citizens taking to public transportation and bicycles, and with urban planning proactively encouraging such options. People Cities recognize climate change as a serious problem, and they have less environmental degradation in their residents' backyards. Students almost always attend public schools in People Cities, and higher education is often free or inexpensive. Diversity is valued, but for People Cities inclusion of its diverse peoples is stressed, so policies for achieving such are put into place. Interestingly, a strong, monolithic culture can challenge the success of such inclusion policies.

With these descriptions of Market Cities and People Cities in hand, how do these institutions interlock to create the ideal types we posit? We believe that these factors are converging, and overlap in both empirical substance and through a cultural worldview. For example, the overall levels of inequality in a city, the density of the city, and the modes of transportation are related to the crime rate. Higher inequality cities that are sprawling with car-centered transportation will have higher crime rates: disadvantaged neighborhoods are substantially segregated from better neighborhoods by distance and transportation, and this social distance of disinvestment allows the possibility for greater crime rates in the face of little opportunity. In turn, mistrust of fellow residents multiplies when media outlets report their city's high (often violent) crime rate, further contributing to residents isolating themselves in urban space, increasingly behind gates and walls, and furthering metropolitan sprawl.

For People Cities, this relationship works in the opposite direction: crime is low because neighborhoods, while still partly segregated, are closer together, more equal, and located at sheer distances that are a fraction of those in a Market City. This type of milieu also has many eyes on the street, with noncar users populating busy sidewalks and bike paths. All of these—combined with lower inequality—build to a collective social camaraderie that discourages crime through low inequality and frequent social contact.

Government has much to do with how people trust one another, and whether that trust can build to a collective buy-in for a regional vision. The ability to regulate a number of the other institutions can vary substantially in the decentralized market system of governance. Schools may be outstanding in one area and barely functioning in another.

Racial segregation occurs along municipal lines. Police forces may be funded adequately in some municipalities but not in others. Unevenness of urban space rules the Market City, and those who are fortunate enough to make choices within such a city—always for the best neighborhoods with the best schools, the lowest crime, far from the poor—only further heighten the unevenness.

In People Cities, much of the public conversation—and the public funding—occurs across a larger proportion of the metropolitan population. Communities connected by shared tax dollars in addition to shared territory are able to provide for public services that more fully reach all. These shared services, such as school systems and well-kept public parks, provide for the spaces that bridge divides and build public trust.

The key takeaway from these two examples is to note how interrelated urban institutions really are. Crime is not a stand-alone factor but involves inequality, trust, transportation, density, and much more. We argue that this interrelation creates an emergent effect, an effect that exists above and through the institutional mixing that creates it. The emergent effect develops in one of two types: Markets Cities or People Cities.

Three Questions

Three critical questions can aid in further elaborating the Market City and People City framework. An understanding of how the Market City and People City perspective pairs with the important urban questions of our time is essential to explaining why our particular approach to studying cities is needed.

The first question concerns the idea that cities are nested within countries, asking: To what extent are the market and people types actually just reflective of their nation-states? To be clear, the character of a city will depend, in part, on the country in which it is located. We argue, however, that it cannot fully explain a city's trajectory, and a city's way of getting things done. This is easily tested—if both Market and People Cities exist within a nation (we find they do), then something more than the nation-state is determining city outcomes.

Cities are as important now as they ever have been, if not more important—a position we do not hold alone. Saskia Sassen, whose research agenda on global cities is one of the most important academic advances in urban studies, powerfully shows that cities are essential to the global capitalist system's functioning.[3] Urban economist Edward Glaeser believes the city's role in attracting human capital has proved the city triumphant.[4] Urban policy advocates Bruce Katz and Jennifer Bradley argue that we are in the midst of a "metropolitan revolution" where cities will lead the way with policy.[5]

We argue that the city itself possesses a unique role as a distinct place in and of itself.[6] It's neither a snapshot of the nation-state nor a sum of its neighborhoods. The role of structural and institutional global processes creates the economic and political conditions that make cities crucial nodes in our social world. To date, urban experts mostly assume that cities are all playing the same capitalist game for the same outcomes. But we think something even more substantial is occurring. By thinking about the different types of cities that we highlight, we can better enunciate what the outcomes of this metropolitan revolution will be. Indeed, we believe that the historical configurations of power accumulate, thereby creating a citywide culture that affects action in a metropolitan area. Cities remain important not just for the mass migrations to them or because of their place in the globalized economy, but also because they deeply condition the many milieus—and the minds—of their residents.

The second question concerns the changes we have seen in global polity across the last four decades toward deregulation, decentralization, the lessened importance of borders, and a host of other market-fueled shifts. Broadly held under the umbrella term of "neoliberalism," these shifts would seem to suggest that all cities are becoming Market Cities. Few things define the Market City more than ceding urban priorities to any program to compel economic growth. The question begs: Are not all cities becoming Market Cities?

Expecting homogeneity across cities in the form of a global shift to Market Cities, however, is unlikely. Despite the neoliberal turn to what David Harvey calls "the entrepreneurial city," cities are neither deregulating at the same pace nor are they completely ceding their purposes to growth.[7] There is variation in the paths that cities are taking. The speed varies. The substance differs. Reducing the heterogeneity across cities today not only misidentifies the core of People Cities by displacing them under the market framework, but it also means too broad an aegis for Market Cities, thereby losing crucial texture that can describe those cities.

The third question is straightforward: Can cities be both Market Cities and People Cities, somehow striking a balance? Take, for instance, the vision statement for a new general plan for the city of Houston. "We promote healthy and resilient communities through smart civic investments, dynamic partnerships, education, and innovation. Houston is the place where anyone can prosper and feel at home." Or consider a 2015 article that we picked up from the University of Copenhagen's newspaper about how recruiting international students is good for business. These words strike some contradictory tones to the priorities rubric we have outlined for each city: Houston shouldn't be highlighting "healthy and resilient communities" if it's a Market City, and Copenhagen shouldn't think of students as dollar signs.

It is important to note that all Market Cities will have people elements, and all People Cities will have market ones. Nonetheless, we argue—and will show in later chapters—that most cities trend in one direction or the other, toward the market or toward people. The importance of heterogeneity here is critical. Cities, and the people who live in them, are not monoliths: they are diverse places riddled with contradictions. The cultural fulcrum of cities, however, exerts a gravitational pull that centers those ideas in relation to dominant themes of the city.

Perhaps most interesting, these contradictions help us understand how urban social change occurs: movements not in agreement with the priorities rubric can marshal supporters and leverage resources, especially during crises, to alter the placement of that cultural fulcrum and to shift the gravitational pull of the city's culture. It is a daunting task; nevertheless, it is constant, as small-scale shifts occur every day among the city's diverse residents.

Two Journeys

Recognizing the Market City and People City can be as simple as availing yourself of your senses. To introduce the concepts in practice, we encourage you to go out and take a journey in your city and check out the market or people dynamics along way. We did.

A late morning sunrise in a chilly Copenhagen February, our bikes spin off down the hill. We have come from a suburb, Søborg, where Smiley lived, and are riding down Bispebjerg Hill. Crowning the hill was Grundtvig's Church, a towering, yet surprising muted relic of the Danish national church, whose fortunes sway not with the offering plate but with the tax receipt. We pass Bispebjerg Hospital on our left, where the Danish state guarantees free health care for all (even us, temporary immigrants).

At the bottom of the hill, we see the colorful—as in literally painted with all the colors of the rainbow—Mimersparken, a striking park that nonetheless would never rank among the city's most prominent. Next to it is the Mjølnerparken, a public housing project home to approximately 2,500 residents, many of whom are non-Western immigrants. Despite some people's fears over who the residents are, the public housing looks like just another five-story apartment building in a city full of them: it is well taken care of and next to a beautiful park. Picturesque, wonderful Copenhagen it seems.

Parks dot both sides of our bike ride, but Fælledparken ranks as the city's biggest, and it is home to the massive Worker's Day festival for the city, which is also a national holiday. But parks do not tell us the whole story about public spaces. We swing our bikes onto the protected, raised bicycle lanes over to Strøget, and hop off our bikes to take in the shopping street and pedestrian mecca. It was here in 1962 that (now world-famous) architect Jan Gehl convinced city officials to shut down part of the street to car traffic and to open the possibilities to pedestrians. It worked. The city opened even more of the street to pedestrians over time and has mimicked this tactic all across the city—indeed, our bike ride has been more comfortable because cars have been systematically discouraged by city government, simply disappearing in the process.

On the harbor between the mainland of the city center of Copenhagen and the city's development on Amager island, we find an unlikely activity: swimming. While many cities (be it their governments or private companies) are highlighting their river waterfronts by actually getting people out in the water with kayaks and canoes, Copenhagen goes even further by inviting the people themselves into the water. Most of these harbor baths are closed during the winter, but even in these frigid times a dip is possible in select parts. Copenhagen's transition to a postindustrial economy meant shuttering the industries of old, and this meant cleaning up a polluted waterway through the central part of the city. They cleaned it up to the point where it was possible to swim and, or perhaps more crucially, people *perceived* it was possible to swim. Finding a seat on the bench down the way from the baths in the park, we contemplate the open water, the multitudes of bicycles, and how an energetic People City government can even convince cold people to jump into even colder water.

On another day, an early Monday evening in the fall, we roll the car windows down and feel the humid air offering a partial respite from the long, intense summer. We are in downtown Houston. We pass City Hall, some scattered government buildings, and a slew of glistening skyscrapers, taking note that the latter are consistently bigger and nicer than what the city government has. There are not many people on the streets: they appear to have left the skyscrapers and headed home. Looping around, we circle Discovery Green, a signature public space that is privately run. Here we find a smattering of people, many of them doing a program called "bum-ba-toning" to get fit. We notice the Brown Convention Center directly across the street from Discovery Green, its impressive façade meant to connote ships with smokestacks emerging from the top of the structure. Meanwhile, we look north to a nearly finished high-end apartment complex that will be sleek and shiny. A 2014 development subsidy passed by city council is already paying off for emergent downtown living and for developers.

We head out to Navigation Boulevard, through the heart of the East End. On our way there, we pass several new midrise apartment complexes, the early fringes of gentrification creeping in on the East End, both the historic center for Houston Hispanics, and a former industrial area. The new soccer stadium rises high above the neighborhood, itself partly financed with a cool $35 million from city government. Navigation Boulevard is bustling, with residents hanging outside famed restaurants and around picnic tables in the revitalized esplanade. The esplanade's new doodads are one of the first installations from the Greater East End District, a tax increment financing area. The area is "hot" and the young and the hip flock to the area. Vibrant Houston.

We turn left and head to the Fifth Ward, a historically black neighborhood established for freed slaves and of late also shared by Hispanic immigrants. Poverty here is dire, life expectancies resemble those of developing nations, public infrastructure feels nearly absent—apart from a couple of main roads, there are no curbs, no gutters, no sidewalks, minimal trash pickup, small, poorly paved streets, decaying houses on "pier and beams" (stilts), and much of the land sits empty or with dilapidated, boarded-up dwellings long ago abandoned. Public transportation here— the bus—is infrequent, irregular, and without much attention given to those waiting at the stops. Typically, just a pole marks the spot as a stop, with no shelter offered from the intense sun, rain, or other elements. Despite the best efforts of neighborhood residents, this is a neighborhood that few of Houston's elite ever visit, and it is rarely a location for their philanthropic and development efforts. Forgotten Houston.

As we then travel to the Pasadena Freeway, we wonder if we should roll the windows up. Refineries are rising all around us as we enter the area around the Houston Ship Channel. Houston is one of the most polluted metropolitan areas in the United States, and the Ship Channel is its most polluted place. That's the current price of being a global headquarters for the oil and gas industry. City governments' (including not just Houston, but suburbs around the Ship Channel) inattention to measuring air quality in the area has everything to do with the Market City promoting its biggest brands. In Houston, this means energy, and the refineries are a testament to the prowess of the Market City. As we sign off on our journey with a trip on the Lynchburg Ferry across the Ship Channel, we reflect on the beauty of the open water, the incredible hulking commercial facilities all around us, and the sincerity of the men fishing next to signs indicating they shouldn't eat more than one fish from the channel per month.

Go take your trip in a Market City or a People City. The route has already been provided; you just have to follow the signs.

The Direction of the Book

We have roughly outlined our main idea, but the fun is in the story, the process, and the details that we embark upon in the rest of the book. Our approach, hinted at above, is to use "ideal-type" cities that fully embody the very concepts we discuss, cities that are in many ways polar opposites despite being rated similarly in world rankings of cities. By "ideal types" we mean that these cities draw out the extremes of difference in choices, orientations, and actions. We do so to highlight our conceptual distinction in types of cities.

This book is organized into two parts: (1) How It Happens (chapters 1–3), in which we explore the ongoing process by which cities become and re-create being Market or People Cities; and (2) Why It Matters (chapters 4–8), in which we explore the vast and substantial implications of being one type of city or another.

Each of the chapters takes us on part of the journey into the realities of two cities, but always connecting to cities beyond Copenhagen and Houston. In chapter 1, we analyze the role of histories in the development of Market and People Cities, comparing how each has responded to crisis across time, and how their deep pasts contributed to whether a Market City or a People City emerged. Chapter 2 examines how government and civic leaders create and sustain the Market City or People City, especially through the government's design, how its money is spent, and through the leadership's relative influence outside of city hall. Chapter 3 moves away from the government and elites to the residents themselves, who more loosely renew the Market City and People City, and who even at times contest it.

Part 2 of the book investigates the massive implications of living in a Market City or People City. In chapter 4, we illustrate how these dynamics affect land-use policies, especially as they relate to transportation and recreational life: being in one type of city or the other means interacting in distinctive built environments. Chapter 5 turns to the environment, where Market Cities and People Cities have very different approaches to dealing with industry and with climate change mitigation and adaptation. In chapter 6, we show how the Market City and People City navigate through issues of difference and diversity, namely, through public trust, racial and ethnic inequality, and the impact of and on immigration. In chapter 7, we use multiple approaches to see if our arguments hold across cities. We find they do.

We marshal a wide variety of evidence for our arguments, attempting at every turn to root our arguments in measurable facts. Undoubtedly residents and experts of other cities will weigh our arguments against their local experience and knowledge, hopefully finding commonalities but also extending our arguments. We conclude this book by considering what our argument means for our future. For clearly, when the majority of humanity lives in cities, understanding the cities we create means understanding ourselves.

PART I

How It Happens

1

Becoming Market and People Cities

The reason cities exist has changed over time. This is why we must understand what cities are becoming today, and the choices they can make. For much of human history cities were markets, places to gather and trade agricultural and other goods. Not many people lived in cities. Before 1800, never more than 3 percent of humanity did (and less than 1 percent lived in cities of 100,000 or more people). This is simply because growing enough food for humans—and related activities—consumed about 97 percent of the population. Since cities dwellers did not produce their own food, the percentage of people able to live in cities was directly tied to agricultural technology and production. It still is.

Although not many people resided in cities, a great many people accessed them—to sell their agricultural surplus, to buy goods, to visit holy sites, access the region's political apparatus, and, at least in later centuries, to be entertained.[1] Cities were not only markets but also often religious, political, and at times cultural capitals. They were also places of retreat for protection from raiders. Cities had walls and moats and other lines of defense (including, often, a military). Some cities served all these functions (the biggest of them), but others served just a few functions.

Across time, because they had people who could spend their time doing something other than agricultural production, cities became sites for education, cultural production, and entertainment. Cities typically were not planned, at least in urban terms. Walk the streets of any ancient city center and you will find streets that resemble spaghetti. They "criss" and they "cross," they run into squares, they curve and meander, they connect to other streets in unpredictable ways and at times simply dead end. Such patterns developed spontaneously, the simple result of people using the land and over time creating pathways for people and carts. The squares of these ancient cities—rarely square—were almost always the great gathering places for trade, debate, announcements, and entertainment. They too were typically unplanned. They just "happened," and the more they happened, the more they came to be identified as gathering squares, to be preserved as such, since they were where much of city public life occurred.

This helps us understand something else about the functions of cities: planned or not, cities are social spaces. They bring volumes of people into central spots, and people interact. People interact because they need to, and they interact because they like to. Cities left to their own development—away from urban planners, engineers, landscapers, architects, code creators, transportation designers and the like—become great social spaces for people to conduct the functions of life, the good, the bad, the ugly.

Unfortunately, without planning and codes, the ugly can be too visible, deterring the positive functions of cities. Over time, more societies began conceiving of cities as something that must be tamed, something that could be designed, and in so doing emphasize the positives of cities and negate the negatives. Such efforts did not always succeed, but we continue attempting to learn how to best design cities. The original "planned" cities used two main designs—the radial, where there is an expansive center circle or square, and grand avenues radiating out from that center. Think of Paris, for example. The other design, which largely won the day all the way until the 1950s, was the grid pattern. Such a street pattern—running north-south and east-west (think Chicago, for example)—has many advantages: it is orderly, easy to understand and navigate, allows for density and multiple ways to travel to any destination, and can expand almost infinitely in size, given that the pattern is repeatable (the functions of life can always be within a few blocks of all residents). It has some negatives too: it can be repetitive and thus monotonous, and it is not always the most efficient for service provision—such as sewer lines and electrical grids—as redundancy gets built into the system. Since the 1950s, the spine and rib—"American suburban-style development" that has a main transportation road with a multitude of cul-de-sac type roads coming off the spine—has overwhelmingly been the built pattern.

The early planning of cities has led to a growth in city management and development specialists. All sorts of urban planning and management professions now exist to help cities. *But to what end? What is the goal?*

Any time there is planning, policy and code making, budget lines, designers, urban architects and landscapers, waste management specialists, or any of the many other professions and offices of a city, some underlying assumption about what a city is, what it is to do, and where it is heading is suggested. It is true that cities still today spontaneously develop, but this is increasingly less true. More often they are managed, nurtured, developed, advertised, measured, and assessed. They represent a substantial reach of humanity in a (at least semi-) coordinated effort to do something—be that for developing markets and wealth, serving as spiritual centers, wielding political power, improving defense, displaying wealth, consuming, creating beauty, building centers of education and solution incubators, or allowing humans to flourish.

Deep changes have occurred in the very essence of cities. Consider what has changed: (1) the majority of humanity lives in cities, (2) increasingly people no longer live in cities just for a time (say their twenties) but across the entire life course, (3) people born in cities rather than just migrating to them is on the rise, (4) more often families will live in cities for multiple generations rather than just one or two, and (5) whereas for nearly all of human history almost all of humanity lived in rural areas and visited cities to learn of life there and access its uniqueness, now most of humanity lives in cities and visits rural areas to learn of life there and access its uniqueness.

What the sum total of these changes means for humanity and urban life is profound. Cities no longer are limited to specific, specialized functions; they now are *the crucibles of all of human life*. Heading into the future most people, across their entire lifespans, across an ever-increasing number of generations, will spend their lives in cities. Apart from "tourist-like" trips to the countryside, human society is now urban. In light of this profound shift in the meaning of cities, we must fully understand the cities of today—the choices they have, the decisions they are making, the directions they are heading—if we are to understand how to best structure the cities of tomorrow.

In our quest to understand the cities of the modern developed world, we now turn to a historical look at the development of our two case study cities of Copenhagen, Denmark, and Houston, Texas. We provide a selective history to help us understand the backdrop of each city so we can better situate where each is today and, most importantly, move forward in understanding the development of and differences between Market and People Cities.

Copenhagen Awakes

From the late eighth to the mid-eleventh century the Vikings—the people of Denmark, Norway, and Sweden—raided and traded their way through Europe east and west and beyond. Around 965, the Danish Viking King Harald Bluetooth (yes, the Bluetooth technology of today is named after him) did something that ultimately ended the world of the Vikings and brought Scandinavia into the mainstream of European civilization. He converted to Christianity. And as the king goes, so go his subjects.[2]

Nearly two hundred years and sixteen kings later, Valdemar I the Great (1131–82) ruled the Danish kingdom (which included what is today Norway and southern Sweden). During his reign, in 1158, Absalon (1128–1201) was elected bishop of Roskilde (Roskilde was at that time the capital of the Danish kingdom), and Valdemar made him his chief advisor. They became close friends.

In a reflection of the times, Bishop Absalon was also a mighty military leader, bringing many victories for King Valdemar I the Great. In what some say was a gift by the king to his trusted friend Bishop Absalon and what others argue was a strategic military and political move, in 1167 the king gave Bishop Absalon an area of land on the far eastern side of the island of Zealand, the island on which Roskilde was located, and Copenhagen was born.

Based on excavations, a fishing and trading post was located there at the time, and perhaps even a more substantial town with a significant market.[3] Bishop Absalon had a castle built at the site, and it became an important coastal point of defense against the Wends, Slavic peoples from the south with whom the Danish kingdom warred. Just a year later, Bishop Absalon succeeded in conquering the Wends and Christianizing them. This only increased his importance in the eyes of the king, and later he was made both the archbishop of Lund (across the sound from Copenhagen, in modern-day Sweden) and helped lead the development of Copenhagen as a key military and merchant site within the larger kingdom.[4] Indeed, the old Danish words for Copenhagen literally mean "merchant's harbor."

The city continued to develop, and it remained a military stronghold.[5] And having such a stronghold meant that the soldiers needed supplies—food, weapons, housing, entertainment. So merchants gathered in Copenhagen to supply the soldiers. Copenhagen, situated in a strategic location to control trade heading in and out of the Baltic Sea, began taxing merchants and passing ships. It grew in wealth. A substantial wall was built in the first half of the 1200s, one far too big for the population of the time, but one that anticipated growth.

And growth came. By the early 1400s Copenhagen became the capital of the Danish kingdom. With the relocation of the court, and with the influential Danish navy having its headquarters in Copenhagen, the city could not help but grow.[6] Mansions needed to be built, the elite needed goods and services, housing for the navy was required, more merchants came, more workers arrived, and Copenhagen's population expanded. In 1479 the University of Copenhagen was founded. With the rise of Denmark's great builder king of the late 1500s and early to mid-1600s, King Christian IV—think of him as the Henry the VIII of Denmark, with similar excess appetites, girth, and influence—Copenhagen became a world city with population growth and massive building projects (to the north of the city, he financed the world's first amusement park in 1583), increasing wealth through taxation of ships passing through the sound between what is now Denmark and southern Sweden.[7] By decree, all population growth was confined within the walls (about 1.5 kilometers in diameter), so significant density of settlement was required.

Most people accessing Copenhagen did not live there or in the surrounding area, though. Just outside of Copenhagen, long lines formed each morning full of travelers and agricultural carts awaiting the long, tedious process of entering through the city gate, one cart at a time. The same process would occur in the evening, as people rushed to leave before the city gates were closed for the night.

After the death of King Christian IV, an absolute monarchy was established and remained in place until 1849. With absolute monarchy, the king was king by birthright, answerable only to God. This concentration of power—and the need to show this power through military might, colonization, and elaborate spending—furthered the growth of Copenhagen, again all within the original walls built many centuries before. Under such a system, Copenhagen was not about the people or the market. It was about the king.

Nearly seventy-five years after the establishment of the United States, the absolute king of Denmark at that time, King Frederik VII, seeing the changing times, agreed to nonviolently establish a democracy, the new government of which would be located in Copenhagen. The Danish royalty of today, in continuous existence for over a thousand years, remain as vital figureheads, occupying a similar role to contemporary British royalty.

The change to a democratic form of government in 1849 was important to the development of Copenhagen. Within a year, Copenhagen was finally allowed to expand beyond its ancient walls (the much-despised gates were the first to be removed). This expansion was desperately needed, as the population within the small confines had swelled to about 150,000 people. Among those walking Copenhagen's crowded city streets of 1849 were residents Hans Christian Andersen (of fairy tales fame) and the father of existential philosophy, Søren Kierkegaard. To put the crowding at that time into perspective, today Copenhagen's vibrant city center has 25,000–30,000 people, the number that also lived there in 1650.

Beginning in 1857, the wall circumscribing the city began coming down. This change in the morphology of Copenhagen, its great expansion in physical size, and the building of entire new sections and neighborhoods was not simply due to a new governmental form but to several interrelated world changes. Having been attacked by the British in the early 1800s, with the British navy using technological advances to lob cannonballs from its ships over the walls into the heart of Copenhagen—causing massive fires, city destruction, homelessness, and death—drove home the point being learned across the world of older cities that walls no longer served their protective role.

What is more, at the time of the change in government, the new economic system of industrialization arrived in Copenhagen. As in so many other places, technological advances were driving peasants and farmers from the countryside into cities. In Denmark, they overwhelmingly arrived en masse in Copenhagen. Thus, the confluence of political, economic, spatial, and social changes served to mutually influence the growth of Copenhagen from a compact medieval city to a rapidly expanding industrial city, complete with wealthy neighborhoods and working-class slums so characteristic of the era. As we will see when we turn to Houston's developmental history, apart from the one-and-a-half-kilometer diameter of Copenhagen's city center, Houston and Copenhagen developed roughly parallel to each other, both being mostly built and settled since 1850.

The latter half of the 1800s brought substantial changes to Copenhagen. Several new neighborhoods developed. In worker districts, to squeeze out profit (and not tamed by adequate codes), developers built reams of tenement blocks constructed with tiny flats stacked upon one another, no bathrooms, and too densely designed to allow for suitable light, air ventilation, or play facilities for children. This is important because this design has had much influence on Copenhagen over subsequent decades. Industrialization continued in full force, and the population grew substantially, from approximately 150,000 in 1850 to 358,000 by 1900. The large growth of the working class and liberal voting laws put in place during the transition to democracy led to the growing influence of workers—who increasingly organized into unions and formed the Social Democratic Party in 1871.[8]

The platform of the party then as now was "liberty, equality, and brotherhood." Fleshed out in more detail, the goal was to create a party of workers that focused on solidarity with the poorest and social welfare for those in need. The party also emphasized the responsibility of citizens to one another and their society. Creating security for workers was an important goal—allowing for universal access to education, health care assurance, and related issues. As part of this, by 1901 Denmark's first kindergarten was established in a working-class neighborhood of Copenhagen. Called Folkebørnhave in Danish, the literal translation into English is the "People's Children Garden," a name reflecting several important values in one Danish word.[9] Though it would take many decades to come to full fruition, a culture "of the people" was beginning to form in Copenhagen, through political parties such as the Social Democrats and through evolving ways of viewing the purpose of city life.

The early 1900s witnessed more population growth, all the way to three-quarters of a million people by 1950. The early period of the 1900s also marked the first time the Social Democrats had gained a majority in the municipal council. In this role, the municipality took on increasingly social tasks: they worked to build more modern, subsidized housing for workers, increase the number of parks (for fresh air, exercise, and gathering spaces), and other amenities. Along with the national government, they moved toward universal health care and retirement pay.

But such movements were halted by the recession of the 1930s and World War II, as the city was occupied by the Nazis from 1940 until the war's end in 1945. Though spared the devastation brought to many European cities, it took time to get back to the work of city building, a process they were just fully entering as the 1950s approached.

A marvel of modern urban planning came to be with the Finger Plan of 1948. With Copenhagen as the hand, the plan called for five train lines (the fingers) to radiate out from Copenhagen, with dense development at each stop along each line (often termed "pearls on a string") and leaving the space between the fingers open for easy access by all to green space—forest, lakes, meadows, farms. This plan has largely guided development of Greater Copenhagen ever since, with an extended version approved in 2007.[10]

The 1950s saw the full emergence of the Scandinavian welfare state, the so-called cradle-to-grave security net. Influenced by the uncertainty of the past nearly twenty years, shaped by a now growing economy and by political parties arguing for a safety net for citizens, the Scandinavian social welfare state became a unique model. Taxes were increased, but as Copenhagen historian Carsten Pape told us in an interview, the rising economy (in the 1960s, unemployment in Copenhagen was just 1 percent to 2 percent) and increased wages meant that higher taxes were not strongly felt. Having health care, free access to education at all levels (including graduate and professional schools), pensions, and other forms of social security was generally viewed as a strong social good. Also during this time, housing reform—put off for at least two decades—began, especially with the need to provide quality housing for an ever-increasing population.

Despite such efforts, Copenhagen continued to have extensive areas of lamentable housing throughout the city and extremely cramped apartment living for workers and their families, typically two rooms and a communal bathroom. Shaped by the unrest in the United States of the 1960s and by the "Right to the City" movement of French philosopher Henri Lefebvre, young people and workers in Copenhagen took to the streets, marching and demonstrating for more influence on redevelopment housing policies, improved working conditions, and better playgrounds for children.[11] What is more, the city had become ever more congested as its policies favored cars and expanded roads. As point in fact, each of the sixteen city center squares—the great social gathering spots for centuries—were now parking lots.

As with so many cities rooted in the global industrial world, the next two decades were not kind to Copenhagen. Though it took many years for cities to realize it, the industrial era of the West had come to an end. Unemployment rose to 15 percent and higher, and with decentralization policies in place, middle-class families poured out of Copenhagen into suburban areas surrounding the city.[12] This trend was exacerbated by Copenhagen's housing policies, which attracted the poor but not concomitantly the middle class. The population loss was dramatic, from a high point of nearly 768,000 to just 467,000 by 1990. Copenhagen was in shambles—a crumbling infrastructure, devoid of substantial development, years of political debate and ineffectiveness, outdated policies created for a different era, and declining revenue. The end result of these negative, co-varying, downward spiraling factors was that by the late 1980s and early 1990s, the city was teetering toward bankruptcy.

At that point—a point of crisis, necessitating a new way of thinking—the People City was born. While a culture had been building over the century, it was not until this point that a fresh approach was undertaken. A new set of political leaders came into office, leaders who found a way to cooperate for a new Copenhagen for a new era, an era that has come to be characterized by the knowledge and service economy.

The main strategy, according to our interview with Carsten Pape and from our discussions with government officials and local experts, was and is to create a city so attractive in terms of livability, so focused on the lives of the people, that it will draw people, energy, and vibrancy to the city. In turn, the market advantages will follow the people advances insofar as the people themselves will thrive in the new knowledge economy. To do this, renewed city-central government cooperation ensued, guided by long-range quality planning directly targeted at improving the lives of all residents. This meant, among many other strategies, that the government would solidify the cradle-to-grave security system, introduce "flexicurity" (liberalized laws for laying off employees but with strong, extended unemployment benefits), provide citizen training and retraining for the new economy, focus on non-car transportation (healthier and friendlier to people's experience of the city than cars), build the Copenhagen metro train system, add more parks, clean the city's central harbor, become increasingly environmentally conscious, establish bold goals (for example, to be the world's first carbon neutral city by 2025), and institute clear measurement assessments to track progress. It also meant a major private development of new housing to attract and retain tens of thousands of educated, middle-class people (in part to generate a higher tax base to meet the other goals), and substantial citizen-influenced urban regeneration.

The protests by residents in the 1960s, 1970s, and 1980s ultimately resulted in amending the Danish Urban Renewal Act in 1993 with the result that the involvement of local residents became a statutory requirement. Thus, a new type of renewal—with built-in citizen involvement—ensued. The result is that today it is a matter of course that residents and other local forces are involved in the process if anything is to occur in their neighborhood or city. This is part of the modern People City that is Copenhagen.

And it has been highly successful according to most measures. Copenhagen's population has rebounded, now growing at a thousand people per month. The quality of life of its citizens has expanded impressively, and organizations that rank such things agree, annually ranking Copenhagen among the most livable cities in the entire world. The global honors do not stop there. Copenhagen has also been named at various points by ranking organizations as "the world's greenest city," "the bike-friendliest city on the planet," one of the top ten "world cities," CNN's ten "healthiest cities," "the sustainable transport mecca" of the globe, Siemens's "Greenest City," the architectural jury's European Prize for Urban Public Space, "Best City in the World" by design magazine *Wallpaper*, and according to one ranking, "the World's Best Metro." The French statistics agency Nantes Applied Research conducted an analysis of the top city rating surveys and combined it with qualitative analysis from social networking sites. Based on their research, they declared Copenhagen "the Most Desirable Best City in the World."[13]

Regardless of how scientific these various rankings are, the sheer total and consistency of the honors means something, and others are taking notice. Tourists, scholars, and government officials increasingly flock to the city to take in the experience, observe the city, and learn its methods. The city, once among the poorest municipalities in Denmark, is now teeming with university students and young families. Copenhagen, despite now being among the world's most expensive cities (a point taken up in a later chapter), has among the lowest levels of inequality—between people and between neighborhoods—of any Western city (see chapter 6). Its benefits and services, by any comparison to other cities, are generous.

The contemporary history unfolding before us is the topic of much of the rest of the book. At this stage, though, it is important to note that modern Copenhagen is possible because it has progressively developed a culture that focuses on people first, on equality, sustainability, trust, and cooperation. As we survey the historic development of Copenhagen, we see that a culture was developed over time—one that could be further developed and drawn upon when crisis hits. Thus we see the culture of the People City come slowly into fruition, put into overdrive by crisis, and now developing fully into a spirit of the People City.

Houston Arises

Positioned on a swampy bayou simmering in heat in a fledgling nation recently beset by revolution, Houston nonetheless set its sights on speculation from its very first moment. Its origins, however, have earlier roots than that speculation: the Akokisa tribe, a subset of the region's Atakapa people, lived in the general Houston area, hunting and gathering plentiful game and vegetation, but the population was hard hit by disease epidemics and had dwindled to just a few hundred members.[14] The threat of incoming white explorers and settlers in the broader region left the remaining early-nineteenth-century Akokisa with few options, with most moving elsewhere and joining other tribes.

In 1836, white settlers, and speculation, came to the swampy bayou. Two brothers, Augustus Chapman and John Kirby, gave their surname—Allen—to a landing on Buffalo Bayou that was to be a great trading center. The bayou, hardly a mighty river but instead a muddy yet navigable stream of water connected to the Gulf of Mexico some fifty miles to the southeast, was to be both the host of a great inland port as well as the new capital of Texas.

These twin aims set ablaze the early development of Houston. The Allen brothers procured the name of "Houston" partly as a reverent nod to General Sam Houston, seen as a hero of the Texas Revolution and a leading politician in the early republic, but also as a political ploy to gain the general's support for the city on the bayou to be the first capital city of Texas. The government came to town in early 1837, only to begin thinking about leaving by October of the same year.[15] Land speculation was rampant in the early days of Houston's first growth spurt. Frustrated with the climate and interested in new land speculation, the government left Houston for Austin in 1839. Houston's twin aims of being a political paragon and an economic entrepôt were to be limited to the latter.

But early Houston leaders did not take this as limiting opportunity. Trade dominated Houston's early decades and it secured Houston's rise as more of a commercial city than a manufacturing one. Transportation was central to this. Railroads increasingly crisscrossed in Houston, with national connections completed by the end of the nineteenth century.[16] Mostly upstaged by its gulf island neighbor to the south, Galveston, Houston in the nineteenth century nonetheless commanded trade up from the Gulf of Mexico via the Buffalo Bayou. This especially increased as railroad connections centered in Houston instead of Galveston, thereby increasing the connectivity of the city with the rest of the country.

The business of trade in the early years was primarily thanks to the extraction of raw materials, most notably the cotton crop. This exploitative economy had at its foundation the labor of Afro-Texans, whose rural work, first as slaves and later as sharecroppers, provided urban capitalists in Houston profits that were not extended to blacks. The heavily wooded forests north of Houston also provided another lucrative trade good, as did sugarcane.

Civic and social life in Houston was unruly at its beginnings. Crime was high, but the outright lawlessness of the frontier town subsided in the period after the American Civil War.[17] Roads were poor, often going to mud in Houston's summer afternoon downpours. Development necessarily clustered in the central business district and the city's small population—only 22,557 people in 1890—did not yet portend the sprawl later to come, although the first housing development outside of the central city, the Heights, was constructed in 1891. Still, the land-use patterns and governance of the city were suspect, at least according to one aggrieved Houston resident of that time: "Houston is an overgrown, dirty village, seemingly blundering along without any policy or defined government or management. . . . I am compelled to say that Houston is the most dirty, slovenly, go-as-you-please vagabond appearing city of which I have knowledge."[18]

In 1901, eighty miles to the east of Houston, a lone watchman at a derrick at Spindletop, near Beaumont, Texas, struck oil. This first major oil find in Texas proved to be the impetus for a massive takeoff in the oil industry. No city was better positioned than Houston to be at the center of this boom. Houston was a city of commerce, pregnant with several emergent banks and a strong tradition in the trade of extractive materials. More important, its centrality as a transportation node was all-important. Railroads lines met in Houston, which brought oil in from throughout Texas. Critical to this transportation network was the Buffalo Bayou. Nearby Galveston, still the major port at the turn of the century, was battered by the deadliest hurricane in American history in the fall of 1900, with the death toll estimated to be 8,000.[19] Galveston was devastated. Houston was spared the worst of the hurricane, and its centrality only increased in Galveston's vacuum. Earlier proposals for the widening and dredging of the Buffalo Bayou to make it viable for oceangoing vessels were now received favorably in the U.S. Congress, which committed federal funds to the project at the urging of local elites.[20] The Houston Ship Channel opened in 1914 and had more than seventy companies along its banks by 1926.[21]

Newcomers came in droves to the city. The population grew from 44,633 to 292,352 between 1900 and 1930, becoming the twenty-sixth biggest city in the country at the time. The city increasingly became segregated during this period. Although Houston lacked formal strictures on residence, such as Jim Crow laws elsewhere in the South, the city's long list of Jim Crow laws is certainly cruelly long. Schools were segregated since the creation of the public school district in 1877 and no public library existed for African Americans until black residents created their own in 1907.[22] Rice University, founded in 1912, incorporated in its charter that the school was only for the "white inhabitants."[23] The list of social spheres that were segregated by law included, to name a few: streetcars, hotels, swimming pools, restaurants, parks, theaters, restrooms, and water fountains. Texas barred blacks from voting in primary elections for Democrats in 1923, effectively eliminating voting for blacks in the one-party state.[24] Hospitals were not segregated by law but instead by tradition, and black doctors could not practice in any medical facility until a hospital for blacks was constructed in 1910.[25] The city's burgeoning Latino population experienced de facto residential segregation into the city's north, east, and southeast sides and, further, were subject to much of the same discrimination via the city's Jim Crow laws.[26]

White economic elites had a firm grip on the city's civic world. Houston was the first major city to move to a commission form of government, which favored elections every two years for a Mayor, and four aldermen elected at large.[27] This type of government continued unabated, with the exception of a five-year interregnum in the 1940s of a city manager government, and had the effect of ensuring white leaders in all major city offices by ensuring minority votes could not be so concentrated to win elections.[28] As sociologist Joe Feagin noted in his study of Houston, "For virtually all of its history, and without any major interruptions since the early 1900s, the local business elites have been able to dominate governmental decisions and nondecisions about most major issues, including determinations on planning and zoning mechanisms."[29]

Houston, however, was not as hard hit in the Great Depression as other major cities. Growth continued. Oil, in particular, was stronger in 1932 than in 1927.[30] Moreover, Houston further consolidated its centrality as the key location for oil, with more companies locating along the Ship Channel, more corporations filling the offices of Houston's emerging skyline, and more pipelines surging to the seemingly endless supplies of oil across Texas. Houston's cultural milieu remained mostly stable, with conveniences such as movie theaters and parks along with civic society organizations and home life representing Houston life at the time.

During World War II, when Copenhagen was occupied by the Nazis, Houston served as a major shipping port, which further aided in the recovery from the Depression even before the United States entered the war. The need for fuel and other raw materials from Houston provided an uptick in jobs along the Ship Channel and in related industries. After the war, the importance of the Ship Channel grew yet more.

Politics from the late 1930s until the mid-1970s was dominated by a particularly strong group of city elites known as the "Suite 8F" crowd. The Suite 8F crowd, named after the high-rise meeting room where the small group of members would gather informally, politicked to raise Houston's national profile, chose political candidates as they saw fit, and ensured a lax, market-centered framework to guide the city's path.[31]

Houston unmistakably transformed beginning in the 1960s. Some of it was an acceleration of existing motifs, such as the immense economic and population growth, the increasing global relevance of Houston as a commercial hub, and the concomitant global and local changes in the centrality of Houston's transportation system. Other transformations, however, were challenges to the racialized systems of power that were enabling the deep racial inequities in the city.[32]

In 1950, Houston had 596,163 residents (about 200,000 less than Copenhagen), a figure that would nearly triple to 1.6 million by 1990 (recall that Copenhagen was at the same time at its modern population nadir of just 467,000). Houston's currency was optimism and opportunism, and optimism and opportunism appeared to yield no end to actual currency. Oil business boomed. The Ship Channel was the trading center for oil being refined and shipped throughout the world. An emergent network of oil pipelines facilitated further movement of the black gold. Through no small political maneuvering, the Manned Spacecraft Center of NASA opened in southeast Houston in 1963. Nearly five thousand workers were employed by NASA when Neil Armstrong and company touched down on the moon. Houstonians are known to ask out-of-towners and transplants: What was the first word ever spoken on the moon? The answer: "Houston."

New residents flocked to Houston, and Houston's transportation systems could hardly keep pace. By the 1960s, the possibilities of mass transit were already hindered by the immense sprawl of the city. The creation of the Gulf Freeway between Houston and Galveston, the nation's first postwar limited access freeway (first opened in 1948 and completed in 1952), provided a model adapted across the United States and much of the world, but the object lesson became a deeply imbued doctrine in Houston to an extent rarely replicated.[33] With the crucial creation of the interstate highway program in 1956, federal aid for highways arrived at just the time that Houston's surge in population necessitated a housing boom. The housing boom primarily took the form of single-family homes in large developments both inside and outside of the city. Conveniences such as air-conditioning, an increasingly popular commodity in middle-class homes in the 1950s, produced the possibility of a comfortable car ride into the city and a cool home to return in the city's stifling heat and humidity.[34] The freeway system in Harris County, where Houston in located, increased from just twenty-six miles in 1950 to nearly three hundred miles by 1985. Freeways were the future, and the future was carrying cars into city fringes previously unthinkable.

The inequalities of postwar Houston, especially beginning in the 1960s, were challenged by the city's racial and ethnic minorities, who had been systematically excluded from the political structures of Houston. These challenges mirrored those occurring throughout the United States, but they also were specific to the historical tradition of the city. Houston historians, while noting some exceptions to the rule, found that Houston did not encourage radical types of social movements seen in other cities.[35] This does not mean, however, that there were no challenges to the foundations of the architecture of power in Houston. There were many challenges, and their successes changed the social and political establishment of Houston.

Blacks in Houston in the 1960s, armed with Supreme Court successes such as the defeat of the all-white primary in *Smith v. Allwright* and the landmark national victory in *Brown v. Board of Education*, sought to destroy Jim Crow in the southern city. Segregation of lunch counters was an early target. In February 1960, students from Texas Southern University, a historically black university located in the city's predominantly black Third Ward, commenced a sit-in at the white-owned Weingarten's grocery near Texas Southern University's campus.[36] Refused service, the sit-ins spread to other lunch counters, including prominent downtown locations and City Hall. Houston's mayor, Lewis Cutrer, threatened arrests of student demonstrators for the sit-ins but, with pressure mounting, created a committee composed of whites and blacks to address the problem, which halted the sit-ins for the time being. With little action from the city or the committee by the summer, sit-ins across the city resumed. On September 1, 1960, nine downtown department stores began serving black customers at their lunch counters.[37] Desegregation would slowly continue at restaurants across the city, with another major victory occurring in January 1961 with the desegregation of eating facilities at City Hall. Two years later, other city facilities such as parks and swimming pools were desegregated.[38] Long fights to decommission educational segregation proved successful from a legal perspective by the early 1980s after much organizing from black and Hispanic (at this time, mostly Mexican American) communities, but white flight to the suburbs served—and still does—as a painful reinstallation of a broken and segregated educational system.[39]

In 1982, the oil boom went bust. The ever-accelerating growth of the post–World War II years had come to a halt. A city that had upward of 80 percent of its workforce directly or indirectly tied to the oil industry found itself sputtering in the crosswinds of the declining local sources of oil, increasing international competition, and its place as a subsidiary corporate center with headquarters elsewhere. Sociologist Joe Feagin, writing in 1988 amid the throes of these difficulties, writes, "Houstonians experienced a major swing from widely heralded prosperity and profitably to unprecedented unemployment and unprofitably."[40] This Market City appeared to be past its zenith. As with Copenhagen, Houston had hit its point of crisis in the postindustrial Western world.

Unlike Copenhagen, however, Houston made very different decisions concerning how to enter the new era. It would double down its efforts to focus on the market, driving it to its present position as a quintessential Market City. Diversifying its economy, focusing more intently on business and job recruitment, and experiencing an upturn in oil prices, Houston's economy began slowly turning upward in the late 1980s. Recent advances in the early 2000s in oil and gas technology with the technique of fracking has opened new lands in Texas and beyond for the extraction of natural gas. The particular boom of this innovation powered Houston when much of the rest of the United States floundered in the Great Recession. Houston experienced job loss in only one year (2009), the only American city to have such limited losses, and by 2013 had two jobs for each one it lost during 2009.[41] At the same time, the economy's diversification has kept abreast of changes typical of a postindustrial economy; for example, Houston now boasts the world's largest medical center. In total, Houston today has an economy that on its own would rank twenty-seventh in the world among countries' GDPs, just ahead of Austria.[42]

Houston's racial and ethnic relations continue to shift as well. Population growth in the Latino community, especially due to immigration, has been substantial. In 2015, Hispanics comprised the largest share of

Houstonians at 45 percent, about three-quarters of whom cite Mexican heritage—a large proportion, but a figure that also reflects a dramatic increase in Central American immigration in this period.[43] The Asian population in the city is also up, with 6 percent of city residents identifying as having heritage or being from one of a diverse set of Asian countries, and substantially higher percentages in suburbs such as Sugar Land. The intensification of global capital that kept Houston's economy humming has not kept pace equally for all racial and ethnic groups, a continuation of a historical trend. To take one snapshot, the poverty rates for blacks and Latinos are approximately triple those of non-Hispanic whites in the Houston metropolitan area, according to recent U.S. Census estimates.[44]

Houston's transportation system continues to explode, both near and far. Globally, the Ship Channel serves as the base point for much of the oil and gas industry in Texas. In 2014, the one hundredth anniversary of the port, it ranked as the second largest port in the United States for total tonnage, and first in U.S. export tonnage. Growing systems of oil pipelines also are centered in the city. Locally, the city continues its outward sprawl. Houston's third ring road, the more than 180-mile Grand Parkway, is being completed in piecemeal fashion and the city's spread toward its corridor may ensure its final installation. The land area of the municipality of Houston means that Chicago, Philadelphia, Denver, and Cincinnati combined could all fit within the city. And the Houston metropolitan region square mileage is larger than that of New Jersey. If urban sprawl has a poster child, it is Houston.

Houston has always been a city with large ambitions, and its global relevance economically has only increased since the 1980s, as Houston now lays claim to being the "energy capital of the world." In transportation, the Ship Channel powers those global ambitions and furnishes the astonishing network of roads that get the city's growing workforce to its employment. Houston surged to become one of the country's most diverse cities in the last thirty years. Known worldwide as the city without zoning, only small changes on this front are proposed or possible.[45]

The city has long had characteristics typical of a Market City that are deeply embedded in its culture and history. From Houston's longtime commitment to the economy and commercial outputs and car-centric transportation systems to the city's ongoing racial inequalities, few land-use policies, and increasing international connectedness, Houston's leaders and residents are already conditioned for the Market City environment and cultural worldview. The oil crisis of the 1980s threw longtime characteristics into relief and accredited anew the market ethos with special zest.

As a Market City, Houston has been highly successful. In recent years it has produced immense job growth, been named one of the top two cities in the United States for creating middle-class jobs, number one for hiring and new jobs, one of the three most business-friendly cities, top two for population growth, a top five immigrant destination, named as the second friendliest city in the United States, and among U.S. cities has the highest annual earnings per job, adjusted for the cost of living.[46] On average the metropolitan region grows by 120,000 to 140,000 people per year, although in the sprawl that is the Houston region, most of that growth is outside Houston's political boundaries. The Houston metropolitan region has grown so large that as of this writing it now has a million more people than all of Denmark. And its GDP is substantially larger than the combined economic output of well-to-do Denmark. The end result? According to market-focused *Forbes* magazine, Houston is America's "coolest city," a ranking given, *Forbes* said, because the city has so many jobs.[47] Houston is the economic growth agenda on steroids.

Conclusion

Drawing on different historical backgrounds, it may seem that only in the twenty-first century could these cities be fodder for comparison. But two historical moments stand out to us to the contrary.

The first is 1850. Houston was small, hot, unruly, and socially oppressive. The population was 2,396, and the "city" was just a smattering of a few blocks. Conversely, Copenhagen was budding, preindustrial, and a beginner at democracy. The population was nearly 150,000, and the city was hemmed inside walls in a space approximately aligned with today's city center. At the same time that Houston was setting out on its first steps as a city, Copenhagen was setting out too, from outside the limiting city walls to develop the countryside beyond. The cities share 1850 as a year when they began to build the city beyond the tiny centers in which they were born. In Copenhagen, this meant the establishment of core neighborhoods, followed decades later by suburban development yet further out. For Houston, this meant the gradual process of expansion, fueled by more white settlers looking for Texas-sized fortunes and black settlers searching for community and economic opportunity, especially after the U.S. Civil War. The year 1850 signifies a preindustrial moment, and indeed lasted but a moment.

The push for the industrial age was coming quickly, especially in Copenhagen, but also in Houston, which was establishing a foundation for an oil future it could not have foreseen. In response to the pressures of the industrial era, each city hedged its bets. Both shared a commitment to industry and industrial jobs as the core of the economy. Copenhagen's geographic growth kept workers close to their jobs, while Houston's spread down the Ship Channel, and the small population prevented much of a need to widely disburse the population.

The second historical moment is the 1980s. Urbanists, students of capitalism everywhere, and residents of the world (whether they would put this historical moment in such terms or not) are attuned to the "neoliberal" turn. Broadly, this refers to the market-minded governance powered by nation-states but intended to flatten their boundaries, and it is best epitomized by the tenures of Ronald Reagan and Margaret Thatcher at the helm of their countries. It put deregulation central to the purposes of governments everywhere. Jobs, especially industrial ones (that had been arriving since that previous moment, 1850), began leaving town, if they hadn't already. Detailing the reason for the neoliberal turn could be—and is—the subject of many good books, but our account seeks to especially hone in on the variation we see in the world's postindustrial cities during and after this important economic change. We think that scholars have too widely construed a singular path that cities take in the neoliberal era, namely, that they deregulate government, loosen tax structures, and make market successes their top achievements, as they compete for "command central" status among the world's cities; that is, they vie to be at the center of the global economic system.

All cities enmeshed in the global capitalist system are indeed part of the system, but they also exercise choice and independence. They are making different choices, choices that must be described, analyzed, and named. We argue that People Cities are an adaptation to the neoliberal era that is typically missed in studies of cities, with the double infraction of oversimplifying Market Cities by homogenizing all cities as having the same experiences.

The neoliberal turn meant crisis. Oil went bust in Houston in 1982, and Copenhagen nearly went bankrupt in the late 1980s and early 1990s. The struggles in the years before and after these crises meant a reorganization of what the city was going to be. Just as in 1850 when the old geographies in each city were thrown out at the same time that factories rose, the 1980s provoked new starts into what the city was supposed to be. By this point, each city carried with it a long history shared by wide swaths of residents and imbued in urban form. Each city doubled down on what it already knew. Houston diversified its economy but kept oil and gas at its center. It developed into previously unseen edges of the urban periphery. And Houston continued to justify itself in the name of making money. Pleasing *markets* made the city work. Copenhagen reorganized itself with its concern for its citizens and famous eye for design, putting people and their built environment even more front and center. Along with Denmark as a whole, it reorganized its welfare system—favoring flexicurity and provisions for poorer newcomers—at the same time that it cemented social support provisions in the public character. Putting people first made the city hum.

The 1980s provoked a crisis in cities. The crises in Copenhagen and Houston were especially severe but were not necessarily atypical of cities of the time either. The crises had long been brewing in the massive relocation of industrial work, the suburbanization of the Western world, and in the claims for justice made by marginalized populations. But the neoliberal turn brought it to a head. And when it did, it produced People Cities and Market Cities. As it happened in our two cases study cities, so it reverberated across the Westernized world.

2

How Government and Leaders Make Cities Work

Sewage is not sexy. And back in mid-nineteenth-century London the not-so-sexy sewage was sent out of sight, and out of mind. Typically sewage was put in cellars and eventually, if all worked well, was sent down the Thames.

That was until hundreds of people got cholera. The trouble was that waste in cellars was quite the nuisance, and those city dwellers who did not regularly get the city to flush their waste down the Thames (still a terrible option, we know now) were left with a cesspit beneath their homes. Along a little street in SoHo called Broad Street, a physician by the name of John Snow pinpointed a particular water pump. He did a spatial study of those who had gotten cholera in the epidemic of 1854, and found that most were clustered in the area around the water pump. Some children who had gotten cholera did not live near the water pump but went to school just around the corner. The only population near the water pump apparently unaffected by cholera were monks at a local monastery, but these monks never imbibed water—only beer.

These results suggested that the water from the Broad Street pump was contaminated. It was eventually discovered that a baby who had contracted cholera had her diapers deposited into a cesspit beneath the house in which her family lived, but that the cesspit had not been excised. The pump was but three feet away from this old cesspit. The baby's diapers had contaminated the water, leading to an epidemic that claimed more than 600 lives, almost all of which related to consumption of the pump water.

Snow's famous findings proved to be the foundation for the field of epidemiology, and this case study is taught to public health students across the world. This classic study is not only meaningful to public health practitioners but also has much to do with city government. Concerns over this case and others like it provoked the United Kingdom to pass the Public Health Act of 1875, which mandated city governments to enforce building codes, hire sanitary officials, and to require running water in residences.

Providing for a healthy living environment has become a major charge of cities, to the point that in the postindustrial cities we study it is taken for granted. Across several decades, municipal government slowly came around to the importance of handling waste and sewage. They have moved from letting it fester under houses like on Broad Street to dumping it in water sources to finally coming up with much more effective systems to keep that which is unclean out of our clean water.

This is what municipal government does: it identifies problems and takes decades to fix it. We are kidding, of course. But our example draws attention to the essential role of municipal governance. We will study the importance of government in this chapter as we examine the active role that it plays in our lives. The active role provides for not only clean water but also city "services," from luring corporations to town to keeping crabgrass out of cracks in tennis courts. City government policies affect individual outcomes: it can mean life or death (as in the case of cholera in the 1850s, or during a natural disaster today), employment or unemployment (can the city ensure a robust economy?), and happiness or dullness (does the city provide for excitement?).

What and how much cities prioritize indicates what cities are capable of. It tells us how their residents will come to know, live, and enjoy their city. Market Cities and People Cities diverge significantly in their takes on city government, and social and economic leaders magnify these differences even further. In this chapter, we explore four facets of these differences by first asking what government is perceived to be, then moving to what priorities rank highest on their urban rubrics. Next we delve into how they pay for it, which is the most important aspect of Market Cities and People Cities you'll find in this book. We finish the analysis by moving beyond the walls of city halls into the burgeoning world of the private sector in public city life, and we will see briefly how city leaders outside of government effect change.

What John Snow taught us as students and residents of cities is that how active a city is in addressing a problem of its own public services is not only an important part of creating healthy environments; it is also a building block for determining the core purpose of what the city is supposed to be.

What Is Government, Anyway?

Let's step back for a minute. We all have suppositions about what municipal government does. We might think of the city as the place that picks up our trash, puts on parades for holidays, attracts companies with well-known names, or is the stop necessary on the way to getting married. But what a city government actually does can vary widely. Celebrating Irish heritage in Chicago, for instance, means the city government sanctions the pouring of green dye into the Chicago River on St. Patrick's Day. Maintaining transportation infrastructure in Venice requires maritime skills. Aside from these admittedly rarer versions of city services, we have to think about the simplistic, but provocative question: what is government?

Before discussing different frameworks of what services are prioritized or how they pay for it, we turn to municipal leaders and government documents to find out the basic terms of engagement. This question completes the rest of the picture by providing different-sized frames for which the city government then paints the portrait of city life.

Let's begin with some brief examples in four different cities of what government is. Our discussion is limited across these four cities, but they produce ideas to stimulate the discussion that follows. Consider Miami. According to its most recent strategic plan, the vision of the city is threefold: "a world-class city with a commitment to public engagement and excellent service delivery; a diverse and vibrant community with a high quality of life; and a global destination for business, culture, and leisure."[1] Mayor Anne Hildago of Paris states the one goal of its municipal government: "service to Parisians in compliance with the Paris values," values that include making Paris "the capital of equality."[2] In Vancouver, the stated mission "is to create a great city of communities that cares about our people, our environment, and our opportunities to live, work, and prosper."[3] And, in Kansas City, a snapshot for a proposed strategic plan argues that "More than anything, what Kansas City residents, business people, and workers told Market Street [a consulting company] is that Kansas City must decide on a vision for its future growth and pursue it efficiently, aggressively, equitably, proactively, and with focused investments that demonstrate sustainable and high-value returns."[4]

A diversity of opinions reigns over what government ought to be in these cities. Miami's import is to be known to export: an international place, with serious civic flavor. Paris desires equality. Vancouver centers on caring for communities. Kansas City says it needs economic progress, as well as a clearer vision for how to get there. These are the sound-bite versions to which each city is boiled down, but the diversity in their composition shows how different city goals can be.

From these first slivers of data, two cities—Miami and Kansas City— suggest a Market City purpose of government, which means foregrounding the economy and finding a vision that can make an international mark. In Miami, this is a measured growth policy because both community and quality of life are important as well. It stems in no small part from its economic position as the southernmost mainland American city and a northern outpost of Latin America, at the same time that it similarly juxtaposes lives of longtime residents alongside those of the many migrants from the south. As urbanist and Miami biographer Jan Nijman puts it while describing the recent rise of the city: "Miami was in the right place, at the right time, to emerge a leading 'world city' in the Americas in the early 1980s, a sort of hyper-node, or massive urban router, connecting business flows between north and south. Its rise owed much to the cross-cultural affinities of Miami's ethnically hybrid workforce, many of whom originated elsewhere."[5] Both the intensity of business and migrants make this Market City oriented to the economy but still sensitive to the importance of quality of life.

In Kansas City, the strategy outlines best practices such as promoting arts and leisure or connectivity and collaboration, but make no mistake, those matter only insofar as they create a strong economy. Here's one take on the Kansas City civic rub: "Kansas City's role in targeted economic development should be to make the City the top urban choice in the nation while supporting regional economic development practitioners. This can be accomplished through managing prospects and projects, making the City more 'business friendly,' supporting workforce development, providing competitive and appropriate incentives, helping existing businesses to expand, researching key trends and indicators, and other key tasks."[6] In this quotation, we see that the first priority—if not also the second and the third—of the city government is to build the economy.

These Market Cities see the purpose of government as making the case for strengthening the economy. Before even thinking about the various divisions of the government and how it spends its money, the Market City lays out in plain words the strategic purpose for why government should get up in the morning and go to work. The economy is key and, if it is strong, all else will follow. Integral to market culture, this often means government needs to stay out of the way of economic forces. When it does enter the fray, it does so with many carrots—in the form of incentive packages for corporations—to supplement and strengthen all things economic.

Our other two example cities—Paris and Vancouver—are governed by People City platforms. With egalitarian possibilities in Paris come hard questions for government, such as the ones posited in a summary of resident viewpoints in a recent strategic plan for the region: "Contrasting aspirations are expressed: how to reconcile the dynamism of a big city and the tranquility of village life? How to reconcile all that demanding everyday use of residents and an overall feeling of well-being?"[7] Paris Mayor Hildago has answers. "By choosing a common destiny with all our neighbors, we will give ourselves the means to build a united metropolis, dynamic and efficient," she argued in her inaugural address, "Paris will take its place in the collective responsibility which imposes new duties and new ambitions, overcoming the traditional political divisions to focus primarily on projects."[8] Build the people—not just individuals, but their collective sum—and the city can achieve striking dynamism.

Vancouver is a leader in sustainability, a city at the forefront in establishing regional cooperation in sustainability and endeavoring to become the world's greenest city by 2020. In an action plan, sustainability meets people priorities: "It's up to everyone to do their part, to rethink, re-evaluate and re-imagine the way Vancouver works and how we lead our lives."[9] Bringing together political issues with collective buy-in epitomizes the People City spirit.

These People Cities find that government is meant to have broad applicability, especially to issues of equity. Collective participation is central in these cities. The crucial goal of municipal government in People Cities is to attain public buy-in and work reciprocally with that buy-in to create policies and places that match the zeal of the citizenry they represent. Broader priorities oriented to social betterment for all require a sincere commitment from many actors. And People Cities often get that commitment.

The what-is-government-anyway question in Copenhagen and Houston provides stark contrasts. For Copenhagen, we start with a counterfactual. We sat down for an interview with Anna Mee Allerslev, the mayor of employment and integration in Copenhagen, who is the city's leading official dedicated to business and the economy. If we were to find evidence of a conception of the purpose of government matched to Market City principles, it would be from Mayor Allerslev.

We found little evidence for that. Instead, her focus on the economy consistently pivoted to lowering unemployment and achieving more equitable social mobility. A successful city to Allerslev meant "high rates of employment for our citizens, an active, rich cultural life, a high degree of social mobility . . . and to be a happy, fulfilled people." Work is considered an individual enterprise but, in hard times for individuals, can be generated by the collective. The model, she says, is this: "You, as a citizen, as part of your social benefits, have the right to get help to get a job and a duty to work." Work is a right and a duty in Copenhagen. The economy, then, functions less as a growth dynamo whose proceeds will filter down to its residents, but instead as a place where dignity and household economic sustenance can be ensured for all.

Municipal goals in Copenhagen reflect People City conceptions of what government ought to be. A recent municipal plan from 2011 foregrounds the need for "a good everyday life in Copenhagen."[10] Simultaneously seeing the need for economic growth and high quality of life for its residents—"growth and prosperity go hand in hand," the plan reports—it settles firmly on government priorities necessitating livability above all else. The plan continues: "By 2025, Copenhagen will still be one of the best cities in the world to live in and be a safe, inspiring and diverse city with its own special and unique character with a mix of old and new buildings, green spaces, and people in the city space."[11]

For all the complexity required for government to actually accomplish the task, the People City model of government is rather simple: create a wonderful city in which to live. The crucial lesson from Copenhagen, and others like Paris and Vancouver, is that People City government is defined by efforts to guarantee a "happy, fulfilled people."

Houston delineates government rather differently. When government succeeds, it is because it met economic aspirations. The buck stops— starts?—with the mayor. Like the mayors before her and the leaders after her, when former mayor Annise Parker, whose term-limited six years at the helm of the city ended in 2015, packaged her biography on the city website or in countless interviews with local and national media, she always led with two items: her job creation record (strong, even through the recessionary environment back in 2008–9), and balancing the budget (she did it six out of six years).[12] She listed these reforms in her 2013 State of the City address: "We've cut waste in the vast city bureaucracy. Put our finances in order. Made city departments more efficient. Balanced the budget without raising taxes. Begun pension reform."[13] Economic growth and fiscal minimalism are often the highlights when arguing for your success in government in a Market City.

The conception of limited government is evinced in other ways too. Houston is a city of no zoning, the only big American city without such laws. Efforts to create a general plan for the city throughout the city's history are curtailed by the connections of a general plan to zoning. The overall effect of this is that Houston lacks the holistic development plan that many other cities have. Even the adoption of the "Plan Houston" effort in 2015, billed as the first general plan in the city's history, is more a laundry list of overall goals (again, often related to the economy) than a strict governing document ready to be applied to urban planning projects throughout the city.

When we consider the metropolitan region as a whole, Market Cities are often fractured metropolitan areas, and in Houston the metropolitan area boasts 112 municipalities. Add in sixty-eight school districts, nine county governments, a separate transit authority, an independent sports authority, municipalities crossing county lines, state and federal funds, and you get a mind-boggling number of government entities (191!) that can never be well coordinated. They were never intended to be.

What is more, nearly two million residents in Houston's home county, Harris County, live in unincorporated areas, unsupervised by any municipal government at all. This is far from typical: for example, every resident of New England states such as Connecticut, Massachusetts, and Rhode Island technically live in a municipality. The unincorporated Harris County residents compose a population larger than Dallas or Philadelphia. It is projected that shortly after this book is published unincorporated Harris County will have more residents than the city of Houston.[14] And these are not rural residents: they are living in the central county, typically in large subdivisions, and see their children off in the morning to school districts, such as the Cypress-Fairbanks School District in the northwest part of the county, which has more than 100,000 students. Houston's decentralized governmental decision making is Market City governance at its zenith: who your government is and what they do *depends on where you live*. The benefits come from localized decision making, as well as from the inherently limited ability to make sweeping changes that might grab too much of private incomes for public programs. Inconsistency of government is the name of the game so much that it also breaks down the rules of the game, paving the way for less government influence and a more unfettered economy.

Contrast this with the municipal plan for Copenhagen, which stresses People City attributes and does so for a metropolitan region that includes two different *countries*—Malmö, Sweden's third biggest city, is forty-four kilometers (twenty-seven miles) away, separated by the Øresund strait. The plans for metropolitan cooperation are ambitious, too. Malmö says in its own municipal plan that they want to create the world's first cross-border carbon neutral zone with Copenhagen.[15] The Copenhagen area on the Denmark side of the Øresund counts a fair number of municipalities at twenty-eight (and another twelve on the Swedish side), but nothing like what's found in many Market Cities. More than this, almost all of these residents live in municipalities.

Simply put, finding out what government is supposed to do in a Market City has much to do with finding out what government is *not* supposed to do. It is not supposed to guarantee social provisions, for fear of recessionary times or serving as a disincentive to economic growth. It is not supposed to go into debt—instead, a balanced budget is lauded. The Market City is not supposed to be unified, and the more and varied governmental bodies there are, the better. Market Cities use the government to make a world-class city by aiding and freeing economic forces.

What Does Government Provide?

Services define a city government. Many cities have similar frameworks for services, not surprising given the historical purposes of cities. For example, cities provide quality water, discard residential waste, build a transportation infrastructure, and steward park spaces.

But there are two major differences in how city governments provide services. First, those services occurring in almost all cities—such as building a transportation infrastructure or water treatment—are not uniform in what they look like across cities. The extent of a given service can vary greatly. They are funded in different ways. Just because two cities have parks does not mean that we would expect the number, quality, design, and effectiveness of the cities' park systems to be the same. Rather, they can be quite different.

Second, some cities pursue services that are not used by most cities or are even totally unique to them. These can be as idiosyncratic as Tampa playing up its coast by supporting a large annual pirate festival, but can be as socially meaningful as efforts by some cities to set ambitious goals for cutting carbon emissions. What a city chooses as a unique service (if at all) has much to say about its priorities, and therefore has much to say about how its government follows a Market City or a People City.

We return to the four example cities above—Miami, Kansas City, Vancouver, and Paris—to compare what government says its purpose is with what that government actually does. Like before, our approach is limited to the introduction of the ideas, but what we see in the examples below is generative. The Market City of Miami stressed its international role in attaining capital and encouraging migration. Miami works both sides of the equation. In terms of working with immigrants, the city provides immigration and refugee assistance to families and individuals as they enter the United States. On the attaining capital side of the equation, Miami is fervent. They have established a Mayor's International Council, which operates as an agency dedicated to "stimulating commercial and residential development and expanding the City's tax base through the promotion of foreign trade and local investment."[16] Jan Nijman, the Miami historian, writes that the city's late development—only five thousand residents lived in the city in 1920—meant that it jumped straight into the postindustrial age, replete with lax governments and diverse migration streams.[17] This meant that trade and tourism were central to the city's economy and to the overall vision of the city itself.

In Kansas City, which seems attuned to themes of growth, growth, growth, we find city services meant to attract corporate capital and jobs. Most cities have tax break policies, dedicated city positions, and public-private programs for attracting jobs, and Kansas City provides an example of what that looks like in a Market City. Attracting investments from tech companies is a major part of cities' efforts in courting corporations, and no tech company gleams quite like Google. So when Google announced in 2010 that they would be initiating a new program called Google Fiber and that they initially would provide it in only one city, cities across the United States jumped at the chance.

Google Fiber provides high-speed broadband access via new technologies at speeds one hundred times faster than the average American's internet speed. Monthly fees for that service would run a customer seventy dollars, but a lesser version would be free. It may be no surprise that 1,100 cities applied to be the first Google Fiber city, but the antics to get the competitive service are surprising: Topeka, Kansas, for one, changed its name briefly to "Google, Kansas," and the mayor of Duluth, Minnesota, took a plunge for publicity into chilly Lake Superior.[18] But Kansas City, Missouri, and neighboring Kansas City, Kansas, won the day. Google Fiber has since expanded to other municipalities in the metropolitan area. Kansas City now encourages tech start-up growth since the Fiber introduction. The city created an "innovations team" to shape Google Fiber's introduction to the community. Zoning has been relaxed so that homes with at least one resident can double as offices for tech start-ups. City priorities reflect the need for investment of private capital; as the mayor pro tem of the city put it, "We're damn lucky to have the private sector do it. . . . There was no way I could get a bond issue passed for this."[19] Market Cities love it when the private sector steps up and facilitates that relationship.

Vancouver has quite the green thumb. People Cities have more ambitious city services when it comes to the environment, a point we return to in depth in chapter 6. Cities are themselves dependent on rural areas such that they are intensified users of natural resources and produce a good deal of waste; in other words, cities are not yet the green world-savers we sometimes expect them to be.[20] This is where a People City with its governmental charge of finding wide-reaching solutions for the betterment of all comes in. Although as a city they serve as a source of environmental degradation, being committed governmentally to doing something about it—as in naming this task as one of its key goals—is a mark of a People City. Vancouver desires to be and works carefully toward being the world's green capital by 2020, a paragon for how public policy can influence greener infrastructure, cleaner air, and a more sustainable planet. Its aggressive goals have meant prioritizing the collective environmental future over that of priorities seen in other cities, such as Kansas City's main focus on economic growth.

A new service in the People City of Paris is popping up in many places: participatory budgeting. Participatory budgeting is a process by which citizens more directly decide how their governmental budget gets spent. According to the Participatory Budgeting Project, an NGO dedicated to the cause, the process of participatory budgeting works something like this: "Though each experience is different, most follow a similar basic process: residents brainstorm spending ideas, volunteer budget delegates develop proposals based on these ideas, residents vote on proposals, and the government implements the top projects."[21] Originally begun in the Brazilian city of Porto Alegre in 1989, participatory budgeting has expanded to 1,500 governments worldwide.

Paris's participatory budgeting is one of the more ambitious schemes in existence: they dedicate 5 percent of the municipal budget to it, more than many cities that offer 1 or 2 percent of their budget to the citizen planning budget. Because Paris is such a large city, it is, in terms of real dollars, the largest participatory budget system in the world ($84.5 million dedicated to it in 2015). Nearly 42,000 Parisians voted for projects in the first go-around in 2014, and more than five thousand proposals were submitted in 2015. The funding went to projects such as using abandoned subway stations for cultural offerings and installing gardens for educational purposes near elementary schools.[22] The purpose of using participatory budgeting as a government service certifies people priorities. This is evidenced in how a deputy mayor (whose office takes up issues of local democracy) assessed the usefulness of the program: "the most important aspect of the Participatory Budget is the fact that it reinforces a sense of community. It is fostering closer interaction between citizens of different ages, origins, modes of living—reminding us that, despite our different ambitions and outlooks, we are all part of a community and citizens of one shared place."[23] People priorities seek stronger communities. In the case of participatory budgeting, it brings citizens directly into the decision making.

In Copenhagen and Houston, what services are offered and how they are prioritized say much about their People City and Market City status. Indeed, this important theme repeats through the book, so we'll take two glances at the assumption that a city's government and leaders heavily favor its model by examining ways in which they seemingly do not. The important theme to remember in these cases is that while People Cities or Market Cities may believe in apparently nonpeople or nonmarket priorities, respectively, it is really just due diligence. Where they find their voice and their passion is in enacting priorities closer to their core beliefs.

One assumption made above is that People Cities like Vancouver prioritize the environment more than Market Cities. A quick tour of Houston suggests evidence that could prove the assertion problematic: the city employs a sustainability director, has more than a dozen Leadership in Energy and Environmental Design (LEED)-certified buildings, and joined ICLEI, an international compact for sustainability in cities. Global climate change has indelibly entered the civic conversation in virtually every city on the globe, and even the most Market City of them all, such as Houston, takes actions to do something about it. Other Market Cities such as Miami and Kansas City do the same: they too have sustainability or chief environmental directors, LEED government buildings, and membership in ICLEI. But the key point of analysis is to see whether Houston goes above and beyond what we expect of a city, especially a Market City, in combating global climate change and unhealthy environments.

The city does not. The menu of environmental reforms in Houston contains more hors d'oeuvres than main dishes. Regulation of industry or car traffic is either not present or not meaningful enough on the municipal level to make the serious inlays into emissions and climate change that People Cities are beginning to achieve. The difference in city government dealing with the environment is that though both Market Cities and People Cities care about the environment, only People Cities go the extra mile to do something about it—making it a top priority, producing strategic plans, enacting the plans, holding themselves accountable in reaching their goals, and funneling resources to the issue.

In contrast, Houston expends its energy on political matters closer to the economy. Faced with the prospect of raising taxes in the recession, Houston opted against it, instead cutting hundreds of millions of dollars from the budget and eliminating 776 city jobs.[24] In 1999, the city ordinances related to land use—*not* zoning, to be sure—were changed so that more homes could be allowed per acre in the central city, which in 2013 was extended to the areas outside central Houston.[25] This relaxation of the already-lax rules enabled a residential development boom in the city that has flowed millions into the coffers of developers and displaced residents through gentrification. Even on noneconomic matters, individualism reigns. A referendum to eliminate red-light cameras to catch automobile speedsters was passed in 2010, and car crashes at intersections that once had the cameras have since doubled.[26] At a public meeting we attended, Mayor Parker lamented not just the loss of life associated with the removal of the cameras—she was opposed to the referendum—but also the loss of income, which brought in some ten million dollars to the city in traffic fines. On both sides of the issue, market values reign—whether it's the need for individual freedom, or the pain felt by the city in lost revenue.

A second assumption made above is that Market Cities such as Kansas City prioritize the economy. Like the counterfactual in Houston, a glance at Copenhagen shows that the city has an agency dedicated to bringing business to town, and creative class frames for economic development show up in city plans.[27] The economy is an integral part of government in Copenhagen. Keeping up with the Jensen's is important for economic matters, but they don't go to lengths beyond what other cities like them do. Indeed, Vancouver and Paris also exhibit similar tendencies with respect to the economy. You may find tax incentives for corporations in these cities, but they're not nearly as ambitious as Market City programs. And, more important, they are not seen as the pathway to city vitality.

Though the economic side of city government remains relevant in Copenhagen, the People City relishes its opportunities to enact people priorities. Copenhagen applies funds early for at-risk children, spending millions in specialized programs that go beyond just the school offerings. And while Houston is eliminating red-light cameras intended to keep drivers honest and safe in the name of government overreach, Copenhagen is installing stoplights that sync up such that cyclists (rather than cars) can have quicker and safer commutes. Not only this, but the city is installing bicycle-only commuting bridges—such as the *cykelslangen*, or "cycle snake"—that are drawing high praise from local residents and admirers around the world.

The difference in governmental priorities is evident in the programs city governments sponsor. Every city inevitably deals with the economy, transportation, sanitation, and a plethora of other services. But which ones climb up the ladder so that they are the most important indicates whether a city is a Market City or a People City. The city services that tell us the most about our city governments are the ones for which cities go the extra mile, instead of just doing enough to keep up with peer cities.

How Does Government Pay for It?

City services are quite different in Market Cities and People Cities. As we have seen, the types and the prioritization of the services depend on the type of city. And the overall themes about what government should do in the first place vary along with these city services. But there's still one more major difference in how government operates: paying for all of it.

Taxes are as boring as they are important. If Robert Penn Warren's *All the King's Men* had been about the minutiae of tax policy changes for creating a state hospital in Louisiana, it would have been in the dustbin, not in the annals of great American classic books. But in understanding cities, we think taxes *are exciting*. Almost more than any other urban indicator, the way a city deals with taxes—the tax structure, the total amount collected, where it spends the money, and attitudes about taxes—is a powerful illustration of People City and Market City dynamics.

Houston and Copenhagen diverge in remarkable ways on the topic of taxes. Even where the taxes come from diverges in the two cities. Houston's municipal budget comes primarily from property taxes, water and sewage taxes, and sales taxes. Property taxes are assessed at about sixty-four cents per one hundred dollars of taxable value on property. Water and sewage taxes generate the next highest amount of taxes collected (about a quarter of the city's total budget), and also are assessed by property (and then sometimes passed on to renters). The overall sales tax rate is 8.25 percent, of which 6.25 percent goes to the state of Texas. Out of the remaining 2 percent, a penny goes to city government, and a penny goes to the Metropolitan Transit Authority.

Copenhagen also uses sales taxes, but this is far from its only source contributing to the city coffers. Income tax is the primary source of municipal funds. The percentage of income that goes solely to municipal government is 23.8 percent, with most households paying twice that total on a progressive tax scale to the national, state, and city government total. Land-use taxes for residences are 2.4 percent, more than three times higher the rate for Houston, and there is a levy for commercial properties too. Not counting those taxes, this means that Copenhageners pay about 25 percent of their income to the city, another 25 percent to other levels of government, and, with what's left over, pay 25 percent sales tax on everything they buy (that money heads to the national government). The national government provides about a third of the city budget, but the majority comes from the income tax and the property taxes. The price is steep, but, as we shall see, it provides a good deal.

Not surprisingly, the cities come up with very different totals for their budgets. In Copenhagen, the 2015 budget came to approximately 47.81 billion Danish kroner (DKK) ($7.27 billion). In Houston, the city budget was $4.79 billion (31.5 billion DKK). The municipal budget is higher in Copenhagen than it is in Houston. Remember, though, that Houston has four times as many residents as Copenhagen. When adding this in, the municipal government pays, in U.S. dollars, about $12,764 per resident in Copenhagen, while Houston manages just $2,181 per resident. Despite the cities being responsible for different levels of services—for examples, schools are underneath the aegis of city government in Copenhagen but are their own government entity in Houston—this gap is a major difference. Even when adding the $1.4 billion of local tax sources that go into the Houston Independent School District budget, Houstonians still only get $2,819 per resident. Copenhagen expends four-and-a-half times as much per resident than does Houston. The difference is powerfully played out in what services are offered in each city.

Copenhagen divides its budget into ten categories. The largest budget category goes to schools, and support for youths in general—about a quarter of the budget. The next three categories—each with approximately one billion U.S. dollars—are employment and integration, disability services, and health care. Interestingly, these health care funds are allocated above and beyond what the regional government allocates, which is the government that administers the country's famed single-payer health care system. That money primarily goes toward care for older citizens, including social services and housing. Even the employment and integration monies are chiefly used for getting out-of-work Copenhageners back to work through training, retooling, and orienting employment opportunities rather than mostly recruiting corporations like a Market City would.

Houston's main areas of expense are for development and maintenance services, and for public safety. The former primarily concerns public works, such as the upkeep of roads, and the latter primarily funds the police, whose budget totals some $809 million. The total school district budget is comparable to Copenhagen's, but it is a fraction per pupil. In the Market City of Houston, the primary function of government is not to be a creative user of space, but instead to maintain order. This occurs by keeping the roads up, providing for basic levels of safety, and sustaining educational programs at the minimum level possible. Also, under the largest budget category of "development and maintenance," a full 40 percent is allocated to "enterprise funds" for attracting businesses and jobs.

TABLE 2.1. Top Four Spending Priorities in City Government

Rank	Copenhagen	Houston
1	Children and youth	Development and maintenance services (40% of which is for business development)
2	Employment training and resident integration	Public safety and order
3	Disability services	Human and cultural services
4	Health care	Schools*

Note: Schools would place a close second in Houston if in city government.

We fear that your eyes have glazed over. We worry that if we speak of *that word* again—in hushed tones, even—we will provoke you. But we must assert again this crucial point: *taxes* really, really matter. Market Cities skimp on taxes, keeping them low (whether by choice or by requirement of some larger political entity), and the taxes they do collect typically are focused on market growth, basic service provision, and maintaining law and order. The idea is to let individuals hold on to more of their money: they are the ones who know how to spend it. And Market Cities believe that innovation strikes individuals. With more money in their pockets, individuals and corporations create economic change that is at once uneven—it is distributed to those who produce the innovation—and also is intended to be, as the rising tide should ultimately lift all boats.

Houston epitomizes this perspective. The city spends its money on basic city services, such as ensuring public safety or fixing existing public infrastructure. Residents do not pay much into the system, but they also do not get much. They instead get to keep much of the money they make, hopefully producing better livelihoods on an individual or household basis, as well as providing social good by innovating for a more robust city economy.

People Cities, however, have substantial taxes—sometimes so high that they can be hard to swallow. Such cities can use those taxes to provide first-rate public services, such as ensuring strong social livelihoods for children, seniors, and the disabled. People Cities thrive on the idea that equity for all is being achieved—even the 2015 budget for Copenhagen has the running theme of "a Copenhagen with room for everyone."

Copenhageners pay dearly for it, with many incomes taxed above 50 percent, when including all levels of taxation, and not yet including the 25 percent value-added sales tax assessed on every purchase with the remaining income. But most Copenhageners, we were told repeatedly by residents and experts alike, do not think it too high a price to pay. Instead, these People City residents find comfort in the social safety net, the array of city services before them, and the feeling that the residents on the busy city streets feel the same way too. Of course, to feel this way, there must be substantial trust that government entities are using the money wisely, rather than for themselves and their friends. Trust is a topic we explore in chapter 6.

When Is Governance Not Done by Government?

Especially in the last thirty years or so, urban scholars have analyzed a fascinating and growing trend: not all that is governmental is done by governments.

Private sponsorship of public services has boomed. This shift and these voices come in many forms. Tax increment financing in neighborhoods uses the increases in tax revenues for revitalization in those specific neighborhoods—meaning that the public dollars intended for the citywide budget stay local. Parks conservancies for specific parks, such as the Central Park Conservancy in New York City, raise private funds for parks, and with the existing public outlays, they run the park separate from the city's park services department, often making eye-opening improvements. Organizations like local chambers of commerce create influential city plans. Cities turn to privately funded charter schools for public education. These are but a few examples of the powerful trend toward privatization of public services.

Many of the voices of leadership about the city come from gleaming skyscrapers and city halls. This occurs in many ways, and links with the privatization of services. Take, for instance, charter schools. The most influential nongovernmental proponents of charter schools are not only housed in nonprofits or think tanks but also come from those funding the schools. The Gates Foundation, for instance, is not a background player in school reforms that donates money and steps away; instead, they're simultaneously policymakers, politicians, and principals. In this case, a global elite—like Bill Gates—has sway, but local elites do too, and while they may not wield quite as much capital as the global ones, their perceived knowledge of local issues makes their influence enormous. They have access to government officials because these people are their friends. They are involved in local civic organizations or economic conveners whose public statements and positions are front-page newspaper fodder. These elites invest money where they see a need, not always waiting for the pesky public go-ahead (too slow, they say—won't spend it right either).

Yet, it is even broader than this. The way in which economic and social elites think about the city will have a greater effect on politics, urban form, the environment—really any urban sphere you can conjure—than efforts by any collective actor or person in the rest of the populace. That's how power works in the capitalist system in which Market Cities and People Cities are embedded—it is purposely uneven, tipped toward the top. When these elites have a vision for the city, they can have a greater impact through such varied platforms as an informal social conversation with an elected official (whom they bankroll come election time) or in speeches to prominent civic organizations or in expending money for public projects. Anytime they act civically, it has an outsized effect.

Many urbanists argue that these trends toward greater privatization and increased influence from the business community for civic priorities, often referred to as part of a broader neoliberal political and economic turn, are increasing everywhere. They are right. But the ways in which it is happening in cities varies. And the variation has everything to do with Market Cities and People Cities.

The main difference is that the privatization turn in city government is part and parcel of twenty-first century Market Cities, but People Cities when involving the private sphere often develop public-private partnerships. Market Cities inherently distrust government—it's in their DNA to do so. And when broader economic forces unravel the impetus for governmental support of public services, Market Cities jump at the chance. Better to have the private sector do what the public sector could do. After all, they're the most efficient bunch around, the reasoning goes.

Elites from outside the government in Copenhagen help to establish what the city is supposed to be. In fact, the very term "People City" is derived from one such influential figure. Jan Gehl, a world-famous architect whose efforts in Copenhagen since the 1960s have transformed the city into the dense, walkable, bikeable urban form we see today, called his 2010 book *Cities for People*.[28] Using Copenhagen as a point of departure, he investigates the ways in which cities find meaning for their residents through the built environment. The book pays close attention to carefully designing the smallest spaces while at the same time forcefully argues that resident-friendly urban form must be integrated into a greater system. The pedestrian, the protagonist of the city to Gehl, must be the first thought at every point in the system. When asked about what type of city Copenhagen is, Gehl responded, "I've had as a Copenhagener this funny feeling that every morning when I woke up I was quite sure that the city was a little bit better than it was yesterday. And I think it's wonderful to live in a city where you can have that feeling. . . . There's been this humanization of the city center. And in the later years they have expanded this. We have decided that Copenhagen shall be the best city for people in the world."[29] With influential voices like this, Copenhagen has developed a vision for what the city should be, even if the vision is encouraged from outside of government. This city is meant for people. The cumulative effect—that little bit better *every day*—is an evocative, powerful feeling. Making spaces more geared to residents' lifeways is a central means to make life better, including by and for a social and cultural elite like Gehl.

Houston elites offer a much different vision. They marry the idea that elites should have more say relative to the government with the practice of doing so. An organization that serves both of these functions—as a loudspeaker and a policy driver—is the Greater Houston Partnership, the local substantiation of the chamber of commerce. At the 2014 annual meeting for the Greater Houston Partnership, Chairman Paul Hobby spoke to thousands of attendees. He offered the Market City vision for the role of nongovernmental organizations and citizens (like himself and the Partnership):

> In Houston we expect a lot of sweat and a lot of money from the private and philanthropic communities. And we get it. The public sector certainly leads where it must—generally this means in public safety and infrastructure.
>
> But in many areas—in performing and visual arts and medical research, in parks, in public and higher education, in clinical healthcare and quality of life, the public sector readily embraces an enabling role and that is not typical behavior for governments in other cities. So, thanks to our elected officials for allowing Houston to be that kind of decentralized meritocracy of ideas and eclectic civic visions.[30]

Nothing epitomizes the cultural basis for the Market City like "decentralized meritocracy." The division between what government does and where the private sector and philanthropy step in matches much of what we've seen throughout the chapter: Market Cities like Houston favor maintaining basic public services such as keeping up funding for police and fire departments. The rest is only supposed to be a limited intervention by the government—and our argument adds that the intervention would be best staged by the private sector. Schools, parks, quality-of-life issues: send them to the private sector, whose gift for ably meeting needs stands head and shoulders above the public sector abilities. Assessing the efficacy of this public-private split is a central tension of the Market City, and the division of labor between these two sectors tells us a lot about how elites think and act about their cities.

The extent of the privatization of urban government is most often studied as a thematic change of governmental functioning—the ways in which people talk about government, and the specific services that are privatized. The examples above illustrate this. But a different starting point—from the vantage point of what private capital puts in instead of what the public sector increasingly does *not* put in—reveals how massive the private investment in public good actually is.

Three billion dollars. That's the amount of money that flows from the coffers of foundations into hundreds of city organizations each year in Houston. Totaling the funds from the six largest foundations in the city, this three-billion-dollar figure is not much less than the total budget of the city government of Houston. According to the *Chronicle of Philanthropy*, almost five billion dollars were given to charities by Houston metropolitan area residents in 2012, some 3.2 percent of their total income.[31] These funds are given to any number of charities for any number of purposes—many of them for religious purposes, and much of those funds did not return into the city, of course. But the sheer generosity of metropolitan residents totals more than even the budget of Houston's city government.

Monetary civic giving is as much a regular practice in Market Cities as participating in public meetings is in People Cities. Collective goods are decided by individuals assessing how they should invest instead of contributing to a government pot of money that is divided up, like in a People City. Civic giving is a main way that city priorities get accomplished.

Houston abounds with examples, but few are as illustrative of the privatization turn as the city's parks. For more than a century, public parks in cities across the world have been seen as the antidote to urban ills, providing a piece of pastoral relaxation right in the middle of urban chaos. Governments readily encouraged such parks, and the most successful parks in a city provoke sincere resident affection.

Houston, though, has long been on the low end of parks services. A 1912 plan for greenways throughout the city was dismissed, only to be resuscitated *a century* later. Today, the city spends just forty-six dollars per resident on parks, according to the Trust for Public Land.[32] This budget total for 2014 was $66 million, about 2 percent of the city's overall budget. The city has a separate and city-sanctioned Houston Parks

Board composed of social and economic elites that leads much of the public policy of parks in Houston. The city's most popular parks—Memorial Park, Hermann Park, and Discovery Green—are all operated either primarily or solely by a parks conservancy through private donations. These parks show it, too: they are far nicer, and far more patronized, than the average city park. Other city parks relying solely on public funds, by contrast, vary greatly, with the worst exhibiting poor maintenance, broken facilities, and a lack of users.[33] A hallmark of privatization in Market Cities is this type of *inequality in urban services*, with users of signature parks getting a good product, and users in more disadvantaged neighborhoods getting a much worse product.

The future of parks in Houston bears out this relationship even further. As Smiley has written elsewhere, greenways—those long, nonroad bicycling and pedestrian paths—are all the rage in many cities as they become a major plank of the economic development agenda.[34] In Houston, this has meant reviving the 1912 plans for paths along bayous and extending it to create the nation's longest system of greenways at 150 total miles of such paths.

The price tag for the greenways, called the Bayou Greenways 2020, is $215 million. The leadership for this effort came from Houston philanthropists, including through the Houston Parks Board. The ideas behind financing the project came from these groups, including the Kinder Foundation, the philanthropic arm of the city's wealthiest residents, Rich and Nancy Kinder.[35] The plan was this: set up a bond election to get $100 million of the $215 million, and the philanthropists will take care of the rest. The Kinders themselves put forth $50 million if the bond was passed, and promised to raise funds from other philanthropists for the remaining $65 million.

Although the residents were not necessarily setting the agenda—as we would expect in a Market City, the city elites hatched the entire plan—they did vote for it in earnest, with 68 percent of voters supporting the bond, the highest percentage ever in support of a city bond put to a referendum. With the $100 million from city voters plus $50 million from the Kinder Foundation, the final fundraising has commenced. Meanwhile, an entirely separate greenway project on the Buffalo Bayou run by a conservancy organization has created the model for other greenways in the city, partly with its design, but also with its organization and fundraising framework (almost entirely private, including another $30 million from the Kinder Foundation).

In efforts dating back less than a decade, public-minded private sources have amassed nearly $200 million in private funds for greenways, alongside $100 million of public funds. They initiated the idea for the project. They moved the political process along expeditiously and successfully. Government did little, mostly using its energy to clear hurdles for the private players. Parks in Houston, particularly with this greenway system, would not have been as successful had government alone done the work.

This is a paradigmatic case of privatization of public services. Parks are something that we deeply associate with cities. Some of our favorite places in our home cities or those we visit are distinctive parks. City governments typically create and maintain the parks. In Market Cities, though, this is not the full picture. Parks are run sometimes by the city and sometimes by park conservancies, who have more funds. Agenda setting may come from outside city hall, such as from a parks board of local elites and from the largest of foundations. The ideas—and the financial backing—for the future of parks in a Market City come from private players. And it is not just parks but also schools, affordable housing, neighborhood reinvestment, and much more.

As a quick study in contrast, the number of parks in Copenhagen that are run by public-private conservancies is zero. What is more, all of the extensive bicycling boulevards in the city are maintained by public funds. A People City often does not need a private push.

Instead, it's public, public, public. Take, for instance, the initiative to create a network of parks so that nine out of ten residents would be within a fifteen-minute walk of a park. The "15 in '15 plan" meant finding fifteen new pocket parks that could serve thousands of residents to get to the 90 percent mark. The city had to get creative in reaching into the nooks and crannies of the built environment to find new green spaces. In a city whose structures are highly regulated, tearing down buildings is a not a plausible option. Pocket parks sprung up around the city in tiny spaces and odd shapes. The municipal government aggressively pursued citizen input, such as with the Superkilen park in the ethnically diverse Nørrebro neighborhood. When designing that park, the designers took five groups of people to a country that meant something to them, in some cases where they or a parent had emigrated from. Following this path led each group to choose objects that even the most creative designers would not have put together on their own: a sound system from Jamaica, bollards with the Ghanaian flag, a statue of a bull from Spain, a boxing ring from Thailand, and a replicated two-story sign from DeAngelis Donut Shop in Rochester, New York.[36] The private influx of interest in the Superkilen park did not come in the form of money (as in the case of Bayou Greenways 2020 in Houston), but instead came with the care taken in the planning process by contracted designers to create a space that made sense to its residents. This case is an exemplar of the Copenhagen approach to parks, but also to public-private partnerships. Architects and designers are the chief private partners, and they work in tandem with local people to make urban space work. This also limits the role that the private sector plays in the long-range planning of city governance, thereby enumerating a clear contrast with Market Cities.

There are two other knots that need to be untied regarding public-private connections in Market Cities and especially People Cities. You may be wondering: if Copenhagen and People Cities everywhere are so thoughtful when it comes to their fellow residents, wouldn't they give more of their private incomes to charity than residents of Market Cities? Taken from the opposite side, if Houstonians give so much in donations, does it not all wash out in the end? Don't both cities contribute equal amounts, but in different ways? It's an intriguing question, and one we have wrestled with. Services in Copenhagen receives about $300 million in donations from large private foundations, certainly not chump change, but both proportionally and in actual dollar amounts it is not nearly at the same level as what is evidenced in Houston.

The fact is that the residents of a People City do in fact give more charitable donations than those in a Market City. They just call them taxes. If Houstonians pay minimal property taxes and sales taxes and another 3.2 percent in charitable donations (that are not even specific to the city), then they have still only given a fraction of the 24 percent that Copenhageners give of their income to their municipal government in the form of income tax. The wide disparity in per capita spending by government seen in the previous section—Copenhagen paying four times per resident what Houston pays—is still lopsided when you add in the foundational giving of Houstonians. In Houston that means that government and foundational giving totals about $3,500 per resident, while the Copenhagen figure for the same calculation inches up to approximately $13,500. Copenhageners do not give because they do not need to—needs are already covered by the government. Houstonians give because they must—social services and public goods such as parks would be highly inadequate otherwise—but they also keep quite a bit in their own pockets, a popular sentiment among residents.

A related knot arises in that our argument rests with the idea that civil society is weaker in Market Cities, but the above examples suggest that civil society is strong in Market Cities, at least in terms of ambition and proportional responsibility. The mosaic of nongovernmental organization such as nonprofits in People Cities can still be very strong, but the difference is in where the locus of power lies and who is the convener for city policy. In Market Cities, it can often be outside of government, but in People Cities it rarely is. If you want to make a difference to the city's park system, in Houston you link up with philanthropic movers and shakers, and in Copenhagen you head to city hall. Having the power in government does not preclude a range of actors outside of it; it just means that the debate convenes inside, not outside. If anything, so goes the belief in People Cities, a strong government encourages a strong citizenry, one that organizes and pushes government to be the best that it can be. They don't necessarily sit back and watch, but the initiators of change and the power to make it happen occur in government and related fields.

Market Cities have different levels of involvement, both in terms of sheer amount of work and in the uneven allocation of power. Social and economic elites do not always choose to get out of the way. Hailing from the Suite 8F tradition (see chapter 1), they intervene to guide the life of the city, usually nothing dramatic, but steady guidance. They see to it that their specific priorities are enacted. This paternalistic system ensures continuity at the same time that it inhibits civil society activity for other sectors of the population.

Conclusion

It is unclear if John Snow, the epidemiologist-cum-city-government-catalyst, foresaw that cities would heed his lessons to the point of eradicating unhealthful water in thousands of cities, and striving to do so in thousands of others. On the one hand, the battle had already begun changing before his time, but, on the other hand, with the immense amount of death on doorsteps all around the Broad Street Pump, it probably did not feel that way. The city government (not to mention other health practitioners) did not directly acknowledge Snow's propositions. They did turn off the pump—and the epidemic cleared—but actual reform was still two decades away.

Today's major debates about city government no longer occur around the water pump but instead in corporate boardrooms and on urban greenways. The city in this perspective has become visionary, not reactionary. As cities compete more and more for global capital, migrants, and prestige, cities lay out frameworks for the future. Policies are guided by this look toward the horizon. At the same time, cities still must deal with the day-to-day minutiae of mowing the grass in parks, taking out the city's trash, and filling in potholes. There is an irony to examining the future while at the same time government funds and officials are mostly just trying to survive the present. In modern times, both the vision for the future and the reactions to everyday urban life can be found the Market City and People City phenomena.

Few places make the distinction between Market Cities and People Cities more clear than city government. Even answering the question "What is government for, anyway?" provokes dramatically different responses. People Cities play up the role; Market Cities play it down. What services government offers varies from city to city, with Market Cities preferring go-getting economic development agendas and People Cities tasking themselves with new, exciting ways to better the lives of residents. How they pay for it is eye-opening. Market Cities use minimal sales taxes as well as low property taxes to finance a no-frills, basic public services–oriented government that also uses a significant proportion of its budget to entice businesses to its municipality. People Cities bring in massive amounts of private income and produce compelling public outcomes. Governments are not all there is to governance, it turns out. Far more than People Cities, Market Cities lean hard on their private sectors to make public services and infrastructure happen.

3

What Residents Think, Believe, and Act Upon

In the pilot episode of the American television show *Parks and Recreation*, parks department officials are hosting a public meeting to hear concerns about the parks in fictional Pawnee, Indiana. As deputy parks director Leslie Knope puts it, public meetings are where "the rubber of government meets the road of actual human beings." We believe that the fact that the rubber-meets-the-road metaphor doesn't actually work is a pretty good indication that a one-to-one ratio between the viewpoints of city leaders and city residents has never existed—especially not in Pawnee, but also not anywhere.

You have probably attended more than a few public meetings in your day. You know the diversity of the viewpoints of city residents. You've seen the iconoclast rail on an issue—perhaps with merit—that will never see the light of day. You've seen organized groups—traditional ones and those new and fired up about the process—challenge their leaders. You may have yourself held a sign, given a speech, or sworn to never vote for those pesky incumbents again.

We know from these instances, and many more, that residents have a lot to say about their city. They do so at public meetings, around the coffee pot at work, at the dinner table, and most virulently while sitting alone in a traffic jam. They don't just do so about their government, although it's an important part. They similarly do so about their neighborhoods, air, churches, parks, and economy. It includes the conversation of an older couple sitting on a bench in an increasingly neglected park wondering how exactly their park went downhill. It's the insurgent core of parents who seek to take over the local PTA. And it's the awe of the child telling her mother that she can't wait to come back to the professional soccer game.

It's a various and sundry collection of comments and actions about the city that residents undertake. Both situational and cumulative, resident beliefs are crucially important. Sometimes they offer sincerely thought-out arguments about how to make their city better. And other times they are just trying to make sense of the continuity or change they witness every day. Often, it's in the middle. The child at the soccer game, for instance, expresses a simple preference for the joy of sport at the same time that her mother's dollars and vote buttresses tens of millions of dollars of public investment toward creating a citywide sports craze.

One of the core arguments of our book is that what residents of cities think, believe, and act upon matter greatly to whether a city is a Market City or a People City, and to their urban future. Depending on one's perspective, this may be obvious or surprising. Some might argue that the cultural beliefs of residents about their city are not so important compared to those of city government and city leaders—covered in chapter 2—and argue that the power pie has been all but eaten up by the time it gets to everyday residents. There's something to this: leaders and elites have more of the power than everyone else—their privileged position puts them at the pinnacle.

Although the city elite pull the strings of the city, residents are not exactly puppets either. The city elites can do what they do because residents believe many of those same things too. Residents' beliefs are shaped by these elites, and they also emerge from below to inform priorities at the top. Residents push back against elites; they critique them. They produce their own ideas. They reinforce the Market City and People City models primarily and shift, change, and reconceptualize those models.

Therefore, one crucial distinction must be made. While city elites in government and elsewhere are remarkably coherent in their set of priorities for the city, residents are far more heterogeneous. So while we think that residents will follow along the lines of their leaders, they definitely will not do so exclusively. The differences will vary by class, race, ethnic group, age, political affiliation, length of residence, and simply because they do not stand to reap the same rewards that the elites reap. They will differ because individuals, families, and groups in the cities do not encounter the same city milieus as their elite counterparts. They eschew the boardroom or backroom for the call center or retail floor. They may not have been on a yacht, but they can see them from their picnic table on the waterfront. People live in immensely different spaces in cities, and the social fabric of these spaces inculcate different beliefs.

What we'll discuss in this chapter are the building blocks of what residents think about their city, and about society in general. These building blocks are attitudes and actions about three major ways of thinking about social life: (1) work and economy, (2) inequality, and (3) government. Each building block underwrites the Market City and People City. In Market Cities, individualism is the core of the economy, why inequality exists, and why government should be limited. In People Cities, a collective mentality links the building blocks together: inequality can be lessened by strong, government-led work programs alongside a humming economy.

Finally, we discuss how the counter-evidence—how residents do *not* represent the Market City or People City—illustrates important heterogeneity and provides for how social change occurs. The difficulty of ideas outside the market or people mainstream to gain currency also provides a window into why the Market City or People City is hegemonic in a given place. Collective ideals in Market Cities exist, but they have less purchase citywide than individual ideals. The opposite is true in People Cities, where individualist viewpoints do not find the People City to be fertile ground for growing their ranks.

Views on Economy, Work, Inequality, and Government

A quick introduction to how we measure what residents think: we'll be using in this chapter, and throughout the remainder of the book, survey data from each city. More on these data can be found in our methodological appendix. In each year of 2014 and 2015, we conducted directly comparable surveys of Copenhagen and Houston. These surveys asked respondents about all sorts of matters, from the issues in this chapter to environmental attitudes to opinions on traffic to religious views. The Copenhagen Area Survey was representative of the Copenhagen metropolitan area, and the Houston Area Survey represented three counties across much of the metropolitan area, including a high number of city residents and suburbanites. We used different surveys for different questions, and footnoted which data were used for a given statistic. The short version is this: our surveys give us more than five thousand respondents in four separate surveys that are statistically representative of the metropolitan area populations.

In the following analysis, we examine five different questions, all of which relate to how residents in both cities think about work, inequality, and their government. The goal is to better understand the political views and cultural beliefs that underwrite Market Cities and People Cities—and to do so from a perspective that listens to the voices of residents. We first examine each of these questions by looking at differences between the cities, and then compare the illuminating differences across income groups between the two cities. Table 3.1 summarizes the first part of these findings.

First, we asked respondents their opinion about a simple statement: if you work hard in your city, eventually you will succeed. Not many in either city disagreed. In our surveys, 28 percent disagreed in Copenhagen, and only 11 percent in Houston did.[1] The major difference occurred in how *strongly* they agreed with the proposition. Eighteen percent of Copenhageners strongly agreed that if you work hard in Copenhagen, you will succeed. But a majority of Houstonians felt that way about Houston: some 59 percent of residents strongly agreed with that proposition.

A second survey question asks: Why are people poor? Is it mostly, as one option put it, because people don't work hard enough, or, as the other option put it, because of circumstances they can't control? An important caveat here is that the question asked why people are poor in the respondents' respective country, that is, Denmark or the United States. A strong majority of respondents did not take the poor-are-lazy choice. Seventy-nine percent of residents in Copenhagen chose circumstances out of the person's control, and 63 percent in Houston chose this answer as well.[2] (Houston residents were also given the option to say both—5 percent did—or neither, chosen by 2 percent of respondents). This agreement across the cities is interesting in and of itself: there is not as much popular support for the notion that the poor are lazy or ineffectual in either city. Even in the Market City, 63 percent saw that larger structures have something to do with being poor. But a corollary should not escape us: despite widespread agreement that being poor primarily has to do with circumstances out of people's control, there is a difference between the two cities. In Houston, it is about three out of five respondents, and in Copenhagen it's four out of five.

Third, even the basic fact of how many things people believe the government should be doing—regardless of what those things are—differs in our People City and our Market City. Only 37 percent of Copenhagen residents felt that the city government is trying to do too many things, while 55 percent of Houston residents felt this way, even though the Copenhagen city government does far more than does the Houston city government, by design.[3] The opposite survey choice given to respondents was that government should be doing more to fix our problems. This option carried a wide majority in Copenhagen but did not do so in Houston.

Fourth, we asked our respondents about government's role in tackling inequality. Residents of both cities agreed that government must reduce inequalities. Four out of five respondents in Copenhagen believe that government should do so, and a narrower majority (52 percent) of Houston residents agreed.[4] Differences are very apparent among those who strongly disagreed with inequality reduction: 34 percent of Houstonians feel that there's no need for government to be in the business of attenuating inequality, but only 8 percent of Copenhageners disagree so strongly.

Fifth, in Copenhagen, 74 percent of residents believe that you can rely on the public authorities, that is, have a little faith in one's government and their services. In Houston, that number is 56 percent.[5] People City residents see the benefit of an energetic government, and Market City residents are, on the aggregate, more equivocal.

TABLE 3.1. Viewpoints of Copenhagen and Houston Residents (by Percent)

Survey question	Copenhagen	Houston
Agree: work hard, succeed	72	89
Agree: poor because of circumstances beyond control	79	63
Agree: government does too many things	37	55
Agree: government should reduce inequalities	81	52
Agree: rely on public authorities	74	56

Across each of these five questions, we found that Houstonians, compared to Copenhageners, are more likely to think those who work hard will succeed, believe that the poor are poor because they don't work hard enough, and think that government is doing too many things, shouldn't reduce inequalities, and can't be trusted. On each of these questions, Copenhageners had higher rates of what we might consider People City cultural beliefs. A vast majority understands that there are structural constraints on the poor and that government should do something about it—not only this, they believe government can be relied upon to carry out the task. The differences between Copenhagen and Houston are not slight, either: the spread from the cities ranges from 16 percentage points (on the "why poor" measure) to 29 percentage points (on the government reducing inequalities question).

What gets really interesting is investigating how different subgroups of the population think about these issues. Take income. There are differences between the cities, but perhaps poorer residents of the cities have similar viewpoints on issues like inequality, no matter what city they are in. For instance, maybe affluent residents share views on the link between hard work and success. If these examples proved to be the case, it would fracture the idea that there is something about the city that structures residents' views on these topics. It would be more class-based than city-based. There is evidence to support this point. For each of the ten possible statistical tests (five questions in two cities), we find five statistically significant relationships by income, meaning that income levels are associated with one's view for half of the tests.[6]

One intriguing way to break down these questions is to compare the highest income quartile in one city to the lowest income quartile in the other city. Perhaps the highest earners in Copenhagen will have more of a Market City viewpoint than the lowest earners in Houston, who might look more like People City residents when it comes to opinions on inequality, work, and the role of government.

But what we found instead is that the differences across income levels show that the most affluent People City residents appear similar to the least affluent Market City residents—and that the most affluent Market City residents are radically different from the least affluent People City residents. Table 3.2 showcases these findings.

Seventy-seven percent of Copenhageners in the top income quartile agree that working hard will get ahead, but this is ten percentage points lower than the *bottom* income quartile in Houston. Perhaps more surprisingly, the poor and near-poor in Houston and the wealthiest folks in Copenhagen have an almost identical rate (66 percent) of believing that being poor is caused by circumstances you can't control. This high degree of similarity (in the form of a one- or two-percentage-point difference between the top quartile in Copenhagen and the lowest in Houston) is also found for both questions about the role of government. For the faith in public authorities measure, you can flip it. You might think that the highest earners in Houston could trust the government more than the lowest income quartile in Copenhagen. This is not the case: 58 percent of Houstonians in that upper income bracket have faith in their public services, but a much greater rate—71 percent—of Copenhageners in the lowest income bracket have this faith.

One implication of these relationships is that high earners across the cities do not look alike at all, and neither do earners on the lower end. As table 3.2 shows, the differences are wide for almost every question between earners in the same quartile in the cities, with the average difference coming in at about nineteen percentage points. This means that for residents who make about the same amount of money (relative to the rest of residents in the metropolitan area), we would expect the rate of their agreement with each of these five questions to be nineteen percentage points higher or lower, depending on if they are living in Copenhagen or Houston. While income certainly shapes one's views, the city in which one lives also deeply conditions how one thinks about social issues like inequality and government.

The goal of this analysis is to center the idea that the viewpoints of residents matter. These views can go a long way to understanding how they underwrite social action in their city. This matrix of viewpoints, together with the actions of elites and ongoing institutional processes, justifies the Market City and the People City. It provides the cultural beliefs that guide the types of actions residents might take, or even the cognitions that they might consider about their city. While there are dominant belief systems at work in the cities, the next section shows that there is critical variation too.

TABLE 3.2. Viewpoints of Copenhagen and Houston Residents by Income

Survey Question	Copenhagen		Houston	
	Bottom quartile (%)	Top quartile (%)	Bottom quartile (%)	Top quartile (%)
Agree: Work hard, succeed	70	77	87	92
Agree: Poor because of circumstances can't control	84	67	66	60
Agree: Government does too many things	27	47	46	67
Agree: Government should reduce inequalities	89	70	68	40
Agree: Rely on public authorities	71	82	52	58

Resistance

Residents never agree cleanly and clearly with their leaders. For every measure in our surveys above, there are a substantial number of respondents who simply disagree with their fellow residents.

The reason this occurs is, broadly, because social life is messy. And, more specifically, because cities are heterogeneous. The vast range of people and spaces in a city is partly what makes cities cities.[7] It is where we all come together in an untidy confluence of ideas and experiences. This untidiness is what draws urbanists, including us, to cities. It is seeing what happens when all of social life takes place in these relatively compact spaces.

A key argument in this book is that residents' cultural beliefs play an important role in buttressing the Market City and People City. But there's still this question of heterogeneity. So far, our framework accounts for variation between cities (that's the Market City and People City distinction), but it has not accounted for the variation within cities.

Cities are contested.[8] In Market Cities, advocates for a more egalitarian city push for better social services from the city. They seek to create more useful and meaningful public spaces. They question inequality. In People Cities, many argue for economic engines to be the primary catalyst of community change. They seek to open up the markets to such change, and to get the government out of conditioning behavior in transportation, public space, and all over the city. In both types of cities, this advocating occurs opposite the dominant ideology of the market or the people.

These beliefs are not as effective as those in the mainstream of the Market City or People City. Their effectiveness depends on a number of factors. The chief factor is how close the agenda being advocated for is to the mainstream. This will affect a number of other secondary factors, such as coalition building, resource mobilization, and ability to strike at moments of prime leverage.

To understand the effectiveness as linked to the people or market mainstream, think of the city's policies and residents' cultural beliefs as constituting a solar system. The sun represents the people or market ideologies, policies, urban form, and history. It exerts a powerful gravitational pull. Planets of other types of belief agendas are grabbed by the gravitational pull of that sun and made a part of the solar system. Belief systems that have more affinities with the market or people themes can be thought of as more closely pulled in by the sun; these are the planets closest to the sun. Other ideological and political agendas that do not have so many affinities with the dominant core of the city are less pulled in by the gravity of the sun; these are the planets furthest away from the sun.

Those closer to the sun have more political possibility because they can speak the language of the Market City or People City. But, by being closer to the sun, they are blinded by the dominant ideology such that changes proposed are more moderate than radical in orientation. They may change the market or people status of the city, but it's more of a shift than a revolt.

Those further away from the sun have less political possibility because they are further outside of the city mainstream. At the same time, their proposals carry the greatest potential for social change. They can work more creatively to rethink what their city should stand for. They will have a good deal more trouble enacting any sort of social change than their more moderate planets closer to the market or people sun, but, when they succeed, they offer profound critiques to the Market City or People City.

Notice the phrase "social change." Our model of cities would seemingly have you believe that Market Cities and People Cities always have been Market Cities and People Cities. Not true. Cities are the products of continuing contestations. As we saw in chapter 1, several lifetimes of contestations have gone into structuring Houston and Copenhagen into the Market City and People City of today. These contestations are, of course, ongoing. There is consistent churning in the urban system, and those sitting outside of the people and market mainstream are trying to change their city. They seek to create serious social change. The difficulty of their task is due to them not being the sun, and it's difficult for a new solar system to rise and take hold.

But the difficulty stops them not. This portion of the chapter looks at four different urban tales of transformation. We tackle four so we can examine two contestations in each type of city, and we chose two different examples within each type of city to sketch what contestations look like that are closer to the sun, and ones that are further away. We focus on what heterogeneity looks like by analyzing social change on those planets closer to the sun for both the Market City and People City using examples outside of Houston and Copenhagen. And then we step back and examine what it looks like for those further out in Houston and Copenhagen by seeing what those planets on the outer ring of the solar system are doing.

Closer-In Planets

Our first tale examines urban transformation in Memphis with an unexpected type of infrastructure: bicycling. Memphis is known for its barbecue, or for being the home of FedEx and Elvis. It is certainly not known for bicycling. It's hot, humid, and sprawling—not necessarily any fun for those who bike such cities. As recently as 2008, the city had *zero* miles of dedicated bicycling infrastructure: no bicycle lanes or greenways. There were only a few signs telling car drivers to be friendly on the road to the two-wheeled crowd.

By 2015, there were more than one hundred miles of bicycling lanes and greenways.[9] The city was certified as the most improved bicycle city in the country by *Bicycling Magazine* in 2012, and drew favorable coverage in outlets like the *New York Times* and the *Atlantic's CityLab*.[10] Grants were flowing in by the millions for bicyclists and pedestrians. A city councilman who was initially opposed the creation of a popular greenway rated that project a "twelve" on a scale of one to ten, and now goes for rides with his family.[11]

The question begs: so how did that happen in Memphis?

We often associate bicycling with People Cities. This is not a clean supposition, however. Bicycling can be associated with People Cities insofar as it is about building out methods of transportation that help the environment, promote quality public spaces with eyes on the street, and aid in an urban region's public health.

But that's not the only reason to take up bicycling. We identify Memphis as a Market City. It has all the characteristics. A major function of government is luring corporations to the city. Local government and business spends serious dollars on attracting tourists rather than building infrastructure for its own people. The city is sprawling. Inequality, especially along racial lines, is high. Schools are segregated.

Bicycling fits the market model in Memphis because primary reasons for advancing bicycling in the city concern attracting creative class entrepreneurs and tourists, in other words, market arguments. As Smiley showed in a coauthored article, the arguments proffered by bicycling advocates primarily hit on these themes.[12] It fits with a wider notion of urban change unveiled by urban sociologist Terry Clark and others who talk of the new "citizen-consumers" who power an urban model of economic growth based on an "entertainment machine."[13] Connecting this framework to Memphis and our work here, urban amenities such as bicycling lanes and greenways are not People City attributes primarily geared toward improving life for residents but, rather, efforts aimed at generating economic prowess. The bicycling infrastructure will do so by improving quality-of-life attributes; however, that is not the be-all, end-all goal. Instead, it is improving the local economy to attract corporations and workers. But it is not a strictly economic line of argumentation, which is what separates some of the bicycling advocates from the dominant ideologies of the Market City. Changes to bicycling prompted smaller shifts in the city of Memphis, but shifts nonetheless. The change makers partly had more power to do so by orienting arguments more closely to the Market City ideology of the city.

Change from closer-in planets in People Cities invokes market mechanisms. Because there are more Market Cities in the postindustrial world and, relatedly, there has been a long arc toward neoliberal policies in recent decades, People Cities are under particular pressure from initiatives that are driven to fracture the People City consensus.

In the People City of Helsinki, public education has long been a bastion of egalitarian ideals. Not just in theory, either: as data from the Program for International Student Assessment (PISA) through the Organisation for Economic Co-operation and Development (OECD) indicates, not only do Finnish children excel compared to their counterparts around the world, the gaps between the highest achieving and lowest achieving children are relatively narrow. These outcomes are directly in line with the egalitarian ideals widely held by Helsinki residents.[14]

Research from scholars at the University of Helsinki demonstrates that the vaunted equality in the Finnish educational system has come under criticism in Helsinki.[15] The mechanism of the critiques was a series of changes to school choice laws in the 1990s, which introduced neoliberal reforms that allowed parents to choose different schools other than their local neighborhood school. Most often, privileged parents take advantage of these opportunities. In the time since these changes were instituted, Helsinki experienced another striking trend: the city went from having very few immigrants to now having about one in five residents who are foreign-born.

These trends intersect to produce measurable increases in inequality in educational outcomes in Helsinki. As the authors demonstrate, school choice played a pivotal role in the new enactment of inequality. With residential segregation also on the rise, some parents, especially ethnic Finns and economically privileged parents, are opting to send their children to better schools elsewhere in the city.[16] This means that the quality of schools is increasingly uneven, which thereby leads to more inequality across students and social groups in the city. For instance, the PISA data for 2015 estimates that immigrants in Finland do not perform as well as the OECD average of immigrants in other countries.[17]

The pragmatic results of school choice laws in Helsinki meant that individualistic opportunities fomented structural change in the social system. Instead of the sole goal of providing a quality education to all, school choice in Helsinki offered some parents the possibility to provide a quality education by switching their student to a more successful school. Success according to market models often relies on the individual, and school choice offers individuals the opportunity to seize the best that the educational system can offer them. In this case, it also engenders inequalities. While this might be normal in a Market City, it instead fractures a People City ethos that encourages egalitarian education. At the same time, it is not a radical reform that might come from a farther-out planet: the importance of public education remains largely unquestioned, and it has not invoked charter-style schools, which might have cropped up had these initiatives come in a Market City.

Helsinki is not alone in dealing with these tensions. Similar trends are found in Copenhagen, with parents in neighborhoods in Denmark seeing a large proportion of immigrants opting for schools outside of their neighborhoods at higher rates than families living in relatively homogeneous neighborhoods.[18] With new data uncovering the changes in People City Helsinki, what local government officials as well as families across the city decide to do in the coming years will closely determine if the People City provisions for education are recalibrated or further eroded.

Farther-Out Planets

"We can't all be students or unemployed or retired. We need people who will get up and go to work and pay their taxes."[19] So decries Lars Berg Dueholm, the candidate of the Liberal Alliance Party for mayor in Copenhagen in 2013. His party went on to a poor showing in the election, and he was one of but two Liberal Alliance members in the fifty-five-member municipal council. Dueholm himself left the party and his council post by 2016, leaving just one Liberal Alliance office-holder on the Copenhagen City Council in 2017.

The Liberal Alliance is an example of a group far outside the mainstream of People City Copenhagen. The party shares "socially liberal" sentiments with many others across the Danish political spectrum, but the similarities end there. The Liberal Alliance is the only major Danish political party to consistently call for cutting taxes. They call for a flat income tax, a regressive tax policy unseen in People Cities. It is worth mentioning, though, that the fairly large tax cut toward a flat tax would lower the overall tax rate to 40 percent. They support nuclear power, the only Danish party to do so. It is considered a smaller political party in the nation as a whole, but it is not a party to be dismissed either: they are among the eight or so main parties that have currency in the country, with most of that support coming from elsewhere in Denmark, rather than in Copenhagen.[20]

But first and foremost comes the idea of strengthening the private sector, and cutting the public sector. In the preview to the 2015 Danish general elections, a video with their election platform begins by proclaiming the need for fewer employees in the public sector and many more in the private sector.[21] City vitality comes from opening the doors for business—and getting government to take a lesser role. The party was (until 2015) actually the youngest on the Danish political scene, having begun in 2007; this is partly to blame for their lack of success. But their goal after crushing early losses was to reposition their focus primarily on liberalizing the economy as much as possible, playing down the public sector and installing libertarian ideas as policy whenever possible.

The Liberal Alliance has not been successful in the People City. In elections in 2011 and 2015, the party finished seventh and sixth, respectively, among voters in the municipality in Copenhagen.[22] They finished eighth in the elections for European Parliament in 2009 and 2014. For local elections in 2009 and 2013, they also finished eighth. They poll poorly in Copenhagen but fare a little better outside of it. These are not exactly impressive figures. Remember: there are really only eight main political parties.

On the policy front, none championed by the Liberal Alliance have made it into law. Nationally, they have some say in the anti-immigrant debate, where they team up with other right-leaning parties in decrying how many refugees and immigrants the country is taking in. But in the city of Copenhagen specifically, the Liberal Alliance sits outside of the center of debates in the city council chambers, and well outside the offices of the mayors—as remote as the now debunked planet Pluto.

The People City denizens with Market City principles must feel lonely. They must wait for a key moment of leverage: perhaps parties on both sides of the political spectrum become ineffectual or are exposed to a corruption crisis. The inability to break through primarily concerns the distance between their vision and the People City way of life. The ways in which residents view place-based characteristics condition the realm of the possible. What might become true is not limitless. For the Liberal Alliance, they sit outside those city limits.

In Houston, we turn to the history of local education to examine what more radical movements offer in understanding social change in the Market City. Public schooling is, in a way, one of America's (and perhaps the world's) great socialist experiments. Launched on a broad scale in a progressive age of the late nineteenth and early twentieth century, the core ideal behind schools is inherently a distributional one: every child deserves the right to a quality education.

As far as experiments go, this one has without question experienced more than a little trial and error. Houston is a clear example. Undermined from the beginning by racially segregated and unequal institutions of learning, stakeholders from diverse ranges of perspectives wrestled with desegregation in the mid- to late twentieth century. Changes and challenges remain afoot. In a Market City, the complex forces behind home values, schools, municipal boundaries, racial discrimination, and class disparities amalgamate in ways that often confound effective and equal public schooling.

Therefore, for the analysis of a "farther-out" planet in a Market City, we investigate a famous movement for school equality by Houston Hispanics in the early 1970s, and pair it with a discussion of public education and spatial inequality in Houston today. In doing so, we highlight how more radical movements push deeply against the grain of the Market City and yet how distinctions and disparities all too easily remain.

In his book *Brown, Not White*, historian Guadalupe San Miguel Jr. documents the rise of the Chicano movement in Houston and how it was catalyzed during school desegregation efforts there.[23] Until 1970, little movement had been made to desegregate the Houston public school system. A court order in that year required that Houston must desegregate its schools, and so a plan was put forward to do so.

Although the plan proposed the desegregation of black schools, it did so by integrating these schools with primarily Mexican American pupils. The function of this was not latent: it was a deliberate attempt to maintain segregation for white schools. The way in which this could work was because Mexican American students were defined as white by school officials. For decades, Mexican American groups in Houston (and often nationally) had lobbied to be considered white rather than a distinct racial category.[24] The desegregation plan provoked opposition in the Mexican American and black communities in Houston. Black leaders, such as the head of the local NAACP, saw it as a continuation of separate and unequal, and therefore not the full measure of school desegregation that the previous law and court decisions required. Mexican Americans similarly saw the outrage over the apparent inequality in school desegregation. With their schools also segregated primarily not by law but by residential segregation, Houston's desegregation plans hardly provided an antidote to school inequalities.

Young and working-class Mexican American persons activated interest in the cause, and a number of organizations flew into action to promote real school desegregation. The most influential of these concerned a boycott of schools. Keeping children out of their regularly scheduled classes was an absolute and major shock to the Houston system. In place of school, boycotting teachers taught their own classes at quickly assembled *huelga* (or "strike") schools, and everyday citizens pitched in with everything from childcare to transportation to preparing lunches. Boycotts, at times lasting weeks, took place across 1970 and 1971. While continuously reticent and seemingly intractable, school officials eventually budged, partly because of court decisions that recognized Mexican Americans as a distinct ethnic group. This paved the way for the formal desegregation of the Houston independent school district. Unlike the example of the Liberal Alliance in Copenhagen, this farther-out planet had real resonance, and because its ideals were further away, it was able to exact a more serious blow to the unequal education system at that time.

These efforts, however, come up against both overt discrimination and the machinations of the Market City. The first—overt discrimination—we have already documented: the segregated system, desegregated plans, and more. In the absence of these legal mechanisms, Market Cities are particularly susceptible to "laissez-faire racism" that often operates with "color-blind" viewpoints.[25] These themes operate in and through cities to systematically disadvantage people of color even though the mechanisms themselves may not overtly smack of racial discrimination.

In the case of schools and Houston, segregation remains alive and well thanks to these mechanisms. In ways that go beyond a full telling here, a constellation of factors contribute to school inequality. Private schools arose especially at the time of desegregation and are primarily composed of children from affluent families. Suburbanization meant the creation of separate school districts that could keep property taxes at home for local schools, and create the decentralized, hyperlocalized governance patchwork that we see with municipalities as well as school districts. More recently, charter schools perfect the Market City fix by invoking the private sector as the foundation and model for public education. At the same time, many continue to contest the inequalities in public education.

The end result is deep economic segregation, and a complex web of racial desegregation and segregation. School districts like Houston's and suburban ones like Aldine, Galena Park, and Alief serve populations where more than 30 percent of students come from families in poverty. Districts in Humble, Katy, and Pearland all have childhood poverty rates of less than 10 percent, a rate but a third of the other districts.[26] This racial segregation shows that the plan's original goal to keep whites separate from schools with students of color in the Houston school district was perhaps realized, albeit through different mechanisms. In the end, there are few white students left in the massive Houston school district to integrate: just 8 percent of students in the Houston district are white. Segregation, then, is not so much within the district, but across districts: some districts have almost no white students, while others do in comparably diverse districts.

When it comes to fighting for dramatic, large-scale change, the story of school segregation in Houston shows that such a change in a Market City or a People City is often best achieved by groups who are dedicated to the most radical change. It also means that their change is often of a fledgling nature and can be toppled by the dominant norms and resources marshalled to preserve the status quo. In the case of Mexican American civic organizations in the early 1970s, operating well outside the confining norms of public education in the city, helped to upend an entire system of legal school segregation. It is impressive, inspiring, and lasting change. Market City mechanisms through intensive suburbanization and economic segregation (among others) ensured that school inequality would remain in spite of such efforts, and that some students would have access to a higher quality education than others.

Conclusion

This chapter foregrounds how residents—not just elites, but folks representative of the whole population of a city—are a part of the Market City and People City dynamic. We highlighted four critical areas that undergird the city type: work and economy, inequality, government, and resistance. In and through all four, we sought to discover how Market Cities and People Cities condition their residents and how their residents shape them.

A few important points emerge from this chapter's findings. First, the beliefs of the wide swath of Copenhageners or Houstonians often match what we would expect in a Market City and a People City. Market City residents expect greater levels of inequality in their city, and People City residents do not. They also have less faith in their government compared to the Copenhagen counterparts. Not only would we expect government policies (see chapter 2) or urban institutions (see the second part of the book) to be different in Market Cities and People Cities, we similarly see that residents also differ in what they believe.

Second, and in part a contradiction to the first point, they do not always strictly match what you would expect to find in a Market City and a People City. Simply put, 100 percent of our respondents do not line up on the exact same side on issues of work, inequality, or government. Rather, there is disagreement, or what some would probably refer to most closely as "humanity." Cities are places of diversity, including of views on their own city. We aver that elites are more likely to be homogeneous in their expectations and beliefs compared to residents who are a much more heterogeneous lot.

Third, it is not just that the views of respondents in surveys do not always align with the Market City and People City thematic frames, but that instead the misalignment is generative. It creates contestation, resistance—constantly and consistently shifting the ethos that undergirds a Market City or People City. Examining the orbits of different organizations and initiatives in Market Cities and People Cities reveals a critical paradox. The closer the idea is to the existing ethos of the city (i.e., for markets or for people), the more likely it is to be successful, but also the more likely it is to not be overwhelming change because of the intense gravitational pull of the market or people culture. By contrast, if the idea is further away from the guiding principles of the city, then the likelihood for success will be attenuated at the same time the successes will be greater in their ability to puncture long-held norms.

This chapter's wider goal is to explore the simple idea that residents matter in how they support and contest their cities. Keeping residents alongside government and elites is integral to the analysis that follows. In this second part of the book, we analyze broad urban institutions—from land use to the environment to diversity—from an array of perspectives to detail a narrative of how these institutions vary greatly between Market Cities and People Cities. And residents are essential to these differences.

PART II

Why It Matters

4

Getting There, Being There

Transportation and Land Use

Transportation and land use provide some of the most illustrative differences in Market Cities and People Cities. One of Emerson's personal comparisons can illustrate the point. In his year in the Market City of Houston—celebrated for its low cost of living—before moving to Copenhagen, he and his family spent $17,200 on car expenses. This was the sum total of owning two cars (and making payments on one of them), paying insurance costs for the two cars and four drivers, gas, oil, tags, license plate fees, tolls, repair costs, and miscellaneous costs—parking fees (a monthly deduction from his paycheck for the right to search for a parking space on the campus where he worked), wipers, replacing a broken windshield, and two broken lights.

He and his family then moved to People City Copenhagen. His family's total transportation cost was $1,800 for the year, which included monthly train passes and a few bicycle expenses. Suddenly, they had $15,400 at their disposal, more than covering the extra money paid for food and shopping. (And, as an aside, it goes further: they had no health insurance costs, providing an additional $800 per month, and because they had a child under 18 living with them, the City of Copenhagen actually deposited money into their bank account, as the city's contribution to supporting the raising of their child, even though the child was an American citizen).

And that's just the differences in transportation costs. We have not yet mentioned distinctions in time, neighborhood form, suburban sprawl, and mixed-use development versus development for single-family homes, zoning, or rent control. Investigating these will be our journey in this chapter.

In chapter 4, two simple questions motivate us. The first—How do you get there?—focuses on transportation. We will detail how Market

Cities foreground cars and People Cities prioritize alternative forms of transportation. This means making a shrine to cars in Houston—in the form of a few hundred miles of twelve-lane highway. In Copenhagen, it means an aggressive approach that favors bicycles and public transportation but, perhaps more than anything and more importantly, is anti-car.

The second—What do you do once you go there?—fills in the important blanks between our transportation corridors. As Helle Søholt, founding partner of Gehl Architects, noted in our interview with her, "Who chooses a city because you can get around quickly in it? Rather, we want mobility for the sake of getting places." These urban spaces are where everyday life occurs, but in Market Cities and People Cities those lives are lived differently. We show how two important parts of "there" are housing and urban scale. Owning dominates in Houston, and housing is cheaper. Renting dominates in Copenhagen, and is kept somewhat affordable through a complex, but mostly effective governmental system. We show how the cumulative effect of transportation and housing leads to different visions of urban scale that fundamentally affect how residents experience their cities.

How Do You Get There? Transportation

In the introduction to this book, we took you on two journeys to show how government is found throughout the urban landscape. You may very well have noticed an immediate difference in those journeys: the mode of transportation. In Houston, we motored in a car; in Copenhagen, we zoomed on a bike.

The difference is deeply pragmatic, and also representative of each city. It is simply easier to get by in a car in Houston and on a bike in Copenhagen. This is not our own supposition but rather that of residents. A vast majority of Houstonians agree—nearly 90 percent take a motor vehicle to work—and a plurality of Copenhageners bike—about 49 percent of commuters, according to our surveys, take the bicycle to work. In this section, we detail three types of transportation to show how a Market City and a People City take radically different approaches to transportation. We discuss cars, bikes and two feet, and public transportation

But we first start with statistics from the census bureaus in each country that provide an indication of the magnitude of commuting differences. Time spent on these journeys is important because it is the least favorite part of a person's day, according to surveys.[1] In the city of Copenhagen, the average commute distance to work is 7.7 miles.[2] All but two municipalities in Greater Copenhagen have average commute distances under 10 miles (the longest, from the southern town of Dragør, is 10.4 miles).

The distances are longer in Houston. The commute distance for Houston city residents is double that of Copenhagen residents, at 18.8 miles.[3] It climbs to more than 20 miles in suburban cities like Sugar Land and averages 20.5 miles for the overall metropolitan area. The mean distance traveled for a Houston commute is almost always at least twice as long as the average commute distance in Copenhagen.

To put this into perspective, it is integral to recall that these figures are for one-way journeys—the journey *to or from* work, not *both*. Taking this into account means that the average resident of the Houston municipality travels approximately 22.2 miles more per day than the average Copenhagen resident. In a year, this extra travel distance is approximately equal to the same distance if you traveled between Washington, D.C., and Los Angeles *and back*.[4] Because Market Cities are sprawling and People Cities are dense, commutes provoke a major contrast.

Four Wheels

The history of the interstate highway system in the United States typically begins in 1956, when President Dwight D. Eisenhower signed the Federal-Aid Highway Act. It created a system of roadways connecting America's far-flung cities to one another with wide roads that provided for easy exits and fluid travel. Before this time, road standards varied by state or city, maintenance was often poor, and car journeys were long affairs. The interstate improved each of these points, and together with projects like it across the globe, fundamentally changed transportation both between and within cities.

The interstate's history, though, has an important forebearer in Houston. The first limited-access highway built in the United States was the Gulf Freeway, begun in 1945 and completed by 1952. The highway, still in existence today as Interstate 45, links seaside Galveston to downtown Houston fifty miles inland. The highway was immediately and immensely popular, and was heavily used even prior to its full opening. Houstonians jumped at the ability to take a quick cruise to the beach, or even just to cruise at high speeds for the sake of cruising. Whatever the reason, the initiation of the Gulf Freeway was perhaps metro Houston's most important infrastructure project in the first decade after World War II.[5]

The main reason for the importance of the Gulf Freeway is that it provided an object lesson for how to quickly move people across expansive distances. The limited-access freeway model—think on- and off-ramps and no stoplights—revolutionized intra-urban transportation. Remembering that the Houston area's population would increase from a little less than one million residents in 1950 to 6.6 million in 2015, the development of the freeway and the booming population growth trend proved to be two intertwined trends. The millions of new residents in the post–World War II era would need somewhere to live, and, throughout the world and especially in Market Cities, people flocked to suburbs for big abodes, green lawns, and an escape from an urban life perceived to be unsafe.

In these ways, Houston embraced the car. At present, two ring roads circumnavigate the city, with a third mostly completed, and a fourth proposed. Twelve-lane highways serve as aortic valves that pump residents from outer suburbs to the heart of downtown and vice versa. In the era of the highway, a city sixty miles across in any direction is not only possible but also an indicator of a large Market City.

If the history of Houston shows decades of car-centric growth, and if residents indicate that that growth must be managed more closely, then we should not be surprised to see the future of the physical plant of Houston reach further and further out.

Cue Conroe. This once sleepy suburb is forty miles (sixty-four kilometers) north of Houston. Not only is there the sheer problem of distance, there's the trouble of the ultra-busy I-45 corridor—the Gulf Freeway's continuation north to Dallas—or the need to pay tolls to downtown or elsewhere along the Hardy toll road. And yet the town is booming. The population of Conroe in 1970 was 11,969. The population more than doubled by 1990, and doubled again by 2010.

A mark of a Market City may be the paradox of creating distance to diminish distance. Let us explain what we mean, taking Conroe as the example. We might expect that Conroe residents spend more time commuting than residents more centrally located in the metropolitan area. This is the age-old story of commuter suburbs that sends affluent workers to the central city. If Conroe fits the profile in some ways (such as rapid population growth, exurban location, and lots of single-family homes), it does not in terms of commuting. The median commute time to work for Conroe residents is twenty-six minutes and thirty-six seconds, only half a minute longer than Houston residents, and a full minute quicker than the median for Harris County (which contains Houston) residents.[6]

Conroe, together with the nearby powerhouse suburb of The Woodlands, composes what Joel Garreau calls "edge cities." Edge cities are suburban and exurban places that once served as commuter suburbs with little economic relevance but, as suburbs have grown in population and economically, have become employment centers all their own. In Garreau's work, he identifies many edge cities in Houston, including these northern outposts. In these suburbs, Conroe and The Woodlands are experiencing population growth, increasing affluence, and they host the headquarters of major corporations such as Chevron Phillips, Andarko Petroleum, and the Huntsman Corporation.

We would expect Market Cities to encourage many and prosperous edge cities within the wider metropolitan area. Underwritten by developer dollars spurring far-out construction, the centrality of choice of individuals in the housing market sends families and workers who can afford better schools, safer environments, and larger homes—all in a place with a growing number of good jobs.

Together with these factors, we must add the car. Even if Market Cities lean heavily on cars for transportation, too far away is sometimes just too far away. This is why we don't see any discernible differences in commute time between residents of Conroe commuting to work and residents of central city locations commuting to work—they simply work in different places. Across the last part of the twentieth century and into the twenty-first, the metropolitan areas of Market Cities matured in such a way as to develop edge cities that complement the existing niceties of housing development with economic and consumer opportunities to match. This is emblematic of the decentralized metropolis of the Market City: constellations of edge cities surrounding a distant central city—paved with asphalt by a transportation system fueled with gasoline.

Two Wheels and Two Feet

Copenhagen flirted with the car too, but the romance didn't last. Among the many stories of the early transitions to People City urban development—Jan Gehl's "temporary" pedestrianization of Strøget, the slow, steady rise of bicycling usage across five decades—one of the most fascinating concerns the area known as "søerne," or "the lakes."

Like a surprising number of beautiful places in Copenhagen, the lakes began as a medieval military fortification. It was a sixteenth-century moat that protected the city. The lakes are a little less than two hundred meters across and are a few meters deep. They curve three kilometers across the northwestern edge of the city center. As noted in chapter 1, the city did not develop outside of the lakes until the back half of the nineteenth century, but when outward development began in earnest in the 1950s and 1960s, the almost four-hundred-year-old lakes nearly met their demise.

The potential assailant was a modern urban development of the sort that was sweeping much of the West, the same trend that gave Houston the Gulf Freeway. The plan was to install a twelve-lane highway that would serve as an inner ring road in the city.[7] The lakes were convenient because, unlike other parts of the corridor, which called for massive demolitions as part of the urban renewal scheme, they wouldn't have to demolish so many properties. After the installation of the first segment of a highway in the city in the 1960s, the northern Bispeengbuen expressway, city residents grew wary, tax coffers were shaky, and the 1973 oil crisis combined to permanently shelve the project.

Today, the lakes stand as one of Copenhagen's most popular public spaces. Running trails line the perimeter of each of the three lakes, where the most ardent exercise enthusiasts share the paths with those wandering on a lazy stroll. It's great for those late evening Copenhagen sunsets in the summer. The middle bridge across them ranks as part of Europe's busiest cycling street.[8] And it almost did not exist.

Instead of these highways, urban planners in Copenhagen have made serious inroads by promoting bikes. New nonmotor vehicle pathways have "occurred" steadily since the 1960s, and examples are everywhere from the large and systematic to the small and particular. Two new bike-only bridges now cross Copenhagen's harbor. Stoplights have been engineered to link up for bicyclists, and to go green at some places a little bit early so as to give cyclists an advantage. Tricky maneuvering around bus stops where transit riders walk off the bus and into the bike lane have been solved across much of the city with reengineered stops that are safer for transit riders and cyclists alike. Perhaps most importantly, many of the bicycle lanes on primary roads are protected or dedicated bicycle lanes: the lane itself is raised a few inches from the rest of the road or there is a barrier between the lane and car traffic. Even minute details matter, such as the metal foot rests one can find at busy traffic stops that allow one to easily place one's right foot onto the rest instead of to the ground—a saving grace for cyclists tired of dangling their feet to touch the ground.

Although this section is about bicycling (and walking too), an important clarification is in order. While Market Cities emphasize cars, People Cities emphasize alternatives to cars. There are many ways in which to emphasize alternatives to cars. These include bicycling, walking, and mass transit, in addition to a general attention to a denser urban design that makes those modes of transportation possible. A city with high rates of mass transportation and low use of bicycling and a different city with low rates of mass transportation and high use of bicycling would both be People Cities, at least in terms of transportation.

Additionally, notice the importance of *rates of use*. All sorts of cities these days are emphasizing bicycling and walkability. They build glorious pedestrian bridges, gorgeous greenways, and mixed-use developments. Houston is one of these cities, as we saw in chapter 2 with the example of the Bayou Greenways 2020 plan. But these changes must be cumulative and lasting. As Smiley has written about the city of Memphis, Tennessee (and as discussed in chapter 3), huge changes have come to that city's bicycling infrastructure, but the most recent census estimates for commuting-to-work rates for bicycling remain stuck at a pedestrian (or, more technically, *less* than pedestrian) rate of 0.3 percent.[9]

It is not enough to invest in the transportation; it has to fundamentally change human behavior. This contrasts, for instance, with Richard Florida's ideas about the need for alternative forms of transportation as essential to being a creative city.[10] The core point of such transportation in creative cities is to spur economic innovation, and cities that pick up on the creative ethos more than the people ethos tend to have highly

symbolic efforts that create one or a few brilliant nodes of activity—
think a pedestrian bridge or a few greenways—but such efforts in Market Cities are less about growing rates of bike users, lessening the carbon
footprint from cars, or achieving greater gender equity in bike usage.
This distinction goes back to the priorities rubric of these two city types.
Market Cities start with the project—a bike path for example—whereas
People Cities start with the people—what can we do to encourage more
bike ridership?

Copenhagen is a city with a serious commitment to alternative transportation. It fits both criteria: it has a cumulative effect, and it has lasted
for decades. The rates of transportation showcase this profile. We asked
Copenhagen workers in both surveys which methods of transportation
they use to get to work. Respondents were allowed to choose more than
one option, so long as they took it often (for example, it is common to
ride one's bike to the train station and then take the train). No transportation mode was used by a majority of respondents, but bicycling came
close: 49 percent of respondents biked to work.[11] The second most frequent choice was driving, at 39 percent of respondents (and nine out of
ten of these respondents drove alone). Public transportation was utilized
by 29 percent of Copenhagen workers, and 10 percent walk. Together,
this means that 61 percent of respondents never drove and, when taking into account that respondents could select multiple choices, that 75
percent took some form of non-car transportation often (even if they at
times used a car too).[12] If you are in a city like Copenhagen where three
out of four residents use transportation options outside of the car, you
may be in a People City. In Houston, by contrast, U.S. Census data indicates that in 2015 only about 9 percent of residents used transportation
options outside of a car.[13] The sheer rate of usage is one of the principal
supports upon which the transportation system is built in a Market City
or a People City.

A few more statistics on biking make the point. In the 2015 edition of
our surveys, we ask respondents three straightforward questions about
biking. These questions asked if respondents owned a bicycle, had ridden
it in the last 30 days, and if the respondent wished they could ride their
bike more often in the region. Each question was dichotomous—yes or no.

Not surprisingly, Copenhageners were much more likely to own a
bike than Houstonians: 88 percent owned one in Copenhagen, twice as

likely as in Houston.[14] The difference is even more gaping when it comes to having biked in the last thirty days. Two out of three residents in Copenhagen had, but just 9 percent in Houston had biked at least once in the last month.[15] Finally, even though Copenhageners have plenty of opportunities to bike already, they still have higher rates of wanting to be able to bike more in their city. A slim majority of Copenhagen residents (52 percent) wish they could bike more, and, considering how few own bikes or have biked recently, a minority of Houstonians wish they could bike more (44 percent). These additional statistics about bicycling in the cities reinforce the overall findings in this section: Houstonians love cars, and Copenhageners often take their bikes whither and thither.

Wheels on the Bus

One way to measure a successful public transportation system[16] is to see if everyone uses it. This means not only looking at a snapshot (i.e., the rate of usage) but also seeing if different populations—men and women, different racial groups, the well-off and the working class—use it at the same levels too.

We asked respondents if they had taken a ride on public transportation. Those who did so regularly (once a week or more) were coded in one category, those who rode once a month in another, and a final category consisted of respondents who did not ride public transit at all.

Our findings reveal deep differences between the cities, and within the cities. Between the cities, we see that Copenhageners are much more likely to ride transit than Houstonians. Forty-five percent of Copenhageners use transit at least once a week, and another 49 percent use it once a month.[17] Public transit use is nearly universal in Copenhagen: more than nine in ten respondents took it at least once a month.

Houston is almost exactly the opposite. Seventy-three percent never take public transit. Only 7 percent take it at least once a week, about the same number who *never* use public transit in Copenhagen. A bit more (20 percent) use the system a few times a year.

Within the cities, an interesting factor to focus on is socioeconomic status (or SES). Sociologists often conceptualize this through education: more education translates to higher SES. Income matters here too: the most traditional marker of class is one's income. Many upper or even middle-class urban residents do not use mass transit because they can afford cars, especially in cities without strong and multimodal transit systems. The primary reason is that transit is perceived by some as the least desirable mode of transportation: it is (often unfairly) stigmatized as dirty, difficult to navigate, less than convenient, and time-consuming. If you have another option (particularly a car), you take that option instead.

This leads to the following question: do residents of different incomes and different education levels use public transportation at different rates? For income, which we divide into quartiles, we see two trends emerge. In Houston, the lowest quartile of income earners is different from respondents in three quartiles above them. The percentage of transit riders in the lowest quartile (15 percent) is twice as high as any other category, and those in the lowest quartile are also 20 percent higher than each of the other quartiles in terms of using the system once a month or so.[18] While all income groups still have a majority that never uses transit, the profile for the lowest quartile suggests that this group must sometimes utilize public transit because of their economic circumstances, and the other groups, having managed some degree of economic advantage, do not do so. Findings for education mirror this: respondents with the lowest levels of education—those without high school degrees—take mass transportation at twice the rate as other education levels.[19]

In Copenhagen, we see more of a graduated difference, and differences that are deeply influenced by the overall presence of more transit users. Like Houston, the lowest quartile has the most transit users, with the lower middle quartile an in-between category between the upper half of the income distribution. A majority of the lowest earners (56 percent) use public transportation at least weekly, nearly twenty percentage points more than the upper middle or top income quartile, and almost a majority of the lower middle quartile use it often.[20] Education offers a similar picture, where those with lower education levels are more reliant on public transportation (62 percent taking it weekly); still, at least 90 percent of each education category use public transportation often or once a month.[21] It appears the Copenhagen pattern can be summarized as follows: lower earners and those with lower educational levels rely on public transportation more often than higher earners, and those with higher incomes and SES tend to use it also, although they lean toward occasional usage instead of regular use.

People Cities encourage alternate modes of transportation, including mass transportation. Residents not only use it to commute but also for trips of leisure around the city. While the poor use it more than anyone else, the more well-off use it too, and, what is perhaps most striking, almost everyone (in Copenhagen, more than nine out of ten) use it at least once in a while.

Market Cities were never built with alternative transportation in mind, especially mass transit, which takes a high degree of urban planning, intermunicipality cooperation, and financial support. In the Market City, you get around as best as you can, and this means a car for almost everyone. The exceptions to this are most often poorer residents or those with lower socioeconomic status.

How urban regions approach transportation systems involves many moving parts. In People Cities, the moving parts are diverse—two feet, two wheels, the automobile engine, rail tracks. In Market Cities the only moving parts are those of the cars.

Where Is There?

When discussing land use and urban form, transportation defines the contours of the conversation. But the biggest part remains in between those contours. In this section, we move from analyzing how we get to places to focusing on the places themselves. We take this up by beginning with the smallest unit of interest, home, before expanding to analyzing land use around the home.

Life at Home

One of the proposed benefits of many Market Cities by their advocates is plentiful and cheap housing. Home ownership is more attainable with a greater economic and geographic range of options for housing. People Cities, conversely, might have tighter housing markets because of denser living, more building and preservation restrictions, and perhaps higher costs.

Recent census data from both cities provide some initial peeks into these dynamics. About three out of five residents in Greater Houston own homes as opposed to renting an apartment, including about 44 percent in the municipality of Houston.[22] In the Copenhagen metropolitan area, 35 percent own homes, including just 21 percent in the central cities of Copenhagen and Frederiksberg.[23] Home ownership rates are much higher in the Market City of Houston, and renting is the more common way to go in People City Copenhagen.

All of this prompts two simple questions: why is renting so prevalent in Copenhagen, and why is owning so prevalent in Houston?

The simpler question to answer concerns Houston. The idea of owning a home is one of the quintessential cultural touchstones in the United States, especially in sprawling cities with a large percentage of home ownership. It is also remunerative to do so. Every dollar spent toward home owning instead of toward rent is an investment. If you can make your mortgage payments (and as the subprime mortgage crisis taught us, that's a big and unequal *if*), then you will likely accumulate wealth. Houston residents often choose to live in homes that they own (almost always detached, single-family structures with large attached garages in front of the house for their cars) because it is a realization of a cultural dream, it is an investment in their financial future, and it is relatively inexpensive to do so in Houston compared to other places.

The last claim—it is relatively inexpensive in a Market City like Houston—deserves more unpacking. The claim is a popular one; for example, urbanist Edward Glaeser analyzed Houston's housing market and reported the following: "More than in any other place, Houston's developers have successfully argued that restrictions on development will make the city less affordable to the less successful. These arguments are patently self-interested, but they are also correct. Houston's free-wheeling growth machine has actually done a better job of providing affordable housing than of the progressive reformers on America's East and West coasts."[24] Greater Houston ranks near the national average in housing costs among the twenty biggest metropolitan areas in the country, but the average housing cost for a new 2,400-square-foot house was $288,271 in 2015, which is much lower than Seattle's ($548,187), San Diego's ($755,724), or Washington D.C.'s ($801,674), among others.[25] Indeed, the ratio of the median home price to the median household income in Houston was 3.3 in 2013, comparable to Atlanta or Dallas, but about half that of cities like New York and San Francisco.[26]

The primary reason that affordable housing can be extended to potential homeowners is because, nationally, housing policy has encouraged home ownership, and because, locally, developers have shaped the contours of supply to demand. On the national front, the city's most direct effort, Houston's Homebuyer Assistance Program, which helps lower-income earners purchase a home with grants, is actually mostly financed by the U.S. Department of Housing and Urban Development. The United States encourages home owning through processes like the Houston Homebuyer Assistance Program, a complex set of tax incentives, and the creation of catalyzing transportation infrastructure. Locally, there are lower costs as developers push the city's outskirts yet farther, and leapfrog less valuable land in-between.

A big part of the differences across cities has to do with the pursuit of mammon. This general argument can be found in John Logan and Harvey Molotch's book *Urban Fortunes*, which details how a coalition of elites called "the growth machine" guides cities along toward growth.[27] Financial growth is one of these mechanisms of growth, as is spatial growth. Pair them together and you get sprawl. Not just sprawl for sprawl's sake or because of a lack of government interest or even because of the invisible hand guiding consumers to rational choices. Instead, development in greater Houston is quite purposeful. This purpose is to make money, primarily for developers (and their attendant, overlapping "cousins" in construction, retail and roads), but also for residents, who can turn those old rent checks into wealth-building mortgage payments. As a Houston developer puts it, "We may not have all the scenery of a place like California . . . but growth makes up for a lot of imperfections."[28]

Turning to Copenhagen, we encounter potential challenges to the People City ethos that come with housing. Two stand out to us. The first is that the high rates of renting could be argued to be unfair to residents because they do not encourage wealth accumulation and always leave open the possibility for exploitation by crass landlords. The second is that the housing sector is regarded by economists and laypersons alike as one of the most speculative and uneven parts of the local economy, and People Cities seek to typically rein in the overly speculative and uneven.

Copenhagen seeks to move past these challenges by employing strict renting laws. Unlike in the United States, where cities vary tremendously on the intensity of their rent laws, the primary laws concerning rent are written by the national government. In the wake of the 2000s housing bubble, and with a new jump in property values in Copenhagen in the mid-2010s, a new rent act was adopted. In this rent act, we see how a People City, always looking for central governance and wide-reaching standards (in this case, from the national government), attempts to keep the housing market fair for all participants.

All properties built before 1991 are subject to rental controls. This has long been a practice (since 1937), and remains so in the new act.[29] Historically, the price of rent in Copenhagen is supposed to be tied to costs of upkeep for the flat. Therefore, it is less about an ever-increasing cut for the landlord; simply, the idea is that the landlord should not excessively profit from the renter.[30] What the new act adds are rent controls calculated such that rent may only be increased with inflation, and may not exceed it. While increases in rent payments have always been tightly controlled, this ends a practice of "staircase rent," where pre-established rent increases were the norm in many places. This policy prevents rent increasing too much in the event that economic growth is slow, and also partly protects landlords who are guaranteed a little extra in rent so long as the economy is moving along. More than anything, it neutralizes the speculation in the rent markets. In Houston, especially in the years before a drop in oil prices in 2014, it was not uncommon to see rent increases of double-digit percentages annually in highly desirable neighborhoods, especially when a tenant vacated their apartment unit— the new tenant could pay quite a bit more in rent.[31] But in Copenhagen (and throughout Denmark), that sort of rent increase is impossible. The law prevents it.

Perhaps the most robust check on maintaining affordable rental housing is through the *huslejenævnene*, or the rent committee.[32] An often-used tribunal on all things related to rent, their chief purpose is to settle disputes about how much rent to pay, especially for new tenants. If you think you are about to be charged too much rent for your new apartment in Copenhagen, you don't have to be like Jimmy McMillan in New York City and start a political party whose eponymous standard is "The Rent Is Too Damn High" and run for governor. Instead, you simply fill out some paperwork with the rent committee. Landlords can do this too. Once you have submitted your complaint, the rent committee does the dirty work: they look at nearby properties in the same building and on nearby blocks. If their research shows that the rent is too high, they have the authority to state a new level of rent, which is then binding for both landlord and tenant. People Cities will often have some sort of rent committee—especially one that pairs with strict and far-reaching rental laws. It is, by definition, a People City position: it is engineered to protect residents, tame the excesses of capitalism, and provide a structural solution for a social good.

Case in point: one of the researchers that conducted our Copenhagen Area Surveys told us about his own experience. A few years ago he shared an apartment with three others in Copenhagen. After living there for about two years, they felt their rent was too high. They took their case to the rent committee, who handled the investigation. The committee determined that indeed they had been paying too much rent. Not only was their rent reduced henceforth, but they were awarded the difference in the reduced rent and the previously charged rate for the entire two years they had lived there, plus they received their full deposit back, even though they continued to live in the apartment.

With all this pro-renter rhetoric, did the new rent law give any advantages to landlords? One notable change concerned so-called eternity tenants, who had the right to remain in a leased home no matter what, more or less—even if the owner wished to live there themselves. Now, the law provides that the owner may move back in, but they must give a year's notice.

The other pro-landlord tactic comes with properties built after 1991. In Copenhagen, this corresponds to only about one out of ten private rental properties.[33] (Here's another quick marker of the People Cities and Market Cities: the median year for a single-family home was built in 1959 in Copenhagen, and 1985 in Houston. This is mostly because of history, but Market Cities love to build, and People Cities love to preserve).[34] These changes were made in more dire economic times for the city and the idea was to spur new construction and create jobs, but it did not spur much construction nor create jobs. Why? Because the market was so fundamentally biased toward rent-controlled apartments, new rental units could not compete with the cheaper places.[35]

Copenhageners also have options that can blur the lines between the hierarchical rental relationship and the difficult-to-achieve ownership status. The most well known is cooperative housing, which can be found in many cities around the world but is essentially absent in Houston. The reason that some of these options exist is because owning property is very expensive in Copenhagen. The average single-family home sold in the Houston metropolitan area in 2015 was $281,352, and it was typically about 1,900 square feet.[36] The price per square foot is about $151. In greater Copenhagen, the price per square foot for a home sold in 2015 was about $301.[37] In terms of square feet, Copenhagen homes cost twice as much as those in Houston. Market Cities tend to have cheaper and more plentiful housing for those looking to own, while People Cities are typically more constrained when it comes to home buying opportunities.

In addition to getting around the higher cost of buying a home in Copenhagen, a second way to avoid the financial squeeze is a different squeeze: the squeeze into a smaller home. Therefore, though the price per square foot in Copenhagen is twice that of Houston, the overall price is not twice as high as Houston. The average home size in Copenhagen is about 1,339 square feet, about 30 percent smaller than in Houston.[38] This means that the average home price in Houston is $281,352, and in Copenhagen it is $403,039. This is not as large as the twice-as-high difference that we saw per square foot, but, of course, it comes with the trade-off that the house is simply smaller. In the Market City, you tend to get more bang for your buck: a larger home for a cheaper price. In the People City, you tend to get less credit for your krone: a smaller, more expensive home. It has some advantages—you can be closer to everyday things, like a grocery store and your friends—but the financial differences in housing can be steep.

The second challenge remains more vexing. It concerns whether the housing market, as one of the more capitalist things around, is corralled by a People City priorities rubric that tries to balance the drive for profits with the power of people. Indeed, this has been a central issue in recent years in Copenhagen. The average price per square foot for detached dwellings approximately doubled in value in the municipality of Copenhagen from 2000 to 2015.[39] While this is not dissimilar to Houston's rise in home prices (which saw the median home price rise by 91 percent in the same time period),[40] a housing affordability crunch poses a much greater threat to People Cities. In Houston, it is largely seen as a boon, and usually reported upon positively by local news outlets.

But in Copenhagen, local leaders, like proper People City politicians, readily identify these rising prices as a problem. Jesper Christensen is the mayor for the Social Committee for the city of Copenhagen, and a member of the center-left party in charge of Copenhagen for more than a hundred years, the Social Democrats. The office handles issues relating to social issues for children and adults; imagine an office dedicated to various functions relating to social work in the city.

When we asked Christensen about challenges facing Copenhagen, he said the biggest one was housing: "So even if it's a great city and a lot of things are going the right way . . . I am very concerned that the city is getting more divided. . . . that you will have a problem finding housing for the people who don't have the same possibilities as the ones who sold their last house; [they] gained a lot of money just by selling their property and getting a new one." Christensen is arguing that the home ownership market has priced out those who already do not own homes, and that homeowners in recent years have been the only ones able to reap the rewards of the housing market. Given this great challenge, Christensen and others—almost every government official we talked to mentioned housing as a hot-button issue—are focused on making home buying more affordable and retaining affordability in the renting market. But they also bemoan the lack of tools at their disposal to handle the rising prices and the gentrification it sometimes entails. It creates an awkward situation.

A recent example of this is epitomized by the conflicting rhetoric and decisions surrounding the developments on Papirøen, or Paper Island.[41] The small industrial zone that used to contain paper industries sports a spectacular location: right on the water, opposite the national theater, and adjacent to the opera house. Paper Island, like other spaces along the waterway, was the subject of great speculation, in both the financial and the social sense.

Developers immediately had interest in generating more housing that, even if it included provisions for social housing of poorer Copenhagen residents, would be quite lucrative. Leaders of the Left balked at the idea of losing prime waterfront space to private forces. As Morten Kabell, the technical and environmental mayor, put it: "Copenhagen must not become too mundane and polished. Therefore I will continue the fight to preserve one of the paper island's old industrial halls as a living example of the area's history. . . . We must ensure that those who get the golden opportunity to develop the area give something back to the city and the people of Copenhagen. . . . The area's unique location creates a risk that Papirøen could become a millionaire's ghetto because of sky-high prices for apartments."[42] Kabell and others rallied around a People City idea that Paper Island should remain as a public space to be enjoyed by residents, not as a housing complex whose occupancy would mostly comprise wealthy residents.

The initial compromise in the debate was to stall development for five years, at which point new buildings could be constructed. In the meantime, Paper Island was to be developed as a public space. One of the warehouses was rebooted as a food stall hall, and another housed an "experimentarium city" as a science museum for children. The food bazaar proved to be immensely popular. Dozens of tiny restaurants represent countries from all over the world and are packed in together tightly, as are the people—one can barely move among the happy, satiated throngs.

But the end is coming: by the time this book is published, construction will have begun. Even during our stay in the city in early summer 2016, we saw the experimentarium city close. The food stalls may stay—its own popularity having secured its survival—but other warehouses will be razed to make way for the housing development. And a widely used public space will become partly public, and partly private: an example of how the People City navigates the tricky terrain between its own people-centered beliefs and the capitalist system to which it subscribes.

Life outside the Home

When we think of land-use patterns in cities, we think of two primary archetypes: the city and the suburb. The city is dense, a flurry of humans going hither and thither. It has shops next to apartments next to restaurants next to parks. It is the sidewalk ballet on Jane Jacobs's Hudson Street in Greenwich Village.[43] The suburb is the leafy cul-de-sac and the quiet streets that lead to it. It is a big backyard, a room for every child—a place for families. It is the garden city in Ebenezer Howard's Letchworth and Welwyn.[44] These archetypes are not so simply divided into typology in Market Cities and People Cities. City and suburb do not mean the same thing in Market Cities and People Cities.

Take, for example, the personal urban history of one of us. Smiley has lived in central locations in big Market Cities like Houston and Memphis, Tennessee, and in a suburb of Copenhagen, Søborg, in the municipality of Gladsaxe. The densest place he has ever lived was in suburban Copenhagen. The highest number of locally useful places—places like grocery stores, pharmacies, restaurants, and public spaces—was in suburban Copenhagen. The most elaborate sidewalk ballet was in Søborg, not Houston's Montrose neighborhood. To be sure, a few neighborhoods in Houston are relatively dense and full of mixed-use development, and some neighborhoods in Copenhagen (rarely in the city proper) are low-density places full of single-family homes and little else. But the lines are plenty blurred: a suburb in Market City Houston is not really the same thing as a suburb in People City Copenhagen.

To this end, we analyze the preferences of city dwellers and suburban residents in both cities, and the degree of satisfaction with where they choose to live. We asked respondents about their interest in moving to a different part of the city: suburbanites were asked about the city, and city residents were queried about their interest in the suburbs. They were given the options of not interested, somewhat interested, or very interested.

While the number of those satisfied with their current location are essentially the same (62 percent of Houstonians and 62 percent of Copenhageners are not at all interested in moving), differences emerge when you split the analysis by location within the city.[45] About 18 percent of city residents in Houston are very interested in moving to the suburbs, compared to 10 percent from the suburbs who are very interested in moving to the city. This same pattern holds for those who are somewhat interested: 26 percent picked that category among city dwellers, 21 percent picked it among suburbanites.[46] In Houston, those living in the city have a greater interest in moving compared to those living in the suburbs.

In Copenhagen, the relationship is flipped. Keeping in mind that the *overall* level of satisfaction is the same between the two cities, it is suburban residents, *not* city residents, who wish to move at a higher clip. Some 17 percent of suburbanites are very interested in moving to the city, six points higher than the number from the city wishing to live in the suburbs. There is a smaller difference among the somewhat interested groups (a three-point difference).[47]

In those questions, though, we are taking for granted that respondents differentiate cities and suburbs by their densities and patterns of land use. They may not do this, though. Therefore, we also analyze whether respondents would prefer to live in areas with a lot of single-family homes, or one with a mix of developments. The descriptive pattern in Copenhagen is unequivocal. About three-fourths of respondents chose the mixed-use area over the single-family residential area. Houstonians were more mixed, but they favored the single-family residential area 57 percent to the 43 percent for the mixed-use developments.[48] The difference between the cities is about *thirty* percentage points.

It gets particularly interesting when broken down by whether you live in the city or suburbs. We see some expected results: 84 percent of urban Copenhagen respondents want mixed-use development, and 62 percent of suburban Houston residents want a single-family residential area, which, while a majority, is still a little lower than one might think. It should logically follow that suburban residents in Copenhagen want single-family residential areas, and urban residents in Houston want mixed-use areas. It does not work this way, though. Houstonians in the central city are split nearly down the middle whether they want a single-family area (52 percent of respondents) or an area with mixed-use development (48 percent). More suburban Copenhageners prefer the mixed-use infrastructure (58 percent) to the single-family residential area (42 percent).[49]

These last two findings run a bit contrary to conventional thinking. Shouldn't the urbane among us desire the mix of coffeehouses, restaurants, and shops? Shouldn't suburbanites enjoy a green lawn? Not in these cases. This is because Market Cities and People Cities have such different built environments that even suburban lifers in Copenhagen still like walkability, and Houstonians in the central city crave space. Significantly, both cities allow for those types of choices. You can live, even in a single-family home, in a Copenhagen suburb and still get around rather easily by foot to the bakery or corner store. In Houston, many neighborhoods close to the central city have a suburban aesthetic. The municipality of Houston, and even within the confines of the inner ring road (Interstate 610), there are hundreds of thousands of plots for single-family homes. Many are just minutes from downtown.

One of the primary reasons for the difference in development is from land-use policies in each metropolitan region. Copenhagen is famous for its attentiveness to urban design, and yet Houston may be even more well known as the only American city without zoning laws. We saw in chapter 1 how much of the urban form came to be across each city's history, but how does each city regulate its urban form?

A hallmark of strong zoning is regional planning. In chapter 2, we discussed how governance in the form of splintered jurisdictional control is characteristic of Market Cities, and more cohesive regional governance is typical of People Cities. One way this powerfully plays out is through regional-level land-use planning.

At the beginning of the 2000s, a movement was afoot in Denmark to reshape local governmental control. Denmark was governed by too many municipalities, the thinking went, and regional plans, existent since the late 1960s, had been defined in eras that were no longer relevant as the region had grown substantially in terms of its physical plant and population. By 2007, a dramatic new plan was put into place. Overnight, the number of municipalities in Denmark was slashed from 271 to 98. Twelve counties were abolished and reworked into five regions. For American readers, this would serve as the equivalent of reworking all fifty states into twenty new states. (For a second, just imagine Bostonians and New Yorkers in the same state—oh my). In one fell swoop, Copenhagen and its suburbs were comprised by only 28 municipalities and fell under one region, Hovedstaden.

Land-use planning is now organized through the regions, and specific urban design policies by municipality, but in accordance with the regional plan. These changes (in addition to a national law to such an effect) prompted the Hovedstaden region to create a new "finger plan," a nod to continuity and to the finger plan of the postwar region discussed in chapter 1.[50] The finger plan refers to the central cities of Copenhagen and Frederiksberg as the palm, with distinct lines of development going out in the shape of fingers from the palm; areas on the opposite end of the palm were the sea, and areas between the fingers were to serve as greener, less developed spaces. Debuting in 2007 and continuously maintained by the minister of the environment in the national government, it established different types of planning for each section of the region. Inner cities like Copenhagen and Frederiksberg were to emphasize density and connectedness to public transportation, especially trains; this has led to the massive construction of a new rail line cutting across the outskirts of Copenhagen's city limits. Outer municipalities are required to intensify development around central parts of municipalities and their train station, and to maintain "green wedges" by disallowing development between the fingers.

All of that planning, and we still have yet only begun discussing planning within individual municipalities or on a block-by-block basis. There are many examples of land-use policies and urban design principles in Copenhagen that go further down in scale. Ranging from wide-reaching historic preservation to a ban on tall buildings in the city center and the Christianshavn neighborhood to the installation of raised foot rests at stoplights for bicycles, these specifics matter.

One fascinating example comes from the recent finger plan. To encourage commercial infrastructure near transportation stations, the rules set a six-hundred-meter radius that governs land use within and beyond it. If you want to build a larger commercial structure (150,000 square feet or larger) outside of that radius, you will suffer a parking penalty. For places in the central city, this means a maximum of one parking spot per one hundred square meters of floor space, and one parking spot per seventy-five square meters in outer municipalities. By comparison, a similar rule in Houston allows about 2.5 spaces for most commercial locations for each square meter of floor space (higher for some industries than others—financial services get four spaces, for instance).[51] In other words, if you want to ignore the city regulations encouraging you to build around transit stations, then you will not only lose out on the usefulness of public transportation corridors and bicycling boulevards, but also on car parking. People Cities have more and harsher disincentives to try to corral capitalist enterprise into the zones they want.

In contrast to all that planning in Copenhagen, Houston has *no* zoning laws. Theoretically, you could transform your house into a palace for oranges, complete with small amusement park rides, tours, and just about every brick, railing, and door painted bright orange. Or not so theoretically: visit the Orange Show in Houston to see the shrine-to-oranges-*cum*-folk-art-masterpiece that is smack dab in the middle of a residential neighborhood.

Houston's long history without zoning is littered with failed initiatives across the twentieth century that stretch to the mostly thematic "Plan Houston" effort installed in 2015, which we discussed in chapter 2. The developers win every time, even with intrigued citizens and some business elites lining up to support zoning.

This is not to say, however, that Houston is totally without land-use laws. This is a confusing point, perhaps best indicated in a 2015 blog post from Rice University's Kinder Institute for Urban Research that appended the phrase "(Sort Of)" in the title of a post otherwise titled "Forget What You've Heard: Houston Really Does Have Zoning."

In that article, Matthew Festa, a law professor who studies land use at the South Texas College of Law in Houston, details the "sort of" zoning. It's Festa's position that Houston's laundry list of zoning-like laws is, in fact, zoning. "We've got a lot of regulations that in other cities would be in the zoning code," Festa says. "When we use it here, we just don't use the 'z' word."[52] These include deed restricted neighborhoods, tax increment refinancing zones (what some cities call "business improvement districts"), historic preservation, rules preventing too big lot sizes and rules that keep tall buildings near other tall buildings, and a mayor-appointed planning commission. Indeed, these are the sorts of items that comprise the land-use policy in cities across the world. Even further, some suburban municipalities have their own zoning laws.

Understanding Market City land-use patterns should not begin by determining whether the city has zoning laws or not. Not only would that yield an incredibly small number of cities (probably just Houston), but it may not be relevant in other national contexts, where cities nested in those countries may have a patchwork of zoning-like laws such as Houston's or perhaps even much stronger than Houston's.

Instead, the key to understanding land-use policy and patterns of urban form comes down to two observations. The first is specific and the second is general.

First, the specific one: if you want to determine if your city is a Market City or People City, take a long look at the litany of policies on the books for the municipality. And then look at how they seem to be enforced.

In Houston, all those policies may be on the books, but little rules are often flaunted: sidewalks not built to the width specified by policy or exceptions made for (especially lucrative) taller buildings. Former Mayor Annise Parker even started a specific initiative just to punish developers who were taking down trees that were supposed to be, according to municipal law, preserved or moved. When systemic deregulation is responded to in a piecemeal fashion (like going after developers who uproot trees that are part of a cultural system of disinterest in land-use regulation), you are probably in a Market City.

The land-use policies are also inconsistent. One example of this is Houston's recent move to disavow density restrictions past the I-610 loop, the city's inner ring road. The restrictions had previously specified that neighborhoods beyond the highway could not be dense—they were deliberately zoned to be suburban. This same change was made for several central city neighborhoods in the late 1990s, resulting in a proliferation of larger homes (especially townhomes in neighborhoods like Montrose and the Heights. This actually is an instance of *de*-regulation: previous regulations (that supported sprawl) were scrapped, and the result has increased the depth of developers' pockets.

Market Cities and People Cities may both have enough land-use regulations to fill many a tome, but while Market Cities' tomes will be a patchwork of apparently unrelated policies, the People City tome will have a cumulative quality. There will be guiding ideals that seem to bring the far-flung parts of the tome together.

This leads to the second key to understanding land-use policy in Market Cities and People Cities—the general one. It is informed by two related questions: is the urban form dedicated to mostly mixed-use places? And does existing policy provide for such spaces? Whereas on the first point it is easier to see the Market Cities, here it is easier to showcase the People Cities. It comes back to Jan Gehl's formulation about the need to build cities for people. If the city has mixed-use spaces and orients its laws to a continuation of that form, it is a People City, a place built with the needs of residents' daily rounds—walkable trips to the grocery store or to visit with a friend—in mind. If the city segregates different land uses from one another—necessitating a drive to the park or to a coffee shop—then it is probably a Market City.

Copenhagen exemplifies the mixed-use persona. Even in suburban places, a cheese shop, a plaza, a bar, and a small department store can often be reached in a short walk—and not just one of them, but all of them, and others too. There are not many places in Copenhagen that do not exhibit this. Even though we both lived in rather different parts of town during our longest stay in the city (Emerson in the heart of the city center, and Smiley in a suburb), we came to strikingly similar conclusions about the urban form we saw every day.

These mixed-use spaces did not arise on their own. Stable policy coupled with more recent innovation has played a huge role and, perhaps more important, will continue to do so. The Market City and People City framing is always partly projective: it is about assuming an ethos and using it as a guide in the complex, global world. In this way, strong land-use policies are that projective ethos, a literal guide to how the spaces before us should unfold.

Conclusion

Researchers who study land use typically study *land*, for fairly obvious reasons. But, in cities, we also plan for other types of topographical form. Given that molten lava and quicksand typically are not found in cities, we turn to a topographical form that has gone largely unmentioned: water.

Water is a forgotten resource when it comes to land use. We more often think of water's relation to cities in terms of providing clean and accessible water for its residents. In some cities, like water-starved cities of the American Southwest, water is a central political issue. More and more, though, water is being understood as a land-use issue, prompting questions about how can it be cleaned up, what should we build near it, and who can access it. The wider purchase of such changes is perhaps best recognized in the satirical newspaper *The Onion*, which proclaimed in a 2014 headline: "Mayor Hits on Crazy Idea of Developing Waterfront, Green Spaces."[53] We are witnessing the rising tide of water in cities. And it's not just the waterfront either: it's the water itself. We think that water in cities is one of the best ways with which to see the massive differences between Market Cities and People Cities. By examining each of the main waterways in Copenhagen and Houston, we see in vibrant colors how each city approaches land use.

Smiley took the plunge. During his second stay in Copenhagen, Smiley's roommates were avid swimmers. This was not laps in a heated pool sort of swimming, though. Instead, it involved donning a bathrobe over swim trunks, taking to the city streets for a few blocks past confused tourists, and heading to the Copenhagen harbor. The harbor is a short, river-like waterway that separates the southern portion of the city from the city center and points further north. It is also in Denmark, a place where the latitude is too far north for anyone to ever expect warm water, even in the early summer. Smiley and his roommates headed out in robes and with blankets for the plunge. One of them, with camera ready, commenced a countdown for the others: three, two, one. In jumps one Dane. Out stays one American. Peer pressure in the form of convulsing laughter at the American's ineptitude roiled through his already-chilling veins.

In what felt like a mix of being pelted with frozen bricks and stung by ice hornets, Smiley hated the water. He hated that Copenhagen had taken such a great effort to rid it of pollution, and hated that in Copenhagen the public space was provided for one to easily access places to jump. But sixty seconds or so was enough to abate the hate. The pain rush gave way to a heightened spirit while Smiley took in the scenery: the Opera House and the ever-busy Paper Island across the harbor, and the National Theatre just beside him. Dozens of boats—tourist boats, old-school ships, little speedboats, and even public transit boats—bobbed up and down on the waters a few hundred meters away. It was a scene in Copenhagen he had seen before, but now from a new vantage point: not the land, but the water.

The municipal government of Copenhagen emphasizes not just the green but also the blue. Systematically, the government of Copenhagen transitioned their declining commercial harbor and transferred its most choice locations to the use of water. This is both land beside the water, and the water itself. "You could say that the harbor is the core of the city and lives at its heart," says Morton Kabell, the environment and technical mayor. He continues: "But for so many years we turned our back on the harbor. . . . Everybody likes to get close to the water. And having such huge open areas of water in Copenhagen it really made people think, why don't we use it? And as many things are in Copenhagen about change—bicycles and now the harbor—it was Copenhageners that took the initiative, they wanted to see a change." The transformation is readily evident. Schools of herring populate the harbor, and now even seals wander in from the Baltic Sea. Also populating the harbor? Humans.

Houston too emphasizes the blue. The city, like Copenhagen and a huge number of others like it in the world, was built first and foremost as a center of trade along key waterways. These commercial beginnings of many cities mean that the default way of thinking about urban water is that of a Market City. As city character emerges now and in recent decades, evaluating land-use policies with regard to water will more often show that the market purposes of water will remain so. It takes a greater effort, as is the case with People Cities, to profoundly shift how water is utilized as an urban resource.

The fifty-three-mile-long Buffalo Bayou is coterminous to the Houston Ship Channel for its first portion, before it meanders past downtown and into the western part of the city and out to suburban lands. In all, the Buffalo Bayou has four distinct parts, each of which is telling about the market city approach to water.

Parts one and three are parks: Terry Hershey Park and Buffalo Bayou Park. Each is among the city's jewel parks. Terry Hershey sits far from the city center (it is outside of the second ring road) and near the headwaters of the bayou. Buffalo Bayou Park is a new endeavor that we briefly profiled in chapter 2 along with the rise of Houston's greenways-and-bayous plan to remake itself.

Part two, which splits Terry Hershey Park from Buffalo Bayou Park, is private. Running about nine miles from Beltway 8 to the inner ring road of Interstate 610, the bayou runs through wealthier neighborhoods like Memorial Villages and includes the Houston Country Club. You can access it by kayak or canoe from Terry Hershey or Buffalo Bayou, but there are no walking trails or parks along the bayou in this section. Spacious homes border the bayou, where affluent homeowners have personal access to the water. This is land use in the traditional Market City fashion. Access to water is not only just a public good for some parks, but also a private good that is lucrative and desirable. Keeping this land in private hands allocates access on the basis of market forces, and the highly sought-after land ends up in the hands of some of Houston's affluent residents.

Given that the default is to keep waterways as conduits for markets, the last part of the Buffalo Bayou doubles as Houston area's primary waterway, the Houston Ship Channel. It has been a bustling center of commerce for more than one hundred years. This is perhaps even more the case now than it has ever been. Today, the Ship Channel ranks as the United States' leading port in foreign tonnage, and second in the overall tonnage from the port.[54] The port's tonnage increased by 20 percent from 2003 to 2013.[55] The primary business exploits of the Houston Ship Channel are oil and gas. It sports several large refineries, hundreds of storage tanks for gas and chemicals, and is the center of a nerve system that takes in and beams back out oil and gas for much of the United States.

Not surprisingly, then, it is also very polluted. The air quality around the Houston Ship Channel ranks among the nation's very worst, and the refineries in particular are among the region's highest emitters of carbon. The water quality is also poor. The Texas Parks and Wildlife Commission recommends only eating one eight-ounce fish per month—anything more than that, and you would overexpose yourself to dioxin and even long-banned and highly toxic polychlorinated biphenyl. And *no* fish is recommended for children younger than twelve and women of childbearing age.[56] We will return early and often to the Ship Channel in chapter 5, which concerns the environment.

The Market City's waterways have the imprimatur of commercial interests. Public spaces cover some of the area but are sometimes governed by public-private partnerships led by local economic and political elites. Real estate revels in high property values along a huge swath of Buffalo Bayou. And many of Houston's economic successes come from the masterful—and environmentally exploitative—management of the Ship Channel.

In this chapter, we have shown how land uses in People Cities are dense, encourage interaction, and are generously funded by the public sector. Market Cities open up enormous avenues for growth and movement of people and goods, leaving much of the work of land use to a range of nongovernmental actors. Both visions are compelling, but the similarities end there. In Copenhagen and Houston, the visions of urban form favor different ideals and different day-to-day practices. And most leaders and residents in both cities think they are better for it.

5

Environment/Economy

And or Versus?

Climate change ranks among the most pressing social issues of our time. As far as government responses to climate change go, cities are a primary arena in which climate change matters.[1] There are many reasons for this. On the one hand, cities are ecologically intensive places that chew up resources and depend on the hinterlands in an environmentally unequal way such that cities and urbanization are compounding headaches in the fight against climate change.[2] On the other hand, some urbanists argue that cities are the key to solving these ecological problems because of increased density or the innovation that may result from bright minds in cities working together.[3] That the evidence for the efficacy of this latter perspective is still mostly forthcoming indicates how critical cities are: right now, they're environmentally devastating—but in the future it could change.

The second main reason is that nation-states have had quite a bit of trouble agreeing on binding climate change accords. It took nation-states until December 2015 to finally link up against global warming, and the plan for the United States to exit from the accords just two years later fractures the fragile framework. By contrast, an international network of municipal governments, ICLEI, went live in 1990 and boasted more than 1,000 members by the time ink was put to paper in Paris. The sorts of actions needed to undercut dangerous emissions once and for all must come at many levels—the nation-state probably chief among them—and may need to involve fundamental changes in governance, such as confronting the link between capitalism, energy, and global warming. Our cities are often laboratories of policy and of democracy, and contain a majority of the world's residents. They will be pivotal in the effort to lessen emissions.

And a final reason is pragmatic. Many of the world's cities have been historically located along waterways, for reasons of commerce and connection. The rising seas threaten the physical plant of cities and are creating the need to rethink urban form in low-lying coastal cities across the world. More proximately, cities are making plans to head off the worst and be resilient when it strikes anyways. Major weather events are a chief worry in cities today, and are already occurring: look no further than New Orleans (for Hurricane Katrina), New York (for superstorm Sandy), California (during 2015 droughts), or Europe (during extreme heat in 2015). Major weather events have an outsized effect on cities. In all, 70 percent of cities report experiencing the effects of global climate change.[4] It is no longer just an issue of preventing rising temperatures but also of how to deal with what we have wrought.

In Copenhagen and Houston, we see profoundly different tableaus of how cities are dealing with climate change. It fits to a tee our conceptualizations of Market Cities and People Cities. Copenhagen has raced out to the front of the climate change debate, seeking to become the first large city to be carbon neutral. The region is fundamentally changing urban infrastructure, local consumer habits, and the thinking of residents to combat climate change, thereby preparing for an age where it is an intractable problem. Houston embodies the conflicting logics of environmental-leaning postindustrial populations in a place where fossil fuel resources are widely consumed and energy fortunes are won.

In this chapter, we investigate our cities around issues of environment and energy, and to show how the market model and the people model have vastly contrasting implications for the health of the planet. We divide the chapter into three overall parts: energy, attitudes, and actions. We show that Copenhagen uses its collective ethos to power an aggressive environmental agenda, and that while Houston makes definite advances, it does so around the edges such that the fundamental energy markets that drive Houston continue to do so.

Energy Fortunes

Energy is at the core of the environment. Houston and Copenhagen offer two critical lessons in how cities' economic growth can be tied to the extraction of natural resources for human consumption. Both cities exist, and are even the subjects of a book such as this one, because of energy. The historical similarities turn into contemporary contrasts.

As we saw in chapter 1, Houston has been tied to oil since oil was struck in Texas at the dawn of the twentieth century. Oil took off in Houston when federal funds helped to build the Houston Ship Channel in the 1910s.[5] It helped the city weather the Great Depression and the Great Recession, and fueled a boom in population that has increased sixteen-fold in a century. Even though reorganization reoriented the economy partly in the 1980s thanks to the oil bust of that decade, Houston remains inextricably tied to all things oil and gas.

Today, this means that Houston is the oil capital of the world. It is home to the world's largest petrochemical facility (ExxonMobil's refinery in Baytown), the world's largest pipeline company (Kinder Morgan), and the world's largest oil fields services company (Schlumberger). Estimates suggest that half of the jobs in Houston are tied to the oil industry.[6] The economy is deeply tied to extractive industries in Houston. This fact imprints anything related to the environment in Houston.

Copenhagen has a more complicated history with energy, one that can be more or less divided into three parts. It should be noted that Copenhagen history and Danish history are closely integrated here. Before the early 1970s, Denmark did little to develop its natural resources and therefore was hit badly by the global oil crisis of 1973.[7] In response to this, phase two meant the exploitation of natural resources, especially rich oil reserves in the North Sea. It included coal power plants, and, later, using natural gas for energy throughout the country. The country had used 92 percent of its energy from imported oil in 1972, but by 1997 Denmark had become a net energy *exporter*, a remarkably large change in just a quarter century.[8] It would remain an exporter until 2013. Some of the country's biggest companies remain tied to these industries, such as the largest, Maersk, a shipping specialist headquartered in Copenhagen. The third phase involved a green transition. Renewable energy sources were developed slowly, increasing with the heightened salience of global climate change beginning in the 1990s. Wind power now accounts for 42 percent of electric power in the country.[9] The goal is to be using 100 percent renewable energy in Denmark in 2050, an ambitious plan exceeded only by Copenhagen's 2025 carbon neutral plan.[10]

The cumulative effect of these three phases produces a curious energy history. Copenhagen, and Denmark generally, was not historically linked to fossil fuel energy sources. But, for about a quarter century from the 1980s until very recently, fossil fuels powered the entire country, gave rise to enormous wealth, and created a huge number of contradictions for a place linked as one of the world's greenest. In recent decades, the country has gone again in a new and fundamentally different direction, this time toward renewable resources. Denmark still aims to be an energy powerhouse, but no longer wishes to use nonrenewable sources like North Sea oil deposits and coal-guzzling power plants. At the forefront of this conversation in Denmark has been Copenhagen, which has installed wind turbines and worked to shift its municipal sources of power away from the toxic and carbon-intensive.

Not all Market Cities and People Cities will have energy histories that will match this; in fact, they definitely do not. But what can make for an intriguing point of contrast when analyzing two or more cities is to identify apparent similarities. Energy happens to be that for our two cases. Both cities share a similarity in having strong fossil fuel industries in particular. From this similarity, though, divergence emerges.

Environmental Attitudes

Copenhageners and Houstonians have both similar and different views on the environment. The similarities change to differences as survey questions move from being general to specific. For a general question about the respondent's level of agreement with how important it is to protect the environment, about 83 percent of Copenhagen residents agree that it is important—eight points higher than the number of Houstonians.[11] Interestingly, the proportion of those who "strongly agree" is slightly higher in Houston (43 percent) than in Copenhagen (40 percent).[12] Similar trends emerge when respondents are asked about their level of concern about the environment. Four out of five respondents in each city are very or somewhat concerned about the environment: 86 percent in Copenhagen and 80 percent in Houston.[13] This would make it seem like the cities are rather similar when it comes to pro-environmental beliefs: overwhelming numbers support the environment in both.

But compare these queries to a much more specific survey question, We asked respondents in each city to pick from two options: (1) protecting the environment should be top priority even if it causes lower economic growth and some loss of jobs, or (2) economic growth and creating jobs should be the top priority, even if the environment suffers to some extent. This question moves forward preferences on the environment by pairing preferences with a specific reality concerning the pros and cons of environment and economy.

Unlike questions on the protection of the environment and the level of environmental concern, there are large differences between the two cities. In Copenhagen, 65 percent chose (1) promoting the environment over economy. In Houston, 59 percent chose (2) promoting the economy over the environment. This means that there is a twenty-four-percentage-point gap between the two cities for each category. Copenhageners—by a nearly two-to-one margin—prioritize the environment over the economy. Only approximately two in five Houstonians share those same priorities in favor of the environment.

We also asked respondents what they felt was the primary cause of higher global temperatures; increasing global temperatures, after all, are a primary indicator of climate change. They were given two options: (1) mainly caused by human activities or (2) mainly caused by normal climate cycles.

Again we find a wide gap between respondents. Seventy-eight percent of Copenhagen residents believe that higher global temperatures are mainly caused by human activities, compared to 52 percent of Houston residents.[14] Given the high rates of environmental concern and emphasis on protecting the environment, a number of respondents—especially in Houston—flipped their stances on the environment depending on whether the questions were general to the environment or specific to climate change. For example, two out of five respondents in Houston who agree that the environment is important also think that climate change is the product of normal climate cycles. This "pro-environmental climate change denier" group makes up a quarter of the total respondents in the Houston survey. Among those who are very or somewhat concerned about the environment in Houston, two out of five ascribe climate change to natural causes. This group is about a third of the total respondents in Houston. While a vast majority of Houstonians are in favor of the environment, Houstonians are split on the issue of climate change, with a large group of respondents identifying as pro-environment while at the same time not agreeing with settled science about the causes of climate change.

By contrast, 86 percent of respondents in Copenhagen who agree that the environment is important believe that global warming has anthropogenic roots. Even half of the respondents who disagree about the importance of the environment agree that human activities are the primary contributor to global warming. A pro-environmental stance is more closely connected to the issue of climate change in Copenhagen.

The pathways that predict human-caused climate change denial in the two cities also differ in the two cities. In a previously published analysis, Smiley investigated these issues.[15] Scholars tend to think of political beliefs as operating along a continuum in how they shape levels of climate change denial. This means that Left-leaning party adherents have the lowest levels, Right-leaning party adherents have the highest levels, and political independents and moderates are somewhere in between. Political beliefs are important because they are widely thought of as one of the most important predictors (if not the most) of human-caused climate change denial.[16]

But the analysis found that these differences were not as continuous as previously thought when it came to these city-specific samples. In Copenhagen, and holding all other measures (items like the respondent's income or gender) constant, analyses showed that voters for right-of-center parties had greater rates of human-caused climate change denial compared to the those without a political affiliation. But voters in favor of left-leaning parties were not different from the politically unaffiliated in Copenhagen. The relationship was flipped but parallel in Houston. Democrats have lower rates of human-caused climate change denial compared to the politically unaffiliated, but Republicans did not have higher rates, holding other variables constant.

These findings suggest that there is a wide diffusion of acceptance of human-caused climate change across the political center in Copenhagen. More problematically, they also suggest that in Houston, human-caused climate change denial is diffused across the political center. The importance of thinking through this diffusion is to think about how these ideas might condition the realm of the possible when it comes to environmental issues, most notably climate change. The clear consensus in Copenhagen makes it possible for more ambitious and lasting environmental change. The fractured public opinion in Houston attenuates the range of possible options for change in the city.

Environmental Actions

Climate change is a social and environmental issue that not only necessarily affects everyone (a hurricane does not carve a path with regard for neighborhood desirability), but also can do so unequally (the first part notwithstanding, desirable neighborhoods are often built on higher ground, leaving low-lying areas for poorer residents that are prone to rising floodwaters from hurricanes). And, more than anything, even the tiniest emission from the most remote place in the world contributes to a phenomenon that is truly global in its reach. There is no place on planet earth that is untouched by climate change.

The wide-reaching nature of global warming provokes different reactions in Market Cities and People Cities. People Cities see the connectedness of climate change and respond aggressively. The connectedness fosters the feeling that everyone is in this together, and, if that is the case, everyone has the impetus to get to work. And with a problem as big as climate change, only the collective has a chance of success, goes the People City thinking.

Market Cities are more divided. For one, as we saw in the previous section, not everyone would agree with the title of this section: is there a need to take action on something that is not due to human activities or is not even occurring? Even so, Market Cities are taking action to combat climate change. Insofar as humans do influence climate change, they are also exacerbating it, more so than in People Cities. Market Cities are centered around the idea of growth, and in Houston, energy industries provide growth. If those industries are characterized as heavily polluting or environmentally destructive, then so be it—the trade-off, as we saw in the previous section, is worth it. It may contribute to climate change or be less than ideal for the air, but it also powers the local economy and creates jobs, goes the Market City thinking.

We identify several ways in which cities interface with climate change, but we hone in on four here: climate change governance, levels of carbon emissions, waste disposal, and disaster readiness.

Environmental Governance in the Cities

Social scientific research is clear: to date the growth of capitalism and the growth of carbon emissions are coupled with one another.[17] As countries and cities grow economically, they tend to use up more carbon (and other climate-change-inducing emissions). While some have claimed that eventually this pattern will shift as populations adopt environmentalist positions that decouple economic growth and environmental degradation, research has yet to confirm this position.[18] Capitalism has a carbon problem. How cities conceive of their local configurations of capitalism and govern these systems will deeply affect how large an effect a city will have on global warming.

Copenhagen is famous for its effort to be the first carbon-neutral capital city in the world. National strategies in Denmark emphasize how local places can and should be empowered to organize against climate change, and the country has created a cross-ministerial forum specifically designed for representatives of Danish cities.[19] Copenhagen was an early adherent of adopting climate policy. When ICLEI, the network of cities committed to combatting climate change, started a pilot effort on climate change policy called the Urban Co2 Reduction Project, Copenhagen was one of twenty-four cities to volunteer. The carbon neutral plan came about in advance of hosting the 2009 United Nations Climate Change Conference. Copenhagen is fast-tracking efforts across the city to reach the carbon neutral goal that is less than a decade away. It has already dropped its carbon use by 20 percent, meeting a goal the city had for 2015.[20] Given that cities are inherently intensive users of resources including carbon, it is well worth unpacking how the municipality plans to pull it off.

There are several areas in which they plan to lessen greenhouse gas emissions, which fall into two primary groups: transportation and energy use.[21] Transportation is more straightforward. The point is to lessen dependence on cars. Copenhagen focuses on making it ever more convenient to choose biking. It continuously invests in making it easier and easier to cycle throughout the city. This topic is covered more thoroughly in chapter 4, but the primary takeaway here is that a main goal behind increasing alternatives to cars is to fight climate change.

Decreasing energy use involves the construction of one hundred wind turbines and further reengineering the sources and creation of heating and electricity.[22] The Copenhagen coast is whipped up with wind, and these targeted efforts aim to take advantage of that rich renewable resource, particularly for heat and electricity in the city. About 75 percent of the carbon emissions in Copenhagen are used for these utilities.[23] As discussed in the waste section below, an additional part of plan is to reuse city trash as energy. The plan also partly relies on private economic actors to develop and implement useful new technologies for the effort.[24] It might also be mentioned that the plan's strategy for controlling the emissions of items manufactured elsewhere but used in Copenhagen is not accounted for in the effort, a major drawback not to be overlooked.

Beyond this, energy is also the site of some controversy. Critics have accused Copenhagen of cooking the books by using energy offsets. Because of these offsets, some argue that even Copenhagen's own plan cannot achieve carbon neutrality.[25] Here's the issue: Copenhagen's fruitful location along the coast generates more wind power than is needed for the city, and is in turn sold to other places. That wind power sold to other places counts as lessening the carbon output of Copenhagen. Estimates currently show that Copenhagen cannot halt enough carbon use in its transportation sector to become carbon neutral, but these green investments in wind energy will end carbon use enough outside of municipal borders to make up the difference. Whether this is fair or not is up to you. On the one hand, they will produce enough clean energy and lessen their own output to emit less carbon than they will have produced. It is carbon neutral by that definition. On the other hand, they are freely admitting that they cannot get to that neutral level of emissions on their own, but only through selling the wind power they generate to places that are not Copenhagen. And therefore it does not count by that definition.

Either way, Copenhagen's carbon neutral plans characterize positions being taken up in other People Cities. It is a comprehensive effort that sets about a deliberate and wide-reaching civic vision. It touches on almost every actor in the city: residents and their consumption, businesses and innovation, energy institutions moving to alternative sources, and residents changing their everyday choices about transportation. It is convened by the government, which involves those actors throughout the city. Finally, it does so within the confines of capitalism. It structures possibilities in energy and transportation at the same time that it leaves larger questions aside about how carbon intensity came to be in the first place.[26]

Houston has its plans too, but also its way of working around them. The underlying feeling throughout any climate policy in Houston is that the city has to be very careful about not limiting the rollicking remuneration from the energy sector. The same is true for development that depends on cars. More than this, it should also take care to avoid pointing fingers at these fossil fuel giants and car-centric developers.

Some of Houston's most successful energy policies come through reforms to policies that affect how the municipality runs itself. For example, the municipality of Houston is a national leader in building sustainable government buildings; in 2013, Houston ranked fourth in the country in total number of buildings with LEED designs.[27] Since 2004, Houston has required that new municipal buildings should meet LEED standards for energy efficiency. Other office buildings, especially downtown, are following suit. Houston ranks third overall in terms of total square feet of LEED-certified building space, with fifteen projects achieving the platinum designation.[28] Mayor Annise Parker, head of the city from 2009 to 2015, was a firm advocate of the approach and advanced tree-planting efforts throughout the city, an issue of longstanding interest to the mayor.[29] The city's guiding emissions reduction plan includes a multitude of programs such as adding LED traffic signals, upgrading the municipal fleet of vehicles, or providing public transit passes for city employees.[30] One thing that the plan does not include is the regulation of much of anything that does not directly concern the city government. Among other potential polluters, commercial industry looms large. So does land-use planning, as we saw in chapter 4.

The overall point here is that Houston does not have a plan that is comprehensive in nature to deal with emissions that cause climate change. It has a plan that is comprehensive in nature to deal with the city government's emissions, but not one for the city itself. That a city with such a large carbon footprint (see more below) does not have a plan seems to be no accident. It stands in strong contradistinction to what we saw in Copenhagen, where, even when taking into account the importance of studying the nuance of their plan, it is much more holistic. On pressing social issues we will often see divergence in governmental policy across Market Cities and People Cities. This is certainly the case for policies concerning climate change.

Carbon Emissions in the Cities

Holding large polluters accountable is a major step to decreasing carbon dioxide (CO_2) emissions. It means taking a serious approach to corporate industrial facilities, and making sure that your own municipal energy providers are not becoming overly part of the problem too. But it depends quite a bit on how many large industrial polluters there are in the first place, and how much they are putting into the air.

We examined two databases in each country that keeps track of CO_2 emissions. This is an inexact science because of different reporting requirements for polluters in the different countries, but there are enough similarities between the two reporting systems—and enough differences between the cities in the observed data—to justify the analysis here. To help with the approximation, we limited the analysis to facilities that report at least 120,000 tons of CO_2 emissions in a year.[31]

Using the European Pollutant Release and Transfer Register (E-PRTR) database, we find that large polluting facilities in the Copenhagen capital region emitted about 3.1 million metric tons of CO_2 from industrial and energy facilities in 2013.[32] This sounds like a lot. But, according to 2013 estimates from the U.S. Environmental Protection Agency's Facility Level Information GreenHouse Gases Tool (FLIGHT) database, the amount of CO_2 emissions in the Houston metropolitan area is 122 million metric tons. There is no extra digit or mistaken decimal point: for every metric ton of CO_2 that greater Copenhagen facilities emit, greater Houston facilities emit about forty. Even accounting for population differences between the metropolitan areas, that still means that the emissions ratio from large facilities is about eleven to one in Houston and Copenhagen. Indeed, researchers who undertook the task of determining the most carbon-intensive places in the United States found that Harris County was the worst emitter in the United States among its more than three thousand counties.[33] This also corresponds to a large difference in the sheer number of facilities. In Houston, those 122 metric tons of emissions come from 129 facilities. In Copenhagen, it comes from just five.

The purposes of the facilities vary too. In Copenhagen, all five are related to power: three are run by the state energy company, and the other two are electric facilities for the city. The old smokestacks that tower over parts of the city on the north end of Amager and near the sea in Østerbro are on this list of the biggest polluters. One of the facilities, Amagerforbrændingen, which processes city waste, is one we will return to later in this chapter. Although they would be required to report to the European Union's European Pollutant Release and Transfer Registry (E-PRTR), no commercial facility meets the standards for reporting carbon dioxide emissions, although some report for other types of chemical emissions.

In Houston, though, all types of facilities contribute to carbon emissions. The six worst-polluting facilities in Houston each emitted more than the total of the Copenhagen region in 2013. Chief among them, like Copenhagen, is a large energy facility: a plant for the NRG corporation, which powers much of the region's electricity. It accounted for a staggering 15.8 million tons of carbon dioxide emissions in 2013. That's the equivalent of driving 3.3 million cars for a year.[34] Unlike Copenhagen, though, three of the other five heavy-polluting facilities are related to oil, and a fourth is in the chemical business. The second-highest emitting facility is the ExxonMobil refinery in Baytown. Other names are well known too: Dow, Marathon, and Shell.

Those names are four-letter words in the eyes of many for their use of nonreusable natural resources and energy practices that emit massive amounts of greenhouse gases. But they are not curse words in Houston. NRG's name graces the stadium of the popular football team, the Houston Texans, and Shell sponsors a nationally known golf tournament in the city. Marathon calls downtown Houston home. They're all large employers, generous benefactors in the community, globally important economic juggernauts, and producers of large amounts of intensive emissions. In Market Cities, the first three attributes are more important than the last one. If you're powering the economy, Market Cities often will look the other way on the dirty laundry, whether it's toxic emissions, compromised labor practices, or the potential move of labor abroad. These businesses are too important to the city's image and economic success.

People Cities, however, have largely departed from heavy commercial polluters. It is not totally purposeful: much of it has come as the postindustrial economy has shifted such ventures elsewhere in the world. But cities have known that they are in changing economic times. And when Copenhagen moved toward a services-based economy, they were no doubt aware that a concomitant change would be the loss of heavy manufacturing—and its requisite pollution.

Waste in the Cities

Refusing refuse is an intractable urban issue. It has been for centuries.[35] An article from *Nature* in 2012 estimates that the amount of waste on earth will triple by 2100, even though urban residents in 2000 were already expending nearly three million tons of waste daily.[36]

Where to put all of that waste is a deeply political issue. Landfills are predominantly located in places where marginalized populations reside.[37] They were not put there by accident. How much waste is generated is another political issue. The size of the landfill has something to do with the rate of recycling. New technologies seek to find ways to not waste the waste, instead using it to create power. In Copenhagen and Houston, this effort at creating power out of waste underwrites distinct reactions.

Copenhagen's newest effort for waste sounds made up. Not because it is spectacularly environmentalist—that much is contested—but because it features a *ski slope*. Amager Bakke is a large new facility that dots the north of Amager island, the island which includes two of the five facilities that registered on the carbon emissions list earlier in the chapter. Any picture of the famous Little Mermaid statue in Copenhagen now sports the Amager Bakke facility across the water in the background. The plant is jointly owned by a company run by five municipalities, including the municipality of Copenhagen.

The first goal behind the new facility is to decrease carbon emissions and use electricity in the region more sustainably. The second goal is to advance what the architectural group calls "hedonistic sustainability" by merging entertainment into an otherwise decidedly nonleisure space. On that second point, the project may very well succeed. Amager Bakke is being built with a long slope across the top, a slope that will be packed down with synthetic snow that will make it ready for skiing.[38] It will be 85 meters tall, the "tallest mountain in the city," as a website for the facility puts it.[39] A nature trail wanders up the building as well, for bikers and hikers; the idea is that it will be a park for many purposes, not just skiing. This is a radical turn for a waste facility. Such facilities are usually sequestered so that civilians cannot go to the facility just because they want to.

It also tracks the emissions with a futuristic, art-meets-environment medium. Carbon generated by the facility is stored up in a chamber near the top of the smokestack. Once it reaches a metric ton, it emits the carbon in the form of a ring. At night, it is proposed that the facility will project light onto the ring.[40] Residents would then see that they are wasting quite a bit of materials, and that it is contributing to climate change. The smoking rings both draw attention to the important issue of carbon emissions and serve to distract you from it through a display of entertainment. It could have the effect of also relaxing environmental pressure: if we're the city who highlights carbon emissions with smoke rings, then wouldn't we probably have fewer emissions than other cities?

But about that other half of the form and function equation. The whole purpose of this facility is to deal with waste from more than one million residents. Waste can go in a few directions: to a landfill, to an incineration plant, to a recycling plant, or shipped elsewhere. In Copenhagen, Amager Bakke is a waste-to-energy facility, a new iteration of an old idea of turning the waste in cities into something more useful, like energy. Using technological developments that burn the waste cleaner than other examples of waste-to-energy facilities, the idea is that the waste that homes generate should be pumped right back into those homes in the form of electricity.[41]

This approach is a step forward in that it pushes the city to think about waste more purposefully than Market Cities would, as we will see in Houston. But it also confuses exciting urban design with some potentially problematic environmental implications. One implication is that waste-to-energy often discourages recycling. Instead of pitching plastics in the recycling, it gets burned and contributes to carbon emissions.[42] Even if it is burned cleaner because of new innovations in technologies, it still gets burned. It could also displace green energy alternatives, such as wind power. Finally, the central city location raises concerns that even modest emissions would still have an impact on the health of nearby residents.[43] Incinerating waste remains a middle ground between recycling and landfills: better, not best.

While we are always alert to hearing about Copenhagen-Houston connections, Smiley did a double take as he listened at a forum at Rice University about a new recycling program in Houston. The program would possibly feature the construction of a new facility that could convert some waste back into energy for the grid. As questions circulated about the efficacy of such a proposal, the exasperated speaker and proponent of the potential facility said, "This is the approach they're taking in *Copenhagen*, for god's sake."

Even in Houston, Copenhagen is a byword for green. And if Copenhagen is incinerating waste, Houston should too, argued the speaker. Houston recently investigated new options for how to handle waste in the city. Houston and waste are inextricably linked because the United States' largest waste corporation, Waste Management, is headquartered in the city. In terms of the waste Houston produces, Houston only recycles 6 percent of its waste from homes, with all of the rest heading to landfills. As recently as 2009, the rate had been 2.6 percent, meaning that only a minuscule amount of waste in the city was recycled and reused.[44] Only households are provided with curbside bins, and no apartment buildings in the city are provided with bins. Instead, apartment dwellers and commercial facilities can take their reusable goods to facilities throughout the city; not surprisingly, you would almost always take a car to reach these facilities. With both alacrity and austerity, the recent history of recycling and waste in the city shows both the inherent ambition and innovation that characterizes the city, as well as the harder realities of declining public monies.

The saga begins in March 2013, with Houston winning a major green grant. Bloomberg Philanthropies (the same Bloomberg who was New York City mayor) awarded an inaugural "Mayor's Challenge Prize" to the city for one million dollars.[45] Only five cities won the grant. Houston's project centered on developing potential plans for a "One Bin for All" system. The idea behind the One Bin plan is that Houstonians would no longer manually separate trash and recyclables, but instead put all refuse in the same bin. A new facility would house new technologies able to separate recyclables, and then incinerate the rest of the trash in the same waste-to-energy fashion as Copenhagen.

The single-bin plan came under criticism from some city residents and local environmental organizations. While it seemingly might be able to help increase recycling rates, some worried it'd be more of a front for profit-making in the form of incinerating materials. Unlike Copenhagen, where the constituent cities of the Amager Bakke plant link together to own it, Houston's new plant would be contracted out to a private vendor. And to whom it would be contracted out is anyone's guess—more than two and a half years into planning, the city had yet to release any names associated with bids, nor the winning company.[46]

More than this, the location of a potential new facility was highly criticized. At a community meeting at Texas Southern University, a city representative assured community members that the facility would not be placed in a neighborhood that did not already have a waste facility, like a landfill. No new neighborhood would be affected. This point was, however, very problematic to many attendees. Robert Bullard, a dean at Texas Southern, is known as the father of environmental justice for his work analyzing how Houston, among others, disproportionately puts landfills in communities of color.[47] It follows that if the new facility will be put only in a neighborhood that already has a toxic municipal facility, then the facility would also be put in a neighborhood with mostly residents of color. Externalities from the facility would include air pollution from its incinerators plus toxins from trash that could leak into groundwater or expose workers to environmentally risky work. Bullard, an emcee for the meeting, made this point directly. The One Bin for All proposal also received criticism on the grounds that it arrests the process by which people should consider the amount of waste they produce.[48] Residents who sort recycling have a greater awareness of how much they are using, but the One Bin system would not encourage consciousness in overall use, which could increase or maintain the amount of city waste and thereby create additional air quality problems during incineration.[49]

In the weeks and months after this influential community meeting, the drumbeat for the One Bin plan got quieter. By January 2016, the local public radio station declared in a headline, "What happened to Houston's 'One Bin for All' program?"[50] It was a good question. Mayor Annise Parker, who had championed the possibilities of the One Bin proposal, issued a progress report on the proposal—on her last day in office on New Year's Eve 2015.[51]

Instead of a robust civic conversation on how best to move forward with new initiatives for recycling, the opportunity was wasted. In early

2016, Waste Management, the refuse behemoth headquartered in the city, changed their rate for how much to charge for the trash. The city was being charged sixty-five dollars per ton, but new contract negotiations called for ninety-five dollars a ton.[52] In a city with an ambitious new mayor that was also facing a $126 million shortfall for its upcoming annual budget, allocating a few extra million for anything was going to be difficult. Houston does not have a garbage fee, one of the few major American cities without one.[53] One city councilperson felt the Market City bind: "As much as we are for recycling, I'm also against cutting people that are actually doing city services. . . . It's going to hurt to lay people off and then to tell them we laid them off because, 'Well, we want to recycle.'"[54] There's something to this: in a Market City with little public finances (like no trash fees as a backbone of the sanitation services), these are the intense trade-offs that local policymakers face. Recycling is too easily subject to the whims of budget constraints.

Even though Houston had recently expanded recycling to all of its neighborhoods for the first time, there was a real chance that municipal recycling would end in the city. But a compromise was reached. The contract would be raised to ninety dollars per ton, not ninety-five dollars. The contract held that the city would no longer recycle glass through curbside bins, a more expensive and difficult-to-process material than other recyclables.[55] This was a harsh concession: glass is nearly fully reusable, but also never decomposes.[56] Glass under the new contract goes to landfills.

The politics of waste in each city portrays some telling points about Market Cities and People Cities. Copenhagen recognizes waste as a huge problem, one that is relevant for climate change and the environment. People Cities understand that waste is the least good kind of public good, and feel the need to manage it in some fashion. Market Cities, however, have trouble dealing with a public externality like waste and end up sending a huge proportion to landfills. Houston's attempts at new policies during difficult budget times end up leaving the waste problem hardly resolved.

The issue of waste also showcases a similarity: the tensions of markets in People Cities, and of people principles in Market Cities. In Copenhagen, one of the intractable problems is not just how to deal with waste, but how to provide affordable electricity and heat to residents. The more environmentally responsible solution to waste is to effect "zero waste" strategies that use multifaceted efforts to eliminate waste and any potential carbon outputs from incineration. Copenhagen could have opted for landfills too, but did not. Instead, it's the middle road. The middle road has the latent effect of benefits in providing lower electric costs, for instance, but still exacts tolls on the environment. Houston, however, has voices working to foreground equity and to protect the environment. These voices are not particularly interested in profit motives. They are interested in human health and long-term changes to the globe. And they have occasional successes: the city's newspaper, for instance, has endorsed a city garbage fee, and all neighborhoods now receive recycling services.[57] Small victories have not fundamentally shifted the Houston system—the city has not adopted a garbage fee and glass recycling is out in the city—but Market Cities must deal with the people voices within their own borders, just as market models are discussed in People Cities.

Disasters in the Cities

Smiley used to work some summers as a tour guide to squeeze extra bucks for his studies. One typically does not think of tour guides as being particularly affected by climate change. But in 2010, while working at a cave in southern Kentucky that features a short waterway, a five-hundred-year flood event in nearby Nashville sent enough rain to shut down the cave for three weeks—the rainwater had filled the eighty-foot cavern. Three weeks of work were lost. The following year, having moved to Memphis, Tennessee, a hundred-year flood event swamped low-lying parts of the city, thanks to a wet spring further north along the Mississippi River. It resulted in missed work time for Smiley, this time at a riverside park in that city. Three weeks of pay lost again. What are the odds of that two summers in a row?

As much as we have been accustomed to thinking of weather events in one hundred (or five hundred!) year intervals, the repeated instances worldwide of extreme weather are enough to make us question the numbers. Indeed, climate scientists are too. An article from 2012 in *Nature Climate Change* details how the "100-year flood event" may start to happen anywhere between every three years and every twenty years.[58]

All of this brings us to a simple point: natural disasters are occurring more often than seems appropriate, and they are coming about partly for reasons that aren't "natural." Anthropogenic climate change, according to scientists, is a primary cause.

Much of the discussion around climate change focuses on fighting against it, not ways to cope with it. But both are increasingly relevant. The effects of climate change are especially thrown into relief with extreme weather events. These storms test cities that were not built to withstand them. They also test more than just the physical infrastructure, but the social infrastructure too. Scholars in this field discuss the "resilience" of cities to climate change, and to extreme weather events.[59]

Copenhagen and Houston are both low-lying coastal cities, and flooding is the primary worry, whether from a sudden downpour or a terrifying hurricane. We profile two disasters, one in each city: the rainstorm of July 2, 2011, in Copenhagen, and Hurricane Ike in Houston in September 2008. These are not the only disasters we could profile; the 2015 Memorial Day floods (as well as repeated floods since) and tropical storm Allison in 2001 also come to mind for Houston. We analyze these two disasters because each had a devastating effect on the respective urban area, and because there has been ample time since the events to investigate new strategies for resilience to climate change in each city.

They knew it was going to rain, but not like this. Business owners with shops at basement level could not have foreseen how quickly the water would come down in the Copenhagen storm of July 2, 2011. For that matter, the Danish Meteorological Institute (DMI) did not issue their highest degree of warning because the storm did not look so bad as it moved from Sweden. One part of the city measured 3.1 millimeters of rain *per minute*, 25 percent more than had ever been recorded in the Copenhagen area.[60] The storm brought the most rainfall in a twenty-four-hour period since the DMI had begun tracking it in the mid-1950s.[61] It was the equivalent of two ordinary Copenhagen Julys worth of rain.[62]

Floods overtook much of the city, including those shopkeepers' basements. The estimated damage citywide was approximately one billion dollars. Homeowners along with shop owners either scooped out water with buckets or waited for insurance help to begin anew. To compound the whole problem, rats, perhaps hundreds of thousands of rats, died as the sewers overflowed and sat out in street gutters in plain view.[63] Because of rats' propensity for carrying disease, some people became sick, including one resident who died eighteen days after the storm from rat-related sickness, the one death from the terrible storm.[64]

What was clearly the worst storm in the city's modern history prompted a political reckoning. Meteorologists, engineers, and politicians agreed that while it had been really bad, it could very well happen again, and that the city would be every bit as unprepared the next time as it was this time. Unless they did something different.

Copenhagen's disaster plan was born out of that July chaos. As Morten Kabell, the technical and environmental mayor for Copenhagen, told us in an interview, the city was presented with two choices. Choice number one: build much larger sewer systems. This was how humans dealt with this problem in the last century or two. If we can engineer enough places to put the water, then that should work. The water would then be sent out to nearby waterways. The price tag would be pretty high, some two billion dollars or so, and it would take twenty years; it would mean digging up the whole underground throughout the city. This is the conventional path, the way most cities would do it.

Which of course means Copenhagen took choice number two. This second choice also shares the importance of underground water catchment areas—or, less nicely, *sewers*—by renovating existing infrastructure. But alongside this focus are equally important priorities that look for places on land to put the water.[65] The point of departure is that the floods of today are not the floods of yesterday, as today they are exacerbated by urbanization. Asphalt is a big culprit, but also think of historic streams that were paved over decades ago or the grass-to-home ratio for where people live versus what the land was like before buildings and pavement were there. The way the water flows off of a parking lot is not the same way it would have flowed when it was not a parking lot. Nature had a better way of taking care of it, and we humans are just trying to keep our heads above water.

The idea, then, is to incorporate green design that meshes the natural with the urban. This means that we use the water on the surface instead of letting it go down to the sewers, where it can bubble up in ways that we're never quite prepared for. Using the water on the surface means installing more water features in parks, ones that are explicitly designed to channel water to them in the event of a storm. Or even just sending water to large fields that are not in use when it's pouring rain anyway, like soccer fields.[66] It means that every bit of concrete—stones in backyards, overly wide sidewalks—that might be able to become green gets grass.[67] And it includes networking the green infrastructure of paths, parks, roofs, and the like, so they all connect a little more, instead of an arrangement of urban islands that are forced to bear a disproportionate burden.[68] When the water runs off of the pavement of the city, the new Copenhagen way seeks to harness the water back into the city, instead of rushing it underground.

There's also one other benefit: cost. The project cost of $868 million comes in at under half of the predicted price of the first option of enhanced and new sewers. It is not why Copenhagen is taking this route—again, most other cities in dire financial straits adapt more ambitious, expensive sewer plans—but it is a nice silver lining.

One final point is that Copenhagen's flood resiliency efforts, like its residents, take global warming as a real threat, and a serious one at that. It's not just something to acknowledge so the city can then move on to higher priorities. Instead, it factors directly into the planning. The climate adaptation plan discusses meteorological projections of the heaviness of rainfall and notes that the changing climate makes the one-in-one-hundred-year flood events to be more likely than one in a hundred years.[69] By inserting climate change science into government planning alongside resident-friendly infrastructure, the People City of Copenhagen gives a holistic problem a necessarily holistic solution.

Greater Houston's location along the Gulf of Mexico means no mistake can be made: it is in hurricane territory. Major hurricanes have hit southeast Texas throughout the city's history. Most devastating was the Galveston hurricane of 1900, the deadliest hurricane in American history when an estimated six to twelve thousand perished in the storm. Galveston forever ceded regional prominence to Houston in the aftermath of the storm.[70]

Galveston and the Houston region were deeply challenged again in 2008 with the landfall of Hurricane Ike. The water rose ten to fifteen feet across the Galveston peninsula and completely covered the once-sleepy beach areas on Bolivar peninsula.[71] Further inland, Houston got hammered by intense rains and winds reaching 110 miles per hour.[72] Seventy-four people died as a result of the storm.[73] The category 2 hurricane exacted approximately twenty billion dollars in damages to the Houston region.[74]

Ike was an unequivocally terrible storm, the worst hurricane to hit the Houston area in decades, and one of the costliest in American history. But a 2015 in-depth report by the *Texas Tribune* and the nonprofit news source ProPublica details how it could have been even worse. Hurricane Ike actually narrowly avoided the city of Houston and the Ship Channel, instead hitting Galveston more directly and heading out to the eastern edge of the metropolitan area.

The investigation compiles what engineers, climate scientists, and social scientists have been fearful of, and what they have been researching for years. As we have noted, Houston is home to some of the world's largest petrochemical facilities, which have been strategically located along the Houston Ship Channel to maximize the movement of goods for profit. The Ship Channel, with its direct connection to the Gulf of Mexico and bayous further inland that flood all too easily, could be overwhelmed with water. Toxic facilities and neighborhoods sit side by side—and next to the water. It prompts a question: how bad could it get if the storm of the century hits?

Really bad, research shows. If a storm of Ike's strength had hit Houston directly—instead of Ike's trajectory slightly east of the city—it would inundate ten of the country's largest refineries and overwhelm dozens of toxic chemical facilities. It would be a near-mortal blow for the Clear Lake area, which includes NASA's Johnson Space Center (a mere five feet above sea level at its lowest point). The economic effect of this would paralyze Houston for years, perhaps forever, and send aftershocks throughout the U.S. economy, including hikes in gas prices at the pump. The loss of human life along Ship Channel neighborhoods could be very high. Finally, as scientists around the world are now saying, it is not *if* the storm of the century hits, but *when*. Houston, for example, is subjected to a major storm every fifteen years.[75]

This harsh reality demands a thorough response. Scientists have begun to outline such responses, most often taking the form of some sort of flood wall and storm surge mitigation in Galveston Bay and beyond. These measures would help to slow the tide of rising water in Houston's

Ship Channel in the event of a storm. It would also be extremely costly: estimates for one option (a "mid-bay gate" in Galveston Bay) is $2.8 billion, while estimates for another (the "coastal spine" or "Ike Dike" along the Galveston Island coast) is $8 billion.[76]

Enter public officials, and a Market City conundrum. Residents and business are deeply threatened by extreme weather events such as hurricanes. Lives would be lost, the economy permanently fractured, and toxins could poison waterways with repercussions for humans and wildlife for years to come. But what may sound like a problem that needs to be fixed ends up creating problems of its own.

The chief problem is political inaction. "We've been sitting ducks. We've done nothing," said Phil Bedient, who is the head of Rice University's Severe Storm Prediction, Education, and Evacuation from Disasters (SSPEED) center.[77] A spokesperson from the mayor's office says that "only a small portion of the city of Houston is at risk for a major storm surge"—forgetting that that "small portion" has hundreds of thousands of residents, and some extremely toxic and economically valuable industrial facilities.[78] The city looks to the federal government for leadership, but the legislative bodies are struggling with even recognizing climate change, much less the links between it and weather events, or the need to protect against such disasters. At the same time, residents are confused about how much to react to storms, as evidenced in interviews conducted by researchers after Ike.[79]

Indeed, that is its own problem—acknowledging that climate change exists and is a present danger, which runs contrary to many of the Ship Channel's biggest clients. ExxonMobil's Baytown refinery is the biggest refinery in the United States, the same ExxonMobil that—in analyses by the Columbia School of Journalism and the *Los Angeles Times* as well as *Inside Climate News*—was researching the effects of climate change for decades while publicly denying the existence of the environmental threat.[80] In Houston, climate change is the problem that has no shame.

The nexus of politics and science that meets at this problem has yet to converge in a manner that produces a solution. Market Cities are not particularly equipped to deal with large, forward-thinking projects like those required for climate change resiliency. Those projects require intensive central planning, which Market Cities dislike. They require potential market disruptions, which Market Cities avoid.

Despite Copenhagen and Houston having faced terrible disasters and looking at more to come, they have not responded with the same commitment to solutions. For the most part, Houston has chosen to hope for the best or to ignore it altogether. The benefit is that present profits go unsqueezed. Job growth continues apace. Copenhagen felt that the situation was untenable and took action. City officials and residents partnered to build a greener infrastructure that can absorb rains. Extreme weather events as a result of climate change are becoming a defining feature of the twenty-first century city, and whether you live in a Market City or a People City will dramatically affect how your city copes with the cataclysm.

Conclusion

Crucial questions addressed in this chapter will become ever more important in coming decades. Can Market Cities create a more impactful approach to environmental problems? Will People Cities be able to decrease their carbon footprints and reverse the dangerous urbanization–climate change relationship?

This chapter indicates that the answers to these questions are complicated. For Market Cities, environmental issues will only continue to increase in importance, especially as adaptation to climate change becomes an apparent reality. Meanwhile, relatively low levels of pro-environmental beliefs, disparities in exposure to environmental degradation, and uneven governmental commitment condition the possibilities for this adaptation and add a significant layer of environmental problems. The economy and environment relationship, as our survey respondents indicated, prioritizes the economy, and the effects on the environment have been and likely will continue to be devastating.

Market Cities, then, demonstrate the tight relationship between capitalist urbanization and environmental degradation. In urban areas where market forces play a greater role in urbanization, there will be more environmental degradation. Little will be done to alleviate this relationship without radical changes for the Market City. Until such change occurs, health risks from toxic facilities will evince racial disparities, carbon emissions will have an outsized effect on the planet's health, waste will stack higher, wild storms will threaten coasts, and toxic industries will be supported as the core of the local economy.

People Cities are more energetic in their attempts to upend the city's dangerous effects on the environment. Planning foregrounds environmental problems—ranging from planning for unplanned storms to combating climate change—and reaches for bold solutions. Economic foci shift to more postindustrial bases, which attenuate reliance on toxic and extractive industries. Residents believe widely in climate change and prioritize the environment over economy.

But these efforts are simultaneously structured by the relationships among cities, environmental degradation, and capitalism. It stands to reason that a People City would be less environmentally problematic compared to a Market City because they pursue a middle ground between being a full participant in the capitalist system and deliberately safeguarding against some capitalist excesses. This line of reasoning, however, does not extend so far as to suggest that People Cities will soon solve the problem of environmental degradation. As we saw with examples of waste incineration and the carbon offsets in the carbon-neutral plan, real environmental problems remain, even if they are not as large or penetrating as those in Market Cities. As both Market Cities and People Cities face perilous environmental futures, precarious change is just the high-water mark.

6

Life Together and Apart

Diversity and Trust

We heard about Patrick, married and the father of three children, through a connection in Copenhagen. He and his family were Americans from Los Angeles (a Market City). At least they used to be Americans. Seven years prior they uprooted the family to move to Copenhagen, not for a year or even seven, but permanently. They moved for life, figuratively and literally.

We sat down with Patrick at a local coffee shop in his densely settled Copenhagen neighborhood. After some initial greetings and introductions, we asked the questions we were most curious about.

Why did you make the giant move from being an Angeleno to a Copenhagener?

"I got tired of having to argue that health care and education for everyone was good for a society. I got tired of people seemingly no longer interested in intelligent discussions, but simply name calling and taking political sides. I just broke and said that is it. I will find a place to bring my family where those issues are largely settled, and where when debate occurs, people are actually interested in being informed and finding best solutions. That has brought me to Copenhagen."

So how would you compare life here to life in Los Angeles?

"I cannot tell you how much less stress we have in our life. I make less money than I could in the U.S., and I don't miss it a bit. I need less, and our basics are covered—we even receive a quarterly deposit into our bank account for each of our three children. That helps. What is interesting is that people here are not so interested in 'getting ahead.' You come to work, you do your job, and then you go home to be with your family and to enjoy life. I get no kudos from my boss if I come in to work early or stay late. In fact, I get a kick in the pants. 'Go home, live your life' he says. 'The work will be here tomorrow when you return.'"

What else strikes you?

"We have a small place, but daycare is downstairs, the metro is a five-minute walk from here, most every store and place we want to be is within ready walking distance. Our friends are close by. It makes life so much simpler. Compared to living in Los Angeles, living in Copenhagen means less stress, more freedom, more natural exercise, and more good living."

We met Tobias and Katrina, a thirty-something couple from Copenhagen in Houston, where they had moved four years prior. Both had grown up in Copenhagen, but due to their employment in the energy industry, they ended up in Houston. We met them at a local restaurant for lunch and discussion.

How does living in Houston contrast with Copenhagen?

"They do not really compare," said Katrina. "They are so different. First is the scale. Houston is so big physically, spread out. The buildings are bigger, people live in houses even in the city, the houses are huge, and you must drive everywhere, because Houston is built for the car, not for people to walk. It is funny, but Tobias and I were talking a few nights ago, saying in Copenhagen we so often met people outside, on the streets, at the canal, at a park. Here, we mostly meet people inside buildings."

"Another uniqueness is that there are many opportunities for people to be what they want to be," stated Tobias, "if they can get an education and live in a good area of the city. People here can be rich, well, you come to realize that a lot of people here seem to have money, and a lot of people here seem to not have money. It is the contrasts that Katrina and I marvel at most—the difference in neighborhoods and crime, the differences between people, the differences in schools."

Katrina picked up on that thought, saying, "it really seems like you can have—how can I best say this?—a good life here, and you can have exactly the opposite. People must compete hard, trying to succeed. That is a concept we are learning, how important it is here to 'succeed,' which we are learning usually means to have a high-paying job, have things, and live in a nice neighborhood." "And those things," Tobias noted, "give you a nice life and respect from others here. It is almost as if your worth as a person is conditional, depending on whether others judge you a success. We have a good life here, because we are judged by other Houstonians to be successful. And I find it strange, but despite the stress we often feel, life here can be intoxicating. You can get accustomed to the perks of living here. It has so many possibilities."

As the experiences of Patrick, Tobias, and Katrina suggest, life in Market Cities and People Cities is different, fundamentally. The same person, the same family, will experience life uniquely depending on the type of city in which they live. From our interviews and our surveys, we have found many key differences, from stress levels, to trust in others, to time spent socializing, to fear of crime, to what types of people live in the city and where they live. Discussing Market Cities and People Cities is not just some academic exercise in classification; it is rather a means to grasp a myriad of differences in city organization and city life, differences that impact us as humans in divergent ways.

Before we turn to those examinations, we introduce a bit of intrigue. On nearly all of the issues explored in this chapter, to many readers it may seem as if Market Cities got the short end of the stick. But despite less trust of others, higher crime, more inequality, and more segregation, residents of Market City Houston are as happy as the "happiest people on earth" in Copenhagen, and they are as supportive of their city being a wonderful place to live as are Copenhageners. How can this be? Let's dive in.

Trust

It is difficult to overestimate the importance of trust for social life. Most everything we do that involves other people is predicated on trusting (or not) other people. A short thought experiment might help make this point clear. Imagine you are searching online to purchase a used car. You read descriptions of various vehicles for sale, look at the photos, and consider the price and the seller. The latter consideration is essential. Is the seller reputable? Can you trust that the description of the car is accurate? Suppose you find the make and model you are looking for at a better-than-expected price. The description says the following (as we actually have seen advertised): "12 years old, but like new, with only 8,000 miles! A widow owned the vehicle the entire 12 years and other than driving to church once a week, kept the car in her garage!"

Would you believe this description? Or does it sound too good to be true? Since you don't know the seller, you have to rely on what we call generalized trust, that is, trust in people you have not met. In short, trust in strangers. If you think people generally cannot be trusted, you would undoubtedly be suspicious. You might reflect, "Probably some hack who knows how to refurbish old cars and wind back the odometer. I'll pass and keep looking." But if you think most people can be trusted, you may jump at the chance to purchase the vehicle.

Conversely, if you are the seller of the car, if the buyer asked to purchase the car today but pay you tomorrow, would you let the buyer drive the car away? This is an actual thought experiment by trust expert and Aarhus University (Denmark) professor Gert Tinggaard Svendsen. In his classes he asks his Copenhagen (and other Danish city) students this very question. Mostly, they say yes, they would be willing to sell the car today and trust they would receive the promised payment tomorrow. We were curious—what would people in Houston say? Our Houston readers are probably already nervously fidgeting in their seats at the prospect. Our sample was nonrandom—we used the classic person-on-the-street method and asked people we knew. Still, the response was resounding: No way!

This example is a market exchange—buyers and sellers are present. But that is just one type of exchange. We can and often do exchange affection, friendship, teamwork, and other forms of social life with others. Always, we rely on trust. If trust is not present, we either avoid the exchange, or engage in what we might call "social control." We attempt to create laws, rules, and other control systems to make sure people and organizations cooperate fairly.

So in our randomized surveys of thousands of Houstonians and thousands of Copenhageners, we asked an often-used question about trust: would you say that most people can be trusted or you can't be too careful in dealing with people? The results were dramatic. Only about 36 percent of Houstonians said most people could be trusted, whereas *more than 80 percent* of Copenhageners said most people could be trusted. As a result, most Copenhageners go through each day's social interactions trusting others. In Houston, most people go through each day suspicious, cautious, and distrustful of people outside their circle of friends and family. In such a case, generalized social interaction is real work in Houston, a complicated game of trying to figure out if one is going to be "taken" or not, of trying to figure out the real motives of others, and determining if you should engage in the social interaction or avoid it.

The result is that, compared to Copenhagen, Houstonians elect to reduce this complexity by limiting social interaction. In contrast to Copenhageners, Houstonians simply spend less time interacting with real live human beings. In the place of such social interaction, they spend more time alone, more time watching TV, more time on computers, and more time in their homes. For example, in our surveys, we found that in the past year, compared to Copenhageners, Houstonians were only half as likely to have visited any cultural place whatsoever (for example, museum, theater, opera, sporting event).[1]

The consequences of such are quite significant. Humans are social creatures. Others things being equal, they are happier, healthier, and more satisfied with life when they have abundant social interaction and when they feel they can trust others. In cities like Houston, finding affirming groups one can trust becomes essential. If you cannot trust people in general, the main coping mechanism—given that the need for human interaction remains—is to find a smaller group of people that you feel you can trust. This may be one factor at play when we find that a very high percentage of Houstonians attend houses of worship, and the more they attend, the happier they report they are.[2]

As a People City, Copenhagen constantly works toward city designs and policies that will encourage and invite interaction among its citizens, not just in small groups, but also with Copenhageners in general. Such design and policies are extensive, from detailed urban design studies—what shape, width, and placement of benches lead to more people sitting together, what park features lead to families spending more time in the park, what ratio of windows to solid walls leads to greater invitation to enter a coffeehouse—to carefully crafted urban policies intended to reward trust in others and facilitate Copenhageners meeting one another and spending time together, be it at large events or talking for a few moments on a bridge between neighborhoods.

The high levels of generalized trust in Copenhagen are what Svendsen in his book *Trust* calls "Danish Gold." An economist by trade, Svendsen's primary focus is on the economic benefits of trust. As he outlines, these include a greater ability to cooperate, fewer lawsuits, fewer burglar alarms, and less extensive forms of other control (less investment needed in police or security officers, for example), less need for and time spent on comprehensive, formal contracts, and ultimately more economic efficiency. Moving beyond strictly economic benefits, he also highlights how high trust, which increases cooperation, ultimately "makes you a little high."[3] By this he means that through positive social interaction, our brains release oxytocin, a hormone that research finds gives people a feeling of well-being, happiness, and contentment. Truly, living in a Market City or a People City can lead to very different feelings toward and experiences with life.

The high level of trust has far-reaching advantages, from the small to the massive. In high trust Copenhagen, it is common to see babies in prams, outside coffee shops and stores, taking naps (no matter the temperature). That in itself is not so entirely unusual. What *is* unusual is that there are no parents or guardians around. Typically they are inside, having coffee or doing some shopping. For most of the world, that is a level of trust hard to fathom.

We even saw trust displayed when we interviewed the Copenhagen mayors. For example, when we interviewed the mayor of employment and integration, we concluded the interview by telling the mayor that if we quote her in the book, we will first send her the manuscript for her to see. She seemed to appreciate that gesture, but as her assistant was escorting her out of the office to attend another meeting, she stopped, turned around, and said, "There is no need for that. I trust you." Something similar happened when we interviewed the mayor of technical and environmental affairs. As we explained at the end of the interview that we would let him see any text pertaining to him before publishing the book, he smiled and told us, "That is thoughtful, but I am sure there will be no need for that. We can trust each other."

Trust has consequences. Back in 1996 *Reader's Digest* did an experiment. Wallets were left with owners' addresses in them in various cities around the world, places the magazine knew from surveys had differing levels of trust. The magazine reported finding that the more trusting the people were in the survey, the higher the percentage of wallets that were mailed back to their owner. Greater trust was associated with greater positive, honest action.

Reporters at a Danish television station decided to do the same experiment in about 2012 in Copenhagen. They chose one of the busiest sites in the city—Copenhagen Central Station. The experiment did not go too well. As they tried to leave the wallets, people would instantly pick them up and go running after whoever had dropped the wallet. After this happened over and over, they simply gave up trying to do the experiment.[4]

We also know trust and its cousin, cooperation, are essential to creating the cities of the future. As Harvard business professor Amy Edmondson and her colleague Susan Salter Reynolds summarize in their article, "Smart Cities: It Takes More than a Village," creating the city of the future "requires a level of teamwork across industries and areas of expertise rarely seen on the world stage." Because "smart cities" necessarily imply the integration of systems, organizations, industries, units, flows, and networks, there is simply no other way to move in such a direction than to rely on trust, cooperation, and problem solving together. Creating and harnessing trust will be a major objective and requirement of successful, vibrant cities going forward.[5]

Crime

When Emerson was five years old, his family home was broken into on a cold February evening. Windows were destroyed, the house was trashed from top to bottom, his father's gun and ammunition (from his days in the military) were taken, and even the precious snowman he and his brother had built in the front yard was pulverized. But what was more fundamentally stolen was a sense of security. From that point on it seemed clear: have an alarm system if you wish, lock your doors and windows if you wish, but if a burglar wants to get into your home, the burglar will get into your home. How does one feel safe in such a context?

The challenge of safety and the threat of crime are critical parts of cities. Given that cities are by definition a heterogeneous collection of people from many different places—a diverse set of strangers—crime seemingly always has been higher in cities.[6] According to social control theory, crime is lower when people know and are accountable to one another. When they are integrated into society through relationships, and the subsequent commitments, values, and norms to not commit crime, to respect others, and to be law-abiding, they will do exactly that. In addition, several theories of why crime occurs reference inequality and the desire to obtain what society says represents the good life but seems out of reach to a person. Thus trust in others, cooperating, greater social interaction, and reduced social inequality all suggest lower crime rates.

Given what we know so far about Houston and Copenhagen, we would suspect that crime is significantly higher in Houston than it is Copenhagen. This is quite dramatically the case. For decades the city of Houston has had at least 200 murders per year (with the single exception of 2011, when there were 198 murders). In the most recent five-year period for which we have data (2011–15), there were over 1,100 murders in Houston, for a murder rate of 10.2 per 100,000 people. Put more simply, for every 100,000 people in Houston, each year 10 will be murdered. In the same five-year period, there were 40 murders in Copenhagen. The murder rate for Copenhagen is 1.2, meaning for every 100,000 people in Copenhagen, each year there will be on average about one murder. In short, Houstonians are 10 times more likely to be murdered in their city than are Copenhageners to be murdered in theirs.

The differences in actual crime rates are reflected in how citizens of the respective cities feel about crime. We asked Houstonians and Copenhageners how worried they were that they or a member of their family would be a victim of crime. Nearly two-thirds (63 percent) of Houstonians said they were somewhat or very worried. In contrast, just 19 percent of Copenhageners reported that they were somewhat or very worried. What is more, though we were unable to ask the question of Houstonians, we asked Copenhageners how much they agreed with the statement, "Crime is a significant problem in my neighborhood." Only one in seventeen Copenhageners strongly agreed with this statement, and fully three-quarters disagreed.

Again, it is not just that Houstonians and Copenhageners differ in their fear of crime victimization. What matters perhaps even more is that a strong majority of Houstonians fear being a victim of crime, while in contrast a strong majority of Copenhageners have no such fear. As Copenhagen city councilperson John Andersen told us: "We don't have 'no go' neighborhoods. The safety of the city is a wonderful positive for our people." In contrast, we often hear from Houston citizens like resident Dwight Bordelon, who appeared at multiple city council meetings to raise the issue of crime in his neighborhood: "The crime is significant in my neighborhood and it is not being addressed." Bordelon lives in a trendy area of the city, an area with lower crime than many other areas of the city.[7] For the majority of Houston residents with whom we spoke, they said the very opposite of Copenhagen councilperson Andersen. They told us there are several neighborhoods one does not go to in the day due to their perception of danger, even more neighborhoods one does not go to at night, and it would be foolish to ever go outside for a walk at night alone in several neighborhoods. As Houston resident Heather Heinke told reporters at the *Houston Chronicle*: "It seems like [crime has] increased, to [the point of] not being able to leave your home in a peaceful state of mind. You kind of feel helpless . . . you feel you're out there exposed, like you're out there on your own."[8]

Living in these two cities, then, produces divergent experiences in people's mental states. It feels different living in the Market City of Houston than it does living in the People City of Copenhagen. Most people in Houston live with a background fear of being victimized by crime. Most people in Copenhagen have no such fear. And these perceptions (and likely the actual differences in crime levels) directly shape behaviors, such as the freedom to move confidently throughout the city.

Inequality

Market Cities, by definition, accept inequality. While most people in most cities would relish seeing all residents thrive, Market City leaders and most residents accept economic and social inequality as part of the market system. Some people win big, others do not. That is simply the reality. A common ideology that goes along with this reality is that who wins (usually expressed as "who succeeds") and who does not is up to individuals. Are they willing to work hard? Are they willing to make sacrifices to succeed educationally and economically? Do they have the fortitude to stick with their dream when the going gets difficult?

The winners in Market Cities are thought to be those for whom the answer is yes to each of these questions. Those doing less well, though they may have family difficulties or live in less-than-ideal neighborhoods, are thought to be those who have chosen not to succeed, made poor choices, or in some cases do not see the substantial opportunities available to them in Market Cities. As an economically successful Houstonian told us over lunch at an upscale restaurant, though there are children growing up in poor, underserved neighborhoods in the city, each child has a pilot light within that if he or she is willing to set aflame, will succeed, due to the abundant opportunities in the city.

Here we see the single key word used to describe Houston by many Houstonians—both as the city currently is and what it wishes to be: *opportunity*. No other word is used more often, thought to be as important, or seen as the ultimate reality and continued hope for the greatness of Houston. The word "opportunity" represents its essence, its core, its center, its beating heart and pulsating lifeblood. In fact, urbanists Joel Kotkin and Tory Gattis call Houston the quintessential "Opportunity City." By this term they mean cities designed for one fundamental purpose—to offer opportunity for economic success and upward mobility. Gattis lists three main characteristics of the opportunity city: Entrepreneur Friendly (pro-growth, pro-business, no zoning, low regulation, and a vibrant economy, to name a few), Affordable Proximity (affordable living near jobs and the urban scene), and an Energized Community with an Open Culture (diversity, friendliness, openness to outsiders, future oriented, optimistic).[9] Social commentator and *New York Times* syndicated columnist David Brooks echoes this terminology—Houston, Dallas, Charlotte, and the like, he says, are Opportunity Cities, or, we would add, in our more holistic understanding, Market Cities.[10]

As long as there is opportunity—typically, at least as defined by influential Houstonians, meaning lots of jobs or the possibility of creating a successful economic path—then inequality is entirely acceptable, acceptable not just to those at the top end, but it seems to many at the bottom end as well. Though all are encouraged to succeed economically, no one is required to do so. As such, we would expect a fairly high level of inequality, as in large gaps in educational achievement, income, wealth, and neighborhood quality.

According to a June 2016 CityLab article, since the recession of 2008–9, nearly all U.S. metros have increased the number of jobs and economic output, but only eight have seen "across-the-board improvements" in the well-being of middle- and low-income residents. Houston has been in the top three in terms of job gains, economic output gains, and population growth, but it is not among the eight U.S. metros that have seen across-the-board improvement. And that, we see across our data, is just fine. Although it would be nice if all were improving, and if there are any clear barriers to success Houstonians should help reduce them, the city is doing what it is meant to do—increase opportunity. Again, it is up to individuals to take advantage of the opportunities. What is more, the high population growth—and the attracting of many immigrants—means there is always a lag, another form of built-in inequality. People move to Houston for opportunities for economic mobility, but it takes time, and as they begin to rise up the economic ladder, they are continually replaced by a stream of immigrants at the bottom of the ladder seeking to make their climb. For most people in Market Cities, the level of inequality is not a measure of the success of the city. Rather, the true measure is whether people over their life span and across generations rise up the economic ladder. According to urbanist Joel Kotkin, places like Houston excel at doing exactly this.

In People Cities like Copenhagen, which are integrated into the same global capitalist system as Market Cities such as Houston, extensive inequality violates one of its core tenets and aspirations—equality of its citizens. As Andersen, the city council member, told us, "as a city we want social democratic growth, not market-driven growth. . . . We avoid extreme inequality." For People Cities, then, capitalism must be tamed. This is usually done through more extensive redistribution efforts than in Market Cities, and through a more concerted focus to provide for free or at much reduced costs services they consider the "essentials" of life in the modern world—health care, dental care, affordable education access through university and professional schools, safe neighborhoods, mobility access, and clean air and water.[11]

Due to differences in national and local policies concerning taxes, redistribution, benefits, retirement rules, and the like, it is difficult to compare levels of inequality across cities of different nations. But a measure called the Gini coefficient is designed to compare, in one number, the level of income inequality between citizens. Its concept is quite simple. If everyone earned the exact same amount, the Gini coefficient would be zero; if all money was in the hands of just one person, and no one else earned any income, the Gini coefficient would be 1. Obviously, neither value exists in the modern world (not even close), but some places have more inequality—more concentration of income in the hands of a few citizens—than do other places.

In 2014, the Gini coefficient for Copenhagen was 0.32,[12] whereas in Houston it was 0.53.[13] The 0.32 figure means Copenhagen is closer to having its citizens' income distributed evenly across its people than it is to having that income concentrated in the hands of just a few. In contrast, with its 0.53 Gini coefficient Houston is closer to having its citizens' income distributed to just a wealthy few than it is to having that income distributed equally across its citizens.

To give us some context for these numbers, while Copenhagen has a Gini value of 0.32, no U.S. metro has a value less than 0.40. So U.S. places that might seem less like Market Cities, such as Portland, Oregon score low (0.44) compared to places like Houston, but they are still higher than Copenhagen. Conversely, only two localities in Denmark have Gini coefficients of 0.40 or higher (as of 2014). Clearly, national policies matter for cities, but what cities do matters as well (hence why we can find substantial variation between cities within the same nations). The world economy matters too: in the last fifteen years both Copenhagen and Houston have seen a steady climb in their levels of inequality, as greater wealth concentrates in both cities but is not evenly distributed among its citizens.

In Houston, this is not a matter of much concern.[14] Inequality may be growing, but that could simply be due not to the poor getting poorer, but to the rich getting richer. That is part of an economically successful, opportunity city—there are vast sums of money to be made. The only *concern*—and a concern Houston leaders discuss and act upon to some degree—is to ensure that there are enough qualified workers to keep the economic dynamo of Houston propelling forward. And there is one *expectation*—that those who make their millions and billions through the opportunities of the Houston region give money back to the community, usually in the form of creating philanthropic foundations, as we saw in chapter 2.[15]

Conversely, in Copenhagen a fair bit of hand-wringing and self-criticism has accompanied the growth of inequality. We many times heard discussions of ghettos forming, but not for the poor. Instead, there was consternation over the possible reality that Copenhagen was developing ghettos for the wealthy, as we saw with the Paper Island example in chapter 4. This was a true slap in Copenagen's face. Despite having among the lowest levels of inequality in the world, the fact that inequality was increasing—regardless of whether it was also increasing elsewhere—was disturbing, a dirty mark on a green People City striving for equality and a good life for its citizens. Many Copenhagen leaders and citizens fret at what this growing inequality means for their residents' quality of life. They seem to have reason to fret. The book *The Spirit Level* finds that inequality is associated with substantially greater social problems such as lower life expectancy rates, higher murder rates, higher dropout rates, higher teenage pregnancy rates, greater mental illness rates, and breeds depression, resignation, addictions, and even premature aging not just for those at the low end but for those at the high end as well. The book's authors, Richard Wilkinson and Kate Pickett, argue that the relationship between economic inequality and these social problems is not merely association. Instead, they spend their entire book arguing that economic inequality *causes* greater social problems and hurts societies in the long run. They are not alone. Other works, such as Joseph Stiglitz's *The Price of Inequality*, draw similar conclusions.[16]

Residential Segregation

Houston and Copenhagen, as we would expect, not only feel and talk about inequality in different ways, they also attempt (or not) to address it in divergent ways. A big part of this is focusing on the spatial concentration of wealth and poverty—and the spatial concentration of migrants and ethnic minorities—within different areas of the city.

When there is inequality in income between people and households, a few questions face the citizens and leaders of cities. Does it matter where people live by income (or as we will discuss soon, by race, ethnicity, and immigration status)? What is the ideal in such cases? Should leaders of cities strive to reduce segregation by income or not worry about it? Perhaps it is more important to focus on providing opportunity so that those in poor areas who wish to can eventually leave.

It is a simple, long-standing question: Does segregation matter? The answer depends, of course, on who is asking and what they wish to find. And it depends on what consequence we wish to focus upon. We could ask, "Does the spatial segregation of rich and poor people negatively impact the life chances of poor people?" Or we could ask, "Does the spatial segregation of the rich and poor positively impact the life chances of the rich?" Or finally, we might ask, "Is the segregation of the rich and poor bad for a city overall, as in harming social cohesion, mental health rates, or economic growth?"

We can find many studies addressing such questions, and they don't always come to the same conclusion. But taken as a whole, the answer to each of the three questions above seems to be "yes." That is, spatial segregation by income and wealth reduces the life chances of poor families, increases the life chances of well-to-do families, and is an economic and social drain on the city, compared to the case of a more equal distribution by neighborhood of the rich and the poor.[17] Because the distribution of people across a city is fundamental to every city, it is well worth our time to unpack these findings and to examine them in the context of Houston and Copenhagen.

As a People City, Copenhagen values not only equality of its citizens but also equality of its neighborhoods. In 2010, the Danish central government identified ten disadvantaged neighborhoods in Copenhagen. As reported in Copenhagen's 2011 city plan, "The City of Copenhagen and central government have a joint responsibility to lift these areas and at the same time reduce social and health inequalities. The quality of life in troubled residential areas [primarily populated by non-Western immigrants] should be increased by ensuring more integration with the remaining city, both socially and physically."[18]

The city has set out to address neighborhood inequalities with stipulations such as access to public transportation and amenities for all citizens. Specifically, Copenhagen has designated that every citizen should live within a fifteen-minute walk of a train stop (to be achieved upon the completion of the massive circle line project in 2019–20) and within a fifteen-minute walk of a park (achieved in 2015). The city government is working to improve the quality of schools across the city. More focus was placed on integration between social workers, police, social housing, and citizens to reduce youth crime—as noted above, already low compared to most cities of the world—in the troubled neighborhoods.

When we interviewed Copenhagen's mayor of social affairs Jesper Christensen (who lives in one of the identified troubled neighborhoods), he told us that the city government has focused on making their services more accessible by being offered directly in the neighborhoods. The efforts are targeted, whether it involves door-to-door interaction encouraging students to attend school or new programs involving young people training for work with elderly persons. Five years after the goals were set, the Ministry of Housing, Urban, and Rural Affairs reported substantial declines in the crime rate among eighteen- to twenty-nine-year-olds in the identified Copenhagen neighborhoods.[19] When we asked Mayor Christensen why he and the city officials and residents cared so much about reducing inequality, he told us, "It's the right thing to do both for the individual and for the society. . . . If we want to continue to be a livable city . . . and be a city where people have good interactions with each other, we need to do the investments in people who don't have the same possibilities, or otherwise Copenhagen will end up just being a city for the rich."

As we have noted, in Market Cities like Houston inequality is not the focus. Thus, inequality levels may be of some concern: as we saw in chapter 3, nearly two-thirds of Houstonians think the government should act to reduce income inequality (though only 46 percent of white Houstonians agree), but that concern does not rise to a priority.[20] In 2004, Houston voters approved a revenue cap for the city. The cap limits the increase in Houston's property tax collections to 4.5 percent or the combined rates of inflation and population growth, whichever is lower. To put this in perspective, if property values in the city increase by 5 percent, then property tax cuts must occur, or the 4.5 percent cap would be violated. Both the previous and current mayor have asked for a repeal of the law, arguing that the cap constricts what city government can do, including addressing inequality, but to no avail. Several rounds of government layoffs have occurred since 2004 in an effort to balance the budget. In Market Cities, the concern with limiting government is almost always greater than the concern for the government addressing inequality.

Why segregation happens can, at one level, be fairly clear-cut: people have preferences for where they want to live, shaping demand for particular areas. If we use basic economics, where demand is high, prices are high. Thus, only those who can afford the most in-demand neighborhoods will end up living in them. Others will locate in neighborhoods as they are able. The result is economic segregation. The world, of course, is not this straightforward. Many other factors can and do impact the residential patterns by income, but at the root of economic segregation, it can be partially explained in these simple terms.

Most people intuitively understand this. How it is interpreted is the point of divergence. In Market Cities the dominant ideology is that this is both natural and acceptable. As people rise up the economic ranks, they can move into nicer neighborhoods. And having poorer neighborhoods serves a vital function—affordable housing for the less well-off. In People Cities the dominant ideology is that such divisions are antithetical to a city's purpose, which is producing a high quality of life for all citizens and equality between citizens. So segregation is a true cause for concern, one that People Cities search for solutions to overcome. It is a complicated task to be sure, but People Cities do have less residential segregation than do Market Cities.

Part of this difference is that there is less income inequality between individual citizens and families in People Cities. This limits the extremes of neighborhood differences found in Market Cities—there are no neighborhoods as poor and isolated as there are in Market Cities, and there are no neighborhoods as wealthy and exclusive as there are in Market Cities. This is partly what Tobias and Katrina, the Copenhageners living in Houston that we met at the beginning of this chapter, were picking up on when they talked about the extremes they see in Houston.

Despite these substantial differences, segregation still occurs in People Cities, though in muted form. As we have already seen, any segregation is a cause for significant concern in People Cities. For people to be segregated, living only with "people like us," is seen as unproductive, anticreative, and nearly immoral. It is a violation of community. Thus, Copenhagen officials and citizens continually seek to upgrade underresourced neighborhoods and to limit the extent that well-to-do people gather in separate neighborhoods.

We can understand on an intuitive level why economic segregation of neighborhoods happens, and even think of ways—if troubled by it—to reduce the levels of segregation. But another characteristic of cities is segregation by people group—by race, ethnicity, or immigration status or origin. In our experience, the instantaneous explanation people give for segregation by these characteristics is that they are simply proxies for economics, so racial/ethnic/immigrant status segregation occurs because of the differential wealth of these groups.

This has been the topic of much study, and it turns out the common understanding is partly right, partly wrong. That is, if groups were to (or eventually do) have equal wealth, segregation between the groups would decline. But it would not go away. In fact, depending on the groups, substantial segregation can and does remain. Something else is going on.

The "something else" appears to be a combination of preferences (people prefer to live with people like themselves, and they prefer to avoid living with certain groups), structural barriers (differential access to information, access to credit, and the like), and straight-up discrimination.[21] Whatever the reasons, as with economic segregation, racial, ethnic, or immigrant status segregation is largely accepted in Market Cities and resisted in People Cities. And the result is as we would expect—greater ethnic segregation in Market Cities, less ethnic segregation in People Cities.

Immigration and Ethnic Diversity

A city is defined in part by immigration and diversity. People continually move to cities from elsewhere, and thus cities are diverse by definition. Incorporating newly arriving residents is both an inevitable part of city life and one of its most difficult tasks. Prejudice against immigrants to the city, especially from nonculturally similar countries, is not only a risk but all too apparent. This can lead to political movements that seek to limit immigration and curtail rights and programs for immigrants already present.

Nearly all cities of the contemporary Western world in principle welcome and celebrate diversity and immigration. Nearly all cities of the contemporary Western world are ethnically diverse to at least a limited extent and typically growing more so. And nearly all cities of the contemporary Western world have a gap between their values and their actions, with conflict, inequality, ethnic tensions, and forces seeking to limit immigration and ethnic diversity.

Houston and Copenhagen approach issues of immigration and diversity in ways we might expect given their Market City versus People City contrast. Houston has relatively little formal policy regarding diversity. In fact, true to its Market City approach, when we web-searched "policies on diversity city of Houston," the first result was "Office of Business Opportunity—City of Houston." Clicking on that link, we find a description of the office's purpose: "The Office of Business Opportunity is committed to creating a competitive and diverse business environment in the City of Houston by promoting the growth and success of local small businesses, with special emphasis on historically underutilized groups."[22]

When we went to the City of Houston website and searched the key term "diversity," the first listing took us to a matrix that was a study aid for fire department personnel to prepare for a promotion examination.[23] The second listing read, "Champions of Diversity." Clicking on it, we were taken to a celebration (using the language of winning, no less) of a person of color who has succeeded economically, from the Office of Business Opportunity of the City of Houston.[24]

We also found a posting from the relatively newly elected mayor, Sylvester Turner, announcing the creation of the Office of New Americans "to improve access to City Services for all Houstonians." The announcement went on to say a task force was being created to generate recommendations to develop a Welcoming Houston program.[25] Also, the mayor "unveiled 60 welcome signs destined for the city's airports, libraries, and convention center via a tweet saluting the city's diversity: "Welcome to #Houston, the most #diverse city in #America,"[26] based on a report finding that the Houston region was the nation's most racially diverse.[27]

And finally, in late 2015 the Houston City Council approved "Plan Houston," a guiding document for Houston's planning (again, not quite zoning). Its vision statement reads: "Houston offers opportunity for all. We celebrate our diversity of people, ideas, economy, culture, and places. We promote healthy and resilient communities through smart civic investments, dynamic partnerships, education, and innovation. Houston is the place where anyone can prosper and feel at home."[28]

True to its Market City nature, Houston formally welcomes all and celebrates diversity, offering opportunity for all to succeed and thrive. It is, of course, a free market approach: you fit in if you make yourself fit in. All are welcome to come and give it a try. It is largely up to you to try to succeed: the government efforts are not large or wide-reaching. But the opportunity is there.

As we would come to expect by now, Copenhagen's approach to immigration and ethnic diversity is quite different. It opts for an intensive integration program and clear, defined, actionable policies for addressing immigration and ethnic diversity. It has set an ambitious goal: "Copenhagen wants to be the most inclusive metropolis in Europe." As a consequence, immigration and diversity issues are woven into a range of policies and initiatives. True to its people orientation, the city government states, "Copenhagen should be a diverse, coherent and safe city with a place for everyone and where everyone is needed."[29]

Policies for diversity and inclusion are woven into most areas of life, from housing and neighborhood policies to the education system and the labor market to the creation and use of public spaces. According to interviews with government officials and heads of local NGOs, for a diverse city to function well the gap between those best and worst off cannot be too big. Thus policies of redistribution, education, and job training, among others, are in part diversity policies.[30] The city also aims to design public spaces to invite its diversity of people to encounter one another: "Public spaces in the city are where we interact with other people. A short chat on a bench or maybe just eye-contact and a smile enhances the quality of life and increases mutual tolerance and understanding."[31] The city also works hard, often in crosswinds of national politics, to attract immigrants, creating an International House, converting many documents into English, sponsoring a city-supported International School, offering free Danish language training, and related support.

The approach seems to work, at least in part. The Department of Inclusion and Employment each year conducts a survey of Copenhageners. Among the questions asked are whether residents feel like they belong in Copenhagen and whether they feel like they belong in Denmark. The responses of the immigrants are interesting. As one employee of the department stated: "We see quite markedly that . . . ethnic minorities feel the same extent of belonging in Copenhagen as the majority does but that they to a much lesser degree feel like part of Denmark compared with natives."[32]

But this is not rose-colored glass. As interviews with government employees and NGO workers suggest, immigration and diversity does not come without problems, and tolerance toward those who are different from oneself is not always achieved, both in the formation of policies and in the perspectives of individual Copenhageners. As one employee of the Financial Administration noted: "It's easy to say that diversity can be rewarding, but in order to be culturally competent and actually benefit from diversity and not just be like . . . 'do as we do, or leave' . . . then you have to challenge your own way of thinking. . . . And I'm not sure that this is always positive in Copenhagen Municipality, and that it is received in a positive manner."[33]

We see evidence of such perspectives in our surveys. We asked respondents in both cities how they felt about changing trends in immigration. Specifically, we asked their views on two straightforward policies. The first asked whether more, fewer, or about the same number of immigrants should be allowed into the country. The second asked whether they favor or oppose citizenship for undocumented immigrants who speak the dominant language and have no criminal record (and gave the option of strongly or slightly favoring or opposing).[34]

We find that Copenhagen residents are more opposed to pro-immigration policies than are Houston residents. About 36 percent of Copenhageners believe there should be fewer immigrants to Denmark compared to 27 percent of Houstonians.[35] A similar ten-point difference is found between those who strongly oppose citizenship for criteria-meeting immigrants: 29 percent of Copenhageners strongly oppose the position compared to 19 percent of Houstonians.[36] By contrast, almost half of Houstonians—some 46 percent—strongly support extending citizenship to immigrants, but only one in five Copenhagen residents (20 percent) feel the same way. These statistics suggest that Copenhageners are more inclined against immigration than are Houstonians.

But we know that Houston has a more heterogeneous population compared to Copenhagen, which raises the question: do all Copenhageners and Houstonians agree on these questions? If we break the question down by whether the respondent is either (1) an immigrant or child of an immigrant or (2) not an immigrant or a child of an immigrant, we found that, not surprisingly, immigrants in both cities were more accepting of future immigrants and of granting citizenship to immigrants than were nonimmigrants.[37] More telling is a comparison of the findings by race in Houston. One-third of white residents (34%) in Houston desire fewer immigrants, but only 21 percent of nonwhite residents feel that way, with only 16 percent of Hispanics and 13 percent of Asians sharing that position. Similarly, while four in five (82 percent) nonwhite respondents support granting citizenship, including 61 percent strongly in support, only 31 percent of white residents strongly support citizenship, with another 27 percent slightly supporting.

White residents in Houston are more comparable to Copenhageners in their anti-immigration views than they are to their fellow Houstonians. Only a three-point difference exists between white Houstonians and Copenhageners on the question of wanting fewer immigrants, with a two-point difference among those strongly opposed to citizenship (both are slightly higher in Copenhagen).

This suggests an intriguing point: there are often wider differences in beliefs about issues in Houston than there are in Copenhagen. Also, often these differences are structured by race or income. Maybe a hallmark of Market Cities like Houston is less agreement on specific issues such as immigration because of the decentralized ethos of the city. By contrast, public opinion in Copenhagen might be less variable across different groups.

Satisfaction with the City

So far we have seen that People Cities have higher trust and cooperation between citizens, more helping behavior, substantially lower crime rates, more freedom to move about the city, more social interaction among its citizens, and significantly lower inequality and segregation. Such findings would seem to suggest that citizens in People Cities would be more satisfied with their cities than citizens living in Market Cities.

This conclusion is not supported by our data. In our survey data, we find that three-fourths of both Houstonians and Copenhageners rank their city as good or excellent. And about nine out of ten people in both cities believe their city is a better city in which to live than comparison cities (other U.S. cities for Houstonians, other northern European cities for Copenhageners). Not only this, but we examined data (see chapter 7 for a different analysis using the data) on a diverse range of seventy-nine cities in Europe that asked about satisfaction with one's city (a bit of a different question than ours, but a similar idea). Somewhat incredibly, 99 percent of residents in Oslo or Zurich were satisfied with their city, and for another three cities it was 98 percent. Of the 79 cities, only three did not have a rate of satisfaction that was at least 75 percent.[38] How can people in radically different cities all be satisfied with their rather different places?

Crister Garrett is a professor of American Studies at Leipzig University in Germany. He was our host when we presented an earlier version of this work at his university. As we were having dinner the evening after our presentation, he began reflecting on our findings. "Cities," he said, "if effective, are closed-system narratives." OK, we thought, we will take the bait: "What do you mean?" we asked Dr. Garrett. He replied:

> I mean that cities present their narrative for how things work, what matters, and how we should view the world—as you well capture it for our times as Market City and People City narratives. These are highly different narratives. We must realize that despite so much communication technology and travel between places, most people live in relative isolation from other possibilities. And as such, they come to evaluate success and purpose as the local narrative defines it, because apart from holiday, we generally live in a closed system. We don't hear about other possibilities, or if we do they are such faint echoes compared to the resounding local narrative that they are but strange, vaguely visible alternative realities ultimately judged as misguided, or to be for some other kind of people in some other context. This close-system narrative means people overwhelmingly judge their city positively.

He seemed to have a point, but we had questions. We talked more, pushing here and there. But his basic argument appeared to hold quite well. Dominant narratives of city life simply are not something people—no matter how much time they spend on the internet or travel about—can usually grasp. City narratives are just reality, a city's ethos, and come to be accepted. If we don't accept it, if we experience true cognitive dissonance between what we think should be valued and the dominant city narrative, we change our views, we resist, or we move (if at all possible), such as Patrick and his family (whom we met at the opening of this chapter) did. So while city narratives are closed systems, people are not. They come and go. But this only lends strength to the closed-system narrative, as temporary residents find it difficult to know let alone change a seemingly permanent city narrative.

The end result is that the more successful city leaders are in defining a dominant narrative, in declaring what matters and what does not, and the more they can show that the city succeeds in meeting what matters, the more people will judge their city a success, even to the point of feeling pride in it, despite its warts.

In the end, the closed-system narrative can be equally effective in each type of city, be it a People City or a Market City. And people reflect this in their support and contentment with their city and even their stated level of happiness (our surveys show that Houstonians and Copenhageners indicate equal levels of happiness). In short, city satisfaction has less to do with whether people live in a Market City or a People City and more to do with how effective each type of city is in communicating and being its type of city.

Conclusion

Market and People Cities are not just abstract concepts for an academic exercise. Rather, such cities have deep, wide-ranging impacts for our lives. In this chapter we focused on the social—our lives living with and apart from one another. The differences are dramatic. Successful Market Cities produce immense wealth, but that wealth is distributed highly unequally across people and across neighborhoods. People Cities produce immense wealth too, but that wealth is distributed much more equally across its citizens and its neighborhoods. As such one will not find the grand, upscale neighborhoods of mansions surrounded by plush landscaping behind gates and walls nearly as frequently in People Cities as in Market Cities. And one will not find deep poverty in tenement and ghetto housing within largely forgotten neighborhoods nearly as frequently in People Cities as in Market Cities.

People trust one another much more in People Cities than in Market Cities. And trust leads to more cooperation and social interaction between people. People help one another more in People Cities than in Market Cities. These facts have implications for doing business (more time, effort, and money must be spent on securing contracts, on litigation, and the like in Market Cities), on crime levels such as murder rates (substantially higher in Market Cities), for how people spend their time (in Market Cities, more time is spent with technological devices and in smaller, homogeneous groups), and even for stress levels. As such, compared to citizens of Market Cities, citizens in People Cities move about more freely and in a more wide-ranging fashion, as there is less fear of being a crime victim or of off-limits areas of the city full of un-trustworthy others.

Valuing immigration and ethnic diversity is not necessarily associ-ated with which type of city a local will prefer. But how immigration and diversity are approached at the city level is associated. Market Cities view their task as offering opportunity for all to succeed and make their way. People Cities view their task as seeking the inclusion of its diverse residents, and so they focus attention on doing so. Which approach ac-tually works best is an empirical question yet to be studied, but ripe for analysis.

Despite all the differences examined in this chapter, they have rela-tively little to do with how residents rate their respective cities. Given what we termed the closed-system narrative, what appears to matter for a positive view of one's city is how effective a city is in communicating and actualizing its status as a Market or People City. In short, be good at being a Market or People City, and people will more likely than not judge the city a success.

7

Across Cities

We have focused almost exclusively on Houston and Copenhagen, although we did sprinkle information about other cities throughout for good measure. We used the two-city approach for clarity and depth. Our aim has been to articulate a way of thinking about cities that reveals the range of choices cities encounter, and the divergent paths they take.

But our perspective has yet to be widely applied to a larger number of cities outside of Copenhagen and Houston, or in depth concerning other cities. The task of this chapter is to dive into other cities and to explore the market and people dynamics further.

While cities like Copenhagen and Houston have obvious dissimilarities, this is not always the case when comparing two cities. Dallas and Houston, for instance, have a similar number of residents, are located in the same state, hold the headquarters of large energy corporations, and are about 250 miles from each other. Similarly, Aarhus and Copenhagen are separated by only a three-hour train ride, are the two largest cities in Denmark, host most of the country's important universities, and each has a percentage of its residents who used to live in the other city.

So these cities are basically the same, right? Do not tell that to their residents. A 2014 book about Dallas and Houston collected interviews from civic and economic leaders. Its title? "Bragging Rights." The first line of the book is: "Dallas and Houston get along like brothers—Cain and Abel."[1] Meanwhile, an online magazine based in Aarhus sums up the (wholly unfair) stereotypes of the cities: "All the people from Aarhus and the rest of Jutland are farmers and all the people from Copenhagen are arrogant."[2]

Admittedly, the differences between these cities may not be large when thinking about them in our book's perspective. Dallas, like Houston, is a Market City, and we think that Aarhus is a People City. But we hope to plant the idea that cities ostensibly more similar than Copenhagen and Houston may yet have profound differences—the type of differences that make urban life remarkably distinct.

We want to explore how a Market City and People City framework might hold up across a different set of cities. We investigate Market Cities and People Cities outside of Copenhagen and Houston in three primary ways. The first analyzes survey data for seventy-nine cities and sketches how levels of trust across a city are related to perceptions of the city. We create a measure that brings together three different variables about trust and find that the city-level average of those variables is associated with more favorable perceptions of city characteristics by city residents. The second section describes a subset of those cities and uses a more in-depth examination of the quantitative data to classify twenty-five cities on the Market City and People City spectrum. The final section details two cities we had classified in the second section: Amsterdam and London. The purpose of analyzing these two cities is to investigate the Market City and People City dynamic in much the same manner as for Copenhagen and Houston.

Trust across Cities

To investigate how our claims hold up across a larger group of cities, we turn to an analysis of seventy-nine European cities. The purpose of this wider analysis is to determine how fundamental levels of trust in a city condition how one thinks about their city. This extends directly to the Market City and People City framework. The web of social ties across an urban space is coupled with an array of other urban institutions, such as crime, the environment, or urban form. The cumulative effect, the dependent pathways, the feedback loops are the processes that make Market Cities and People Cities. And therefore this analysis explores how one element—trust in a city—is related to how individuals perceive their cities on questions ranging from safety to air quality to how many people like their local streets.

The seventy-nine cities are from Europe because there we could find the necessary comparative data for our purposes. The data comes from the "Flash Eurobarometer 419: Quality of Life in European Cities."[3] The survey was conducted by country-specific survey firms under the aegis of the European Union's direction. The cities come from thirty-two countries, and the survey includes all European capitals in the European Union.[4] Each country had between one and six cities surveyed. The cities that were surveyed were not chosen according to the same criteria across countries; in some countries, it was simply a few of the biggest, while in others there were regional counterweights. We used the 2015 iteration of the data. Each city had almost exactly five hundred respondents sampled, for a total of just under 40,000 respondents.

The analysis examines individual-level responses to many of the questions examined above. It also takes up a few important variables at the city level to determine whether higher levels of trust across the city predict satisfaction and agreement with more specific urban attributes at the individual level. An important reason for this analysis is to control for key individual attributes that often structure viewpoints on one's city, such as one's gender, class, and age. The idea is to examine if levels of trust are associated with assorted viewpoints on one's city, even when taking into account a range of other factors. The goal of the analysis is rather simple: to determine whether the way residents of a city trust others conditions how those residents think of their city.

To create this analysis, we analyze individual-level data by utilizing multilevel statistical models. Multilevel models are useful when analyzing social phenomena that often have a contextual component. For instance, multilevel models are often used to assess student success in the classroom: models account not just for attributes of the individual student but also for characteristics at a level of analysis greater than the individual, like the classroom, school, and/or school system. In our case, we are interested in how cities shape perceptions of the city by individuals. Therefore, the contextual factor is the city, and the units of analysis are individuals nested within those cities.

To create our measure of trust, we combine three survey questions about trust for the seventy-nine cities. The three statements concern the agreement (1) that others in general can be trusted, (2) that others in their city can be trusted, and (3) that the public administration of the city can be trusted. We use these to create a factor variable, which takes into account the relative correlations between the three variables to create a new measure that can be thought of as corresponding to the overall level of trust in the city.

We use several variables that "control" for other factors that might influence how one perceives their city. The purpose of this move is to confirm that any relationships we find with the trust variable are not spurious, that is, are not canceled out by the inclusion of a different measure. Perhaps most important among the control variables is the region in which the city is located, such as central Europe, eastern Europe, the Nordic countries, southern Europe, and western Europe. We test directly to see if differences across cities are, in fact, actually differences across regions instead. For instance, is the People City of Copenhagen really just a part of a wider Nordic "People Region?" Evidence might also be found for both the city-level trust and regional trust or, as we shall see, for some regions of Europe and not others. Other control variables are individual characteristics such as gender, age, education, how long an individual has lived in the city, whether the respondent is a parent, and if the respondent has trouble paying their bills.

We test to see if the trust in the city variable is associated with six different perceptions of one's city. The six perceptions are: (1) satisfaction with the city's streets and buildings, (2) satisfaction with green space, (3) satisfaction with the city's air quality, (4) agreement that the city is combating climate change, (5) agreement that the respondent's neighborhood is safe, and (6) agreement that the city is safe. To analyze these, we turn to logistic regression techniques that can measure the relative effect of city-level trust and the control variable on each of these six measures.

Our primary hypothesis is that cities with higher levels of overall trust will have greater satisfaction or agreement on each of the six measures. Further, we believe that places with these levels of trust are indicative of People Cities. In turn, as we claimed in earlier chapters, we would expect People Cities to have stronger public spaces and urban form (such as streets, buildings, and green spaces), more attention to the environment (more highly rated air quality and a stronger commitment to mitigating climate change), and less crime (evinced in greater feelings of safety both in the immediate local environment as well as throughout the city). Market Cities, by contrast, would have less satisfaction or agreement on these variables because public investment and civic involvement is lower, as is trust of others.

The results for our analysis find consistent support for the importance of city trust. The more trusting people in a city are, the more satisfied they are with the city's streets, buildings, green space, and air quality. The more trusting the people in a city are, the more they agree that their city is working to combat climate change and that their neighborhoods and the entire city are safe. Trust, then, shapes a great deal of how people feel and perceive their city, just like we found to be the case in the previous chapter for residents of Houston and Copenhagen.

As an example, consider the relationship between city-level trust and satisfaction with the streets and buildings in that city. Our analysis suggests that for each one point increase in the five-point trust measure, the odds that the residents of the city will be satisfied with their city's streets and buildings double. In short, more trust equals substantially more satisfaction with the built environment of the city. These are sizable differences and are found at similar rates across many of the variables. The exception are the two variables relating to safety, where the odds ratios are even higher, meaning that trust and feelings of safety are even more strongly linked.

While the findings about trust remain important even when holding the region constant, there are some important regional differences. Our analysis used the western European region as the comparison group, meaning that all of the relationships below are relative to levels for western European cities. For five of the six dependent variables (all except the perception of safety in the city), cities in southern Europe experience less satisfaction or agreement with items such as the city's streets or buildings or its air quality. Eastern European cities agree that their city is safe compared to western European ones—but they are not particularly distinguished from western European countries on the other four measures. Copenhagen's central position in the Nordic region might lead to curiosity about whether regional differences supersede local ones (i.e., perhaps People City dynamics are instead fully regional, Nordic ones), but the variable for Nordic cities is found for only one of the dependent variables (Nordic city residents believe their cities are more safe). Finally, while we also find evidence for individual-level differences, the city-level trust variable remains a pivotal predictor of satisfaction with the diverse range of city characteristics.[5] In summary, the regional differences are found mostly for southern European cities, are inconsistent for other regions, and the city-level trust is robust to all of these regional distinctions.

TABLE 7.1. Odds Ratios for Logistic Regression Predicting Satisfaction or Agreement on City Characteristics[a]

Dependent Variable	City-Level Trust Odds Ratio[b]
Green space—satisfaction	1.88
Streets and buildings—satisfaction	2.01
Air quality—satisfaction	1.87
Climate change commitment—agreement[c]	2.05
Safe neighborhood—agreement	4.34
Safe city—agreement	4.45

a. Data: 2015 Flash Eurobarometer 419.
b. Each association for city-level trust is significant at the $p < 0.05$ level.
c. The analysis for the climate change variable does not include five cities that had more than 20 percent missing values for the dependent variable.

Perhaps most intriguing, though, is that the findings about city trust hold even when accounting for all of these theoretically important factors at the individual level and for any regional differences. This variable—a combination of generalized trust of others, trust of others in their particular city, and trust of their government—is a consistent, powerful factor in structuring the respondents' satisfaction across a diverse array of city attributes.

Finally, this analysis has some limitations. The most important is that we could not pursue a full slate of city-level characteristics, such as data on the city's economy or on urban inequalities. This was largely because of data limitations: reporting across all of these cities and countries varies, and, while the European Union has a fascinating resource called the "Urban Audit," where they collate such resources, they are far from uniform across variables and across time. Future research might explore these relationships with different data that could account for some of these limitations.

Classifying across Cities

In an initial attempt to classify cities, we examined a smaller number of cities in the Eurobarometer survey. Because the survey data had large samples that are representative of residents, we felt it was important to ascertain data about the priorities rubric from city leaders and city government. To do so, we collected a limited number of documents from each city: notes on the government structure (such as committee foci and whether there was a regional governance component), two recent municipal budgets, and five additional documents (mostly government reports, but also newspaper articles, city website pages, reports from nongovernmental organizations). Using a common guide to classify cities, we examined the materials for each city and made a classification of the city on a five-point scale: strong market, lean market, a middle category, lean people, or strong people.

We used this qualitative classification as one measure of whether a city is currently a Market City or a People City. But we did not stop there. Employing our quantitative survey data, we took two additional steps to create our classification.

First we created a combined resident attitude measure that included the following nine survey variables, consistent with the previous analysis in this chapter. They are: Satisfaction with the city's (1) streets and building, (2) green spaces, and (3) air quality; and agreement that (4) the city is safe overall, (5) the respondent's neighborhood is safe, (6) the city is combating climate change, (7) others can trusted, (8) others in their city can be trusted, and (9) the public administration of the city can be trusted. According to our arguments, People Cities should get high marks from their residents on these issues. And it turns out in our analysis that this is the case; all of these variables are closely related to one another.[6] For our subsequent analysis, we employed what we call a "supervariable" (a factor variable) that combines information from all nine variables noted above.

Finally, we used the *variation* in the supervariable within each city. Our reasoning went like this: Market Cities are places of contrast—amazing, sparkling neighborhoods full of well-manicured, expansive homes and yards with lots of services and little crime; and broken down, neglected neighborhoods with aging housing stock falling into disrepair, largely devoid of investment, and with more crime. The experience of living in such cities will depend, then, on where one lives within the city and where one is on the socioeconomic scale. People Cities are characterized in part by acting to minimize these extremes. The experience of living in such cities thus will be more uniform. As such, cities where citizens range widely in their assessments of their city and its quality are indicative of Market Cities; cities where citizens don't vary much in their assessments of their city and its quality are indicative of People Cities.

Thus, to classify our Market Cities we combined our qualitative ranking derived from analyzing websites, budgets, government reports, and other statements of the city with two quantitative measures: mean scores on our supervariable assessing city quality and experience, and the amount of variation on this supervariable among a city's residents.

Based on this analysis, we created six categories and populated them with five cities that consistently, across each of our measures, suggest they fit their assigned category.

TABLE 7.2. Classification of 30 European Cities on People to Market City Continuum

Strong People	Lean People	In Between	Lean Market	Strong Market	In Transition
Munich	Antwerp	Berlin	Sofia	Marseille	Rostock
Copenhagen	Leipzig	Dortmund	Rome	Bucharest	Riga
Malmö	Amsterdam	Verona	Malaga	Madrid	Warsaw
Oslo	Rotterdam	Essen	Braga	Torino	Bratislava
Zurich	Paris	Budapest	London	Istanbul	Prague

Strong People Cities have all the hallmarks of People Cities as we have described them. We classified these cities as such in our qualitative study of documents and websites. What is more, in these cities the citizens express high levels of satisfaction with their city, and variation between citizens' responses is low in comparison to the variation found in other cities.[7]

Lean People Cities are classified as such in our qualitative rating when the citizens express above-average levels of satisfaction with their city (but not as high as in Strong People Cities), and variation between the citizens' responses is higher than Strong People Cities but lower than average. After we made a presentation in Leipzig about Market and People Cities, we were invited to meet with a senior city official who wanted to talk to us about Leipzig's priority rubric and foci. He told us that the city had four priority goals: two focused on people, two focused on the market. He said that because of Leipzig's communist past, the city had failed to sufficiently focus on the market. Thus this People City was actually trying to give more focus to having some market-oriented goals, rendering it currently a Lean People City.

Cities classified as "In Between" truly seem to be just that. As we analyzed their official documents and speeches given by officials, they seem to balance both market and people characteristics and goals. And when we analyzed these cities using the citizen surveys, they had average levels of satisfaction with their city and average levels of variation between citizens. So we label these cities as "In Between" Market Cities and People Cities. We do not know if they will stay in this category, or if instead they are in the process of moving from one type of city to another.

Lean Market Cities are classified as such in our qualitative assessment when they have below-average levels of satisfaction with the city expressed by its citizens (but not as low as Strong Market Cities), and have above-average levels of variation in citizens' assessment of their city (but not as high as in Strong Market Cities).

Strong Market Cities are classified as such in our qualitative assessment when they have more below-average levels of satisfaction with the city expressed by its citizens and have high-average levels of variation in citizens' assessment of their city—that is, some think the city wonderful, some think it quite the opposite.[8]

Finally, cities labeled as "In Transition" are cities that have a sizable discrepancy between the citizens' views, the variation in those views, and how we classified the city based on the government and related documents; and such cities are all former Soviet bloc cities, so indeed they can be viewed as being in transition. Given their unique place historically, they do not yet have consistency in what the government and leaders express and what its citizens experience. Not all Soviet bloc cities are in transition, but many currently are.

As we look at this list of cities, we can see that even in limiting our analysis to Europe we have quite a range. There are Strong Market Cities and Strong People Cities and everything in between. These cities range in location across Europe, and we can and do find variation within countries.

We are often asked how certain American cities would be classified. We do not have the quantitative survey data to do a comparative analysis of U.S. cities. However, we did classify several qualitatively, finding less variation in cities than in Europe. That is, while cities like Atlanta and

Dallas join Houston as Strong Market Cities, and cities like Chicago can be classified as Lean Market Cities, we found no Strong People Cities. One possibility is that cities such as Portland and Minneapolis can be classified as Lean People Cities, and they appear to still be in the process of solidifying that status.

Our method of classifying cities in this section of the chapter is of course limited. The best way to classify cities is to take a more comprehensive, holistic approach to understanding a city—its history, trajectory, leaders, citizens, feel, lived reality. Our hope is that scholars will collectively undertake such work.

Two Examples

We end with two cities for the final section of analysis: Amsterdam and London. We dive into these two cities to buttress our overall arguments about Copenhagen and Houston. Thus far in this chapter we did so using statistical data across dozens of cities. Now, we will conduct a side-by-side two-city study. The treatment of these cities will be briefer, as we have not conducted our own surveys in the city nor collected a huge cache of primary sources. But we have consulted other scholars' books and articles, and delved into media and primary sources. Amsterdam and London were chosen because they are relatively well known, rank among the highest echelons of global cities across any number of such rankings, and have been international commercial centers for centuries.[9] In the previous section, we determined that Amsterdam ranked toward the people end of the spectrum and London toward the market end. In the analysis that follows, we highlight three themes that elucidate intriguing differences: urban form, housing, and the role of financial centers.

Urban Form

Situated a short hop across the south end of the North Sea, you might think that Amsterdam and London would have developed rather similar urban forms. But this is not the case. As Susan Fainstein details in her book *The Just City*, which includes detailed cases studies of Amsterdam, London, and New York City, the reason begins with history.[10]

Amsterdam's coastal location means that, for centuries, the issues stem-
ming from drainage and landfill necessitated a large degree of central
planning carried out by local government.[11] As redevelopment occurred
across the twentieth century, attention to affordability and the needs of
the middle and working classes was comparatively higher than in its
English counterpart. London, then, experienced more tepid growth
in post–World War II years, followed by a huge neoliberal push in the
1980s that broke open the floodgates for large urban projects favoring
the wealthy in the city. It also meant a spread of the metropolitan area,
which had roots even earlier. As London historian Peter Ackroyd wrote,
"The suburbs, like the rest of London, were established upon the principles of commercial gain."[12] Ackroyd wrote that sentence in reference to
seventeenth-century development in London. Even centuries back, the
cities had different roots.

This has led to different configurations of power and planning. Fainstein's book centers on the concept of "the just city" and how it is supported through contextually situated and political processes of three
crucial pillars: equity, diversity, and democracy. On these three points,
she argues that: "Amsterdam remains exemplary. Social policy estab-
lishes a floor beneath which people may not sink; and while there is a
numerous well-to-do class, there are few signs of the excesses of wealth
evident in New York and London. Democratic participation is encouraged, and both decision-making authority and resources are sufficiently
decentralized to make it influential. The population of the city is diverse,
and this diversity is evident in most neighborhoods and public spaces."[13]

Fainstein is mostly focused on urban planning but uses a lens that
highlights how this planning should be used for social justice. The focus
is not just on economic growth, as it has been across so many (Market)
cities for so long. By looking at cities like Amsterdam, Fainstein uncov-
ers how governments, alongside civically engaged residents, can plan
cities with its residents' needs chiefly in mind.

Broadly, the differences between Amsterdam and London have led
to different levels of inequalities. Ackroyd writes that "it is one of the
great and continuing paradoxes of London life that the rich global city
contains also the worst examples of poverty and deprivation. But perhaps that comprises the contradictions of the human condition, both as
an example and as a warning."[14] If Ackroyd says that London serves as

a warning, Fainstein says that Amsterdam is an aspiration. It is not as just as it could be. But the commitment to Fainstein's important pillars of equity, diversity, and democracy is most typified by Amsterdam compared to London and New York. As Fainstein writes, "Amsterdam may not be the ideal city, and it is less egalitarian than in the past, but it still represents a model to which others might aspire."[15]

Housing

One of the central issues of cities concerns housing. Housing takes up the plurality of space in a city. For most residents, it is their largest financial outlay: a source of wealth for some and a bank account breaker for others. It is not surprising that in Copenhagen it was the issue most often raised as a challenge for the city in the future, or that affordable housing in Houston is one of the bulwarks of support for the Market City ethos.

One difference between Amsterdam and London is the average price of a home. In 2016, the average price of a home in Amsterdam was about $270,000 dollars.[16] The average price of a home in London in 2016 was approximately $666,000.[17] Even the figures in the comparatively inexpensive outer metropolitan area of London put the price of a home at around $445,000.[18] London's high prices are the product of breakneck growth where prices nearly tripled in just eleven years from 1996 to 2007, and even the Great Recession hardly haltered this growth, with only a short lull in 2008 and 2009. Even Amsterdam prices are getting hotter— the growth in the first quarter of 2016 was higher than London's.[19]

Another difference comes in the percentage of housing that is social housing, that is, housing owned by the government or nonprofit organizations and intended to remain affordable. In Amsterdam, about half of the housing units are social housing, while in London it is about a quarter.[20] While both figures are historically low, this means that not only are home prices higher in London compared to Amsterdam, there are proportionally fewer rental units for middle-class and lower-income residents.

Still, both cities struggle with recent rises in prices, and the accordant worries about gentrification. But what makes the cities different is that Amsterdam, with its overall lower prices and greater share of social housing, is relatively sheltered from coming storms than is London. Academic research on these cities make this very point: Amsterdam is subject to the same market forces that are engaging cities worldwide, but historical and institutional arrangements allay the impact of those forces.[21] London, on the other hand, initiated the term "gentrification" (by Ruth Glass in 1964). Across the last fifty years, rising home values in central city areas—and increasingly even in in-between areas neither near nor far from the city's center—have continued apace, and with enough depth and variety to suggest that this is simply how London does business.[22]

An intriguing implication suggested by this analysis is that Market Cities can have runaway housing values; in our cases here, both Amsterdam and London are highly sought after and big ticket locales. But only one city is able to do enough to keep housing costs reasonable. In our discussion of Copenhagen and Houston, it was the People City that had the higher home values. What is important, then, is the mechanism rather than the price itself. In Houston, prices are driven by intensive home building, with little regard for urban planning or cost control. In London, population growth and international allure combine to drastically drive up costs year after year. In both cases, the apparent mechanisms are different—in Houston, a continuous generation of housing supply, and, in London, intense demand—but the underlying ethos is the same: housing is not to be overly controlled by any central power and should be left up to the markets. By contrast, both Amsterdam and Copenhagen have extensive and wide-reaching programs that limit the influence of the market on housing costs.

Finance

A city does not exist in a vacuum, and it is fascinating when we see the interaction between cities up close. Although operating in a global realm, Copenhagen and Houston do not always have these direct relationships.

Amsterdam and London, by contrast, have more direct links. With the 2016 Brexit vote, the United Kingdom is exiting the European Union. London serves as the de facto financial capital of Europe, but there are questions swirling around Europe about how long London may keep that status. Simply put: will London maintain its central status if it is no longer the nucleus of a European continent populated by five hundred million people, but instead the hub of a single country of sixty-five million residents?

The idea is that financial institutions and attendant industries—as well as companies further afield but attracted to financial centers—may decamp for other major cities in the European Union instead of London to access that much larger market. How many institutions and to what degree they will do so are questions that can only be answered in time. But that is not stopping some cities from openly campaigning for new commerce.

If not London, then where? Leading candidates include Dublin, Frankfurt, Milan, and Paris, among others.[23] They also include Amsterdam. The attractiveness of Amsterdam is readily apparent. English is commonly spoken in the city, keeping it in tune with financial markets in the United States and making an easy transition from the United Kingdom. Standards of living and quality of life measures are high in the city. It is diverse: many global companies already call Amsterdam home or have branches there. Perhaps most important, it is already a premier center of finance; the world's first stock exchange is in Amsterdam.

But while many London denizens will be happy warriors in the pursuit of maintaining their financial centers, Amsterdammers are more mixed in their opinions and not altogether welcoming of becoming Europe's foremost financial center. Russell Shorto wrote of the mood in the *New York Times Magazine* a few months after the Britain's vote to leave the European Union: "While people had a range of opinions, nearly everyone thought it would rattle the city. There has been talk of Amsterdam, with its long history as a financial center, eventually replacing London as the unofficial economic capital of the European Union. No one I met with looked forward to such a thing."[24] This is not market talk. Even the head of the Netherlands Banking Association had doubts about luring finance jobs: "For many companies, we are an excellent gateway to Europe for many countries, but a great center for investment banking Amsterdam is not. The Netherlands has a more restrained salary policy for banks and insurers than other countries and companies will take that into consideration."[25] Keep in mind that those words are coming from someone who works as a chief ambassador for banking in the Netherlands. A person in a comparable position in a Market City would be drooling over the possibility of luring new economic growth, and sticking it to a rival. But this is not the case in Amsterdam.

Meanwhile, other competitor cities are chomping at the bit. A *Financial Times* headline from late 2016 reads, "Dublin jockeys for Brexit spoils."[26] A political party in Germany pasted slogans on the side of trucks in its capital that played on a quintessential British saying: "Dear Start-ups, Keep Calm and Move to Berlin."[27]

What London can do to stem the tide is not yet clear. But initial plans focus on retaining free movement of travel for E.U. country passport holders or on having economic access to the single E.U. market through a new E.U. directive.[28] Free movement, though, is against the grain of the Brexit vote in the first place: one of the core ideas against E.U. membership is the concern about this free movement. Ditto for the belief in a shared economic future. Outside of these legal pathways that are pursued at the national level, local governmental and civic leaders will still campaign closely for retaining London as a hub of finance for decades to come.

Summary of Cases

By examining two cities not named Copenhagen and Houston, we hoped to explore similar distinctions but in different places. Amsterdam and London readily supply those distinctions. Drawing on different histories, the urban form is different in cities, particularly in the purposes behind urban planning in the cities. This leads to distinctions in housing, with London being more unaffordable and unequal, and Amsterdam, even without recent price hikes, maintaining a relative level of affordability. Finally, the dissimilarities played out right in front of our eyes. The Brexit vote threw into relief how the cities are—or, in Amsterdam's case, are sort of not—competing for capital. Together, the differences across Amsterdam and London are generative, just like the ones in Copenhagen and Houston. They illuminate why studying the differences across cities in a globalizing world is an essential task.

Conclusion

The goal of this chapter has been to elucidate this book's fundamental differences by examining a wider array of cities. Different levels of trust across cities condition how individuals perceive characteristics of their city such as its streets and buildings or their safety. We created a preliminary classification of a few dozen cities, arguing that thinking through these cities in these ways can power a new research agenda. Finally, we conducted a deeper analysis of two cities, Amsterdam and London, in an effort to describe in entirely new places many of the relationships in this book.

The aim of this endeavor is to demonstrate how the Market City and People City perspective can aid in understanding the cities in which we live, research, and resist. We have not provided a conclusive or even a full analysis of how to research these topics. It is an exploration. But across the data we highlight here, we find evidence that consistently suggests how our perspective on urban variation can underwrite a better understanding of cities.

8

To Be or Not to Be

The truth about cities is that they are changing. Humans are now urban, and they are busy. City residents—government leaders, business leaders, nonprofit personnel, the clergy, and the average person on the street—have choices and collectively shape the direction of their city, even as not everyone has the same influence as others. A cultural ethos arises over time through the myriad of daily interactions, conflicts, negotiations, and decisions, ultimately leading down one path or another. This culture works to justify the city's priorities rubric, the metric used to make choices amid the diversity of possibilities.

Being a Market City or People City has substantial, cascading, compounding impacts for how the city and life are experienced. How a city is designed, how people move through the city, where they live, who their neighbors will be, the quality of the air they breathe and the water they drink, how they address environmental issues, how they will view opportunity and success, how trusting of each other they are, their perceived and actual levels of crime, the extent of inequality and segregation, and how ethnic diversity and inclusion are approached are but a few consequences of living in Market Cities or People Cities. Truly, understanding these emergent city types means understanding ourselves.

Try as we might to be otherwise, we humans are a normative people. And so we imagine readers want us to answer the question we have thus far not directly answered. That question of course is: What kind of city—Market or People—is better? In other words, which type of city should we strive for?

Our Response

Those who support Market Cities will undoubtedly believe we are biased toward People Cities. Those who support People Cities will undoubtedly expect that we will say People Cities. After all, we have said that People

Cities have more trust between its citizens, less crime, less pollution, less inequality, more people-pleasing urban design, and many other seemingly obvious positives. What is more, we have said that Market Cities are bigger polluters, have more inequality, more crime, less trust, extensive sprawl, and a host of other seemingly clear negatives. And we have *not* said that Market Cities are actually better at producing jobs, luring businesses, and attracting wealth. The jury is actually still out on that, and much more research will need to be done comparing these different types of cities once scholars better classify cities as Market or People Cities.

But rather than answer the question as phrased above, consider the following. This book offers us two vital lessons that, if followed, will improve cities across the globe. First, citizens need to know about the range of cities. Too often, as we noted in chapter 6, citizens are locked in closed narratives. They have not been offered real options to think about the type of city in which they wish to live and work. They need to know about the types of cities, either by reading this book or in some other fashion.

Second, as this book describes, we need to know the risks arising from each type of city and work specifically to mitigate those risks. Let's first consider the risks of Market Cities. Will they find the willpower internally (or externally from regional or national regulations) to reduce pollution and natural resource degradation before it is too late, even if it hinders their economic competitiveness? Is there a way to produce higher trust among its people? Will they address issues of poverty? Will inequality between its citizens and between its neighborhoods ever grow so great that the city will erupt in protest, rebellion, and chaos?

Market Cities—on their own—are tough, even mean places to live for those whose opportunity is constrained. But that meanness is softened, the toughness blunted to some degree by the heroic efforts of nonprofits and the citizens themselves (interestingly, often funded by the foundations of the major economic winners of the local area). Some residents can fashion decent lives, then, even if they don't have substantial incomes. But the struggle is profound.

Relying on nonprofits and the volunteer spirit of local citizens—despite its many advantages for grassroots leadership and civic involvement—never fully succeeds. Not able to generate sufficient monies on their own, nonprofits are always and continually at the mercy of the monies made available through limited (and volatile) government grants, private foundations, and private citizen donations. Nonprofits are in constant competition with one another, forcing them to ever more myopic views of their missions and purposes. The problem here is clear—since there is no one overseeing what services are offered to whom, making sure there is balance and sufficient coverage, the approach whereby the nonprofits provide social services does not cover the full needs of people and neighborhoods. And because this is true, the heroic efforts of the philanthropic, volunteer, and nonprofit communities fall short by design. Some individual and community needs are met, yet the problems remain—poverty, crime, inequality, and pollution among them.

What is more, inequality is reproduced among the nonprofits. Those with leaders most closely connected to wealthy people, foundations, and government officials succeed in obtaining funds at a much higher rate than those with leaders who are not. It doesn't take much imagination to see where this leads. Well-resourced nonprofits are overwhelmingly those led by people who are themselves well-to-do, who are (at least in the United States) mostly white, who speak the language of those with money, and who move in such circles. Well-resourced nonprofits are also the ones that focus on issues and use methods that matter to those who give money (even if it doesn't really matter, or doesn't matter the most). The result is that despite heroic, sacrificial efforts, the very approach of meeting the needs of people and neighborhoods (privatized, competing for limited funds, focused on a specific issue or neighborhood rather than a cohesive, comprehensive approach for the city) produced by the Market City means these efforts always fall short, by design.

Of course, if we are true to Market City principles, falling short in the private, nonprofit world is okay. Market Cities do not exist to reduce inequality, only to produce opportunity through jobs and generate wealth and economic influence. On the surface, at least to sociologists, such a perspective sounds harsh. But people often vote with their feet. And in places like Houston, people are voting early and voting often, moving to the region to a tune of, conservatively, tens of thousands per year (the Houston region grows through immigration and natural increase by well over 100,000 people a year). Why would people move to the region given what we have noted?

This is a question that Harvard economist Edward Glaeser addresses in his book, *The Triumph of Cities*. After analyzing the data, his number one answer to why people move to Houston is because of the combinations of jobs—good paying ones at that, relative to the cost of living—and inexpensive housing. As he notes, "Houston succeeds by providing an affordable, attractive lifestyle for middle-class people,"[1] or as we would add, also for those who aspire to middle-class status. The role of jobs and affordable housing was reiterated to us just a day before writing this chapter. A middle-class Houstonian (a transplant two decades prior from the San Francisco area) told us how glad he was to live in Houston. He and his wife were building a second home for one of their children and spouse, paying about $185,000 for the four-bedroom, 2,700-square-foot house. He told us, "I know there are fancier cities, cleaner cities, cities that do a better job helping out everyone, but I love Houston. Here I, nothing but a middle-class man, can afford two homes, and I can provide for my family." And when Houston transplant and local National Public Radio host Craig Cohen reflected on what he most liked about Houston, he wrote: "#1. The attitude. It's positive, it's uplifting. People here are optimistic about the future. (An economic boom and rising population sure helps.) I've lived in communities on a downturn, and I've lived in communities very slowly on the rise, but this is the first full-fledged boomtown I've had the pleasure to be a part of. There is a palpable sense of excitement about where Houston may be going in the years to come. There's a sense of progress. . . . it's an exciting time to be a Houstonian."[2] Perhaps Glaeser should have entitled his book *The Triumph of "Market" Cities*.

But the lesson we stress for Market Cities is that the emphasis on creating jobs and wealth and luring companies to relocate to the region will always be associated with known costs. Count those costs. Admit that leaving everything beyond the very basics to the private sector and nonprofit world doesn't and cannot work, as currently designed.

Let us speak to Market City proponents. "Market City" is too limiting a concept. Instead the goal should be to become Big-Hearted Market Cities, cities that excel in producing jobs and wealth but have counted the costs and found ways to limit them. The task is to find a different way to meet the needs of those who will always be left behind. No city yet has ever produced enough jobs and educated its people in just the right

way to employ everyone at a livable wage. Such is the reality of a capitalist economy. So drop the obfuscating argument that if, as a Market City,
we simply succeed in producing the jobs, the rest of life will take care
of itself. Take a look at our data and arguments in this book. Market
City people don't trust one another. They fear crime. They experience
crime. They are afraid to go to certain neighborhoods. They live (and
die) with toxins at rates not meant for humans. It is time that Market
Cities face up to the shortcomings of their city type. People Cities deal
with the pressures of Market concerns far more than Market Cities have
to deal with People priorities. Consider that script flipped: Market Cities
should consider the kinds of critiques that People Cities might leverage
against them. It is time to find a way—using ingenuity, creativity, and
can-do-spirit—to create a new generation of Market Cities, what we call
Big-Hearted Market Cities. Big-Hearted Market Cities are Market Cities
that find a way to mitigate their most severe shortcomings.

We now turn to the lessons we think this book offers to People Cities.
In attempting to provide a high quality of life for all its residents and
equality between its citizens, People Cities run the risk of a "one size
fits all" approach. By that we mean the temptation always will be to assume that what constitutes a high quality of life has a singular definition,
that is, the same definition for everyone. For example, a city filled with
cyclists and walkers is certainly better for the environment and people's
health than a city filled with cars. In this case, the People City temptation is to strong-arm such a result—perhaps to the point of outlawing
cars, or bringing social contempt upon those who continue to use a car.
It is easy, in the name of the perceived group good, to run over (pun
intended) individual preference and difference. It is easy because the
alternative is far more complex and time-consuming.

Copenhagen has done a good, but not perfect, job in attempting to
move away from the car without using strong-arm methods. The city's
approach has largely been *not* to say residents cannot use cars, but instead to make the alternatives so attractive that people will choose the alternatives. Hence the city's incredible attention to bike riding detail and
design (often influenced by private organizations located in Copenhagen that exist to improve the biking experience). Creating a network of
walking streets—forbidding cars on certain streets and even the riding
of bikes—does much to encourage walking. The city removing parking

spots to the tune of about 3 percent per year is a gentle, slow approach to making a car less convenient. Placing a high tax on car usage again functions to make other transportation options relatively more appealing, while still allowing those who truly want or need a car to purchase one.

But we met more than one Copenhagener who felt that the city had become too severe against car users, making it punitive to own and use a car. They also expressed feeling ostracized by other Copenhageners for using a car. They clearly knew what the norm was and felt the sting of violating that norm.

As a few scholars and experts with whom we talked wondered, how long can a system built on comparably high taxes and strong social service provisions last? The only way the People City approach can work, they estimate, is because Copenhagen has a thriving, dynamic economy to produce the necessary tax base, and residents and businesses are willing to pay a very high tax rate to make such services available.

But can such a system continue indefinitely? Take restaurant owner Paul, for example. A young Frenchman, he and two of his friends moved to Copenhagen back in 2013 and opened a French café. But in addition to rent, he pays a 25 percent tax on his receipts, and he must pay a fee for each table and chair on the sidewalk outside his restaurant. When we interviewed him he told us he was making money for the first time, had become the sole owner, and his café had become quite popular since a newspaper review of his restaurant gave it high praise. But always looming over his profits are the high taxes he must pay on them. Is there a limit to how much can be funded to provide equality, a strong safety net, and a high quality of life for all residents? Such is a risk of People Cities that seems not yet to be answered. The concern is that, across generations, the weight of the system could collapse in on itself.

The other concern for People Cities is the threat of external forces. People Cities create outcomes that capitalism on its own does not (equality, for example). But People Cities are attempting to ensure egalitarian outcomes while remaining solidly within the capitalist system. People Cities are under assault more than Market Cities. The flattening of national borders and the rise of global cities, coupled with lasting changes in favor of market governance worldwide (what is known as the neoliberal trend), has meant that Market Cities are hegemonic. Indeed, we would expect that there are many more Market Cities in the modern world than People Cities. This is no historical accident but rather a deliberate product of decades of globally relevant and locally specific changes—just as we saw in Houston.

Can People Cities like Copenhagen survive these transformations? We already see some evidence that Copenhagen at times is yielding to market mechanisms. Government sometimes uses the language of global competitiveness and focuses energies on promoting Copenhagen as a place to do business. City hall has at times approved more car parking in Copenhagen and is even considering a harbor tunnel that could bring a flood of cars through the city core.[3] Just as in places like London or New York, outside investors are buying up flats and residential buildings to turn their money into greater profit, driving up prices artificially and putting more pressure on this People City's attempt to keep housing affordable and accessible.

For People Cities to survive, they could take one of two paths (or somewhere in the middle). The first path is to adopt market mechanisms again and again. This would fracture the People City and eventually would mean that the city would no longer be a People City.

The second path would be to double down on the People City priorities. Projecting this path is difficult to do. But our prognostication based on our book's arguments would suggest that the best defense is a good offense. People Cities ought to do what they were made to do and be Strong People Cities, intensely focusing on their residents and finding ways to overcome the larger global forces pushing them toward the market. They ought to encourage and extend people programs. The strength of the city is in its core ideological and pragmatic foundations. Abandoning these foundations would just open the structure to ruination when the next storm arrives.

Can People Cities compete economically against Market Cities, given that Market Cities define their very existence and expend their resources primarily in driving market growth? Copenhagen has made a gamble that People Cities can indeed do so. As we analyzed government reports and documents, transcripts of town hall meetings, and the like, it became clear: Copenhagen is banking that the People City approach will actually be a way to economically compete or even beat Market Cities at their own game.

Their reasoning is twofold. First, by creating an attractive city designed for people and their quality of life, people will stay in Copenhagen, and what is more, people will move from far and wide to live in such a city. As Helle Søholt, founding partner of Gehl Architects told us, "Many cities [such as Copenhagen] seem more aware of the need to compete for people based on their qualities, not just the number of jobs." And those people, attracted by the city qualities, will bring their innovative energy and creativity to the city, leading to start-ups and economic vitality otherwise not possible. Second, city officials believe that the world will desperately need green solutions to many problems that threaten the globe, and so they will be the green capital of the world, the city where green innovators come to innovate, not just for a cleaner, healthier Copenhagen, but to import green industry and green solutions across the world. Just as Detroit specialized in auto production and London in banking, so Copenhagen will specialize in the very industries that fit its People City ethos, green innovation, start-ups, companies, and export.

It seems to be working thus far. Copenhagen grows by about 1,000 people per month, its economy is strong and vibrant, it has a solid start-up rate, entrepreneurs from elsewhere interested in green innovation are relocating there, and the city has many positive features. On a podcast originally aired in October 2016, the host, a transplant from England to Copenhagen, asked Austin Sailsbury, a transplant from the United States to Copenhagen, and author of *The 500 Hidden Secrets of Copenhagen*, "How does the city make you feel?"

> It just feels like if you have to live in a city it's hard to imagine a better one to live in. It seems the reason a lot of people are coming here are the reasons you and I moved here . . . they [the people of Copenhagen] are getting a lot of things right. . . . What I see now is a community, a city, a government who have worked diligently for generations to make the city livable. [For example, the city is now] designed for cycling. I think there's something about biking that keeps the candle of childhood lit inside of us. There's something about hopping on a bike, you can get your heart rate going, the wind is in your face, the rain is in your face, and you feel like a kid again. And I think you've got these candy-colored buildings, you've got these tall-masted ships sailing along the coast of this city every day, the smell of bread is in the air and cake makers (everywhere). It is a city out of a story book.[4]

Such is a lesson for People Cities. They must stay focused on the quality of life and creating a positive experience of living in the city, yet acknowledge the market forces around them and put structures into place to mitigate those costs. The world needs Strong People Cities, cities that exist for equality between residents and creating a high quality of life, combating and resisting market pressures that value profit over people, and finding ways not to collapse under their own weight of social provision.

Blueprint for Change

We have stressed that globally we have a variety of cities, and that we ought to focus on creating Big-Hearted Market Cities and Strong People Cities. We have stressed that we can have such a range insofar as people and companies—with full information—can chose to locate in one type of city or the other.

But we don't buy the second part of our own argument. People (and companies) do not have full freedom to assess the range of cities and then move to the city that best suits them. People never have full knowledge of their options, and even if they did, it does not mean they could or would act upon those options. A simple example: well over 300 million people live in the United States and as far as we can tell, not a single one has the option of living in a Strong People City if they wish to stay in their country of residence. It is foolish to believe that all Americans desiring to live in a Strong People City would be able and willing to pick up and move to another nation, and other nations could not and would not absorb so many people.

This reality leads to a clear implication: *we must understand how to create the city we desire in the city where we reside.* How then might we go about changing a city from one type to another? Although we could focus on moving a city from being a Lean Market to a Strong Market City, or from being a Lean People to a Strong People City, we believe such methods are relatively self-evident given what we have covered in this book. We will focus on the more dramatic change—from being one fundamental type (Market or People) to being the reverse.

To make our point, let's start with what doesn't work. A high quality of life is not achieved by building some nice parks and painting bicycle lines on some streets, any more than getting a facelift makes us young. A market orientation is not achieved by offering some incentives for businesses or creating some new jobs, any more than standing in a garage makes us a car.

To be a Market City or a People City is an ethos, a culture, a way of being, a pulsating lifeblood of a people and their city. As we have noted, it is a guiding spirit. For change to occur, it takes vision, commitment, organization, and, perhaps most of all, time. It often also takes a "crisis moment" that opens city leaders and residents to the possibility of change. As many urban scholars note, cities are contested. They are amazing places of diversity and multiple visions of what should be. As we noted in chapter 3, there are advocates of People Cities living in Market Cities, and there are advocates of Market Cities living in People Cities. Resources for change always exist internally.

In attempting to change from one type of city to another, understanding social movements is essential because almost any large-scale change requires a social movement. We can define a social movement as "collective actions in which the populace is alerted, educated, and mobilized, over years and decades, to challenge the powerholders and the whole society to redress social problems or grievances."[5] Many books and articles have been written analyzing what methods are used by successful social movements (those movements that had clear goals and reached them). Bill Moyer—social change activist, principle organizer of the 1966 Chicago Open Housing Movement, key figure in several other later social movements, and author—invested a good portion of his life to understanding how to generate successful social movements, which he formulated into eight steps.[6] As summarized by writer Gloria Kostadinova, the eight steps are the following:

1. Identify a social problem and its solution
2. Demonstrate institutional failures
3. Prepare nonviolent grassroots
4. Educate the public
5. Acknowledge opposition
6. Dedicate to long-term goals
7. Recognize success
8. Retain success

A successful social movement must identify a problem—in our present case, the problem would be a certain city is not the type of city it should be—and the solution—what type of city should it be and how will that look, feel, and be experienced?

The next step is to carefully identify, in light of the definition of the problem and solution, where the failures are occurring in the system. It is likely that part of the issue is the very undergirding assumption guiding city life—for example, an assumption that we should only spend money on X if it makes us more economically competitive, or equality is a fundamental value so all decisions must be made through the sieve of producing greater equality. In short, the current guiding culture, worldview, and underlying assumptions must be assessed for their role in shaping and limiting change.

In the third step, the work of organizing continues, focuses on the residents themselves, and the means used are to be nonviolent. Although there is certainly disagreement on whether movements should be nonviolent, nonviolence seems to be the only way to move to lasting change that does not simply produce a counter social movement or massive pushback and crackdowns.

A successful movement always effectively educates the public to problematize what often is assumed to be unchangeable, to show the solution, and to recruit more people to the cause. Education is ongoing and often takes years, if not decades. Much social movement literature focuses on what are called "frames." Simply put, successful social movements find a "magic potion"—that is, they find a way to connect the social movement's concern with the felt needs of residents. In short, it is not just what is taught, but how it is taught.

A successful movement also is careful and deliberate in identifying which groups and organizations will resist the change and why and how they will resist the change. It is also careful and deliberate in planning counter actions to such resistance. The sixth step overtly acknowledges this fact: be dedicated to long-term goals. Woman's suffrage did not occur overnight or even over the course of a few years. It took an organized movement of people who worked for many decades until the long-range goal—women having the right to vote—was accomplished.

Importantly, successful social movements—while dedicated to their long-range goals—recognize successes along the way. Doing so builds momentum, encourages the faithful, and serves as marker points for re-cruiting more supporters and resources. Recognizing success also helps to maintain successes. In Copenhagen, for instance, urban planners have literally built on their successes through a decades-long, block-by-block challenge to what the city can be. They are always creating and innovating to retain success. One could say the same about developers in Houston: it is not an overnight project but instead powers success by reenergizing the urban form through the continuous extension of it.

The take-away is that real city change from one type to the other is slow, deliberative, and challenges the status quo even while sometimes working with the status quo. It seeks to change underlying assumptions, create a new city ethos and spirit, alter laws and policies, educate people, and provide clear solutions to clear problems. So much more has been written on the topic of how social change occurs, and the interested reader can pursue such literature in far more depth than we can offer here. Our purpose is merely to outline and highlight the key steps and issues to keep in mind as city change is attempted.

We should note that often organizations already exist to at least in part work for change, which we outlined in chapter 3. For example, if desiring to be a Market City, one might join CEOs for Cities, an organi-zation that helps cities attain increased economic success. Several grass-roots organizations help cities move toward at least aspects of People Cities. Ultimately, such organizations might consider joining forces to either holistically help cities become Big-Hearted Market Cities or be-come Strong People Cities. Such organizations may be most effective if they are internationally organized, sharing best practices across the range of the globe's cities.

Bringing It Home

If this book has done nothing else, we hope it has raised awareness of two essential ideas. First, that across the developed world, cities interlinked in a complex global web are nevertheless staking out unique positions within that web, and those positions are coalescing around what we have termed Market Cities and People Cities. Second, the choices that cities make, and the directions they are headed—be they Market or People orientations—have substantial, cumulative, compounding, intersecting impacts for economics, government, urban form, transportation, the environment, human relations, and human experiences.

Ultimately, we must hold at the forefront that we make the city, and in turn the city makes us. Our plea is a simple one. Take seriously that we have agency in making our cities, and make them well. The future of humanity depends upon it.

Afterword

In late August 2017, Hurricane Harvey battered the Houston region. The system stalled over Houston for days, and by the time it moved on, more than fifty inches of rain had fallen, rain totals so high that Houston experienced the single greatest rainfall on record in the continental United States.

Flooding was devastating, as video on televisions and the internet showed in real time, day after day: images of massively flooded regions of Houston, houses under water, evacuations possible only via boats, and people waiting for rescue on rooftops. Perhaps the image that most poignantly captured the social devastation was a photo of a nursing home where residents in wheelchairs sat in water that was at least waist-deep and were unable to evacuate or go to higher ground. They were rescued only after photos went viral on social media.[1]

At the time of this writing at least ninety people have lost their lives due to the storm, and there has been at least $180 billion worth of damage (and likely more).

Houston will rebuild. Its can-do spirit assures that. But in the wake of the storm, many of the nation's top media outlets ran stories questioning if the extent of the damage from the storm would have been nearly so severe if it weren't for Houston's all-out market approach. The rapid growth and sprawl of Houston has meant reducing the available arable land of the region, as land is paved over for development of far-flung subdivisions, strip malls, office parks, and multi-lane freeways and highways to connect them all. We discussed many of these issues ourselves throughout the book, especially in chapter 5, where we discuss how they relate to disasters.

Many articles and blogs also appeared, urging Houston to use this crisis moment to rethink itself, to consider becoming less of an all-out Market City.

True to Houston's ethos, however, defenders of the Market City soon countered these "outsider" views. The *Wall Street Journal* reported that "Stephen Costello, whose official title is chief resilience officer, but who is known to many as Houston's flood czar, says the go-go culture of growth is here to stay. 'I don't think you're going to see a dramatic change in the way we are developing.' . . .

"Regulating development through, say, a stricter zoning code is a nonstarter," he said. 'Zoning is never going to happen here, not in my lifetime.'"[2]

As we noted in the preceding chapter, there are known costs to the type of city we choose to create. Count the costs. Houston, as is the case for all Market Cities, must strive to become a Big-Hearted Market City. We saw big-hearted actions taken by residents again and again as the waters rose and remained. Their daring is beyond description.

Still, persistent problems will linger. Flooding, segregation, and loss of life are bad for business. More importantly, they are unsustainable: loss of human and natural life is the very definition of unsustainable.

Market Cities will not be able to continue business as usual long-term. Although in the preceding chapter we discussed how People Cities are perceived as more vulnerable to change than Market Cities, perhaps it is actually Market Cities that are more vulnerable. Faced with large problems that necessitate collective action, can they endure? Failure to become a Big-Hearted Market City may result in ultimate failure, the demise of the city altogether. That would do no one any good.

Crisis moments, even in the most harrowing of times, create the space for change. Houston and cities around the world have the opportunity to do exactly that.

ACKNOWLEDGMENTS

This book was several years in the making. We benefitted from amazing support, creative people, and patient families. Our thanks to Rice University's Kinder Institute for Urban Research. Director Bill Fulton was a supporter of the project from the beginning and agreed to funding for many parts of the book—from surveys to travel. We also are indebted to Rice University, North Park University in Chicago, the University at Buffalo, and the Danish Institute for Study Abroad (DIS). In addition to the Kinder Institute for Urban Research, we appreciate the financial support at Rice of the Boniuk Institute for Religious Tolerance and the James T. Wagoner '29 Foreign Study Scholarship.

DIS offered Emerson a teaching position for a year and was incredibly generous in creating the time and space for this research. We especially thank Malene Torp, Carsten Pape, Neringa Vendelbo, Thorsten Wagner, Bianca Hermensen, Charlotte Dalsgaard, Helle Søholt, Jan Gehl, John Andersen, Paul Laurent, the Copenhagen mayors, the Houston mayors, and the FIBC folks, especially Erik Nielsen. We appreciate the comments from audiences at the Kinder Institute for Urban Research, the University of Leipzig, Fudan University, Baylor University, the University of Padua, Loyola University of Chicago, DIS, the Southern Sociological Society, the Natural Hazards Workshop, and the Urban Affairs Association. We also acknowledge the help from anonymous reviewers at journals that published our previous work on Copenhagen and Houston in *Environmental Sociology* and *Sociological Forum*. Smiley would like to also thank Mikael Carleheden, who offered comments on early theoretical arguments that were part of a term paper at the University of Copenhagen. Finally, we are particularly thankful for our faculty and graduate student colleagues at Rice University who discussed and encouraged our ideas. We also thank then-baccalaureate fellow Kiara Douds, who helped greatly with data analysis for chapter 7.

We are deeply indebted to our research assistant, Julie Werner Markussen, who so many times was our eyes and ears in Copenhagen, always willing to help us when we asked. She and her parents also provided a most memorable hygge lunch. We cannot thank Julie enough.

Søren Troldborg and Allen Toft Knudsen of Epinion (and of the Danish Evaluation Institute) are incredibly talented at what they do, and they went far above and beyond to make the Copenhagen Area Surveys successful. Along the way they became treasured friends. We thank them for their willingness to teach us amid our endless questions, and their willingness to simply spend time with us.

We are grateful to our editor, Ilene Kalish and the NYU team who saw the vision of this book and were encouraging throughout the process. And we are grateful to NYU Press, which publishes many an excellent book. We hope this one does not disappoint.

Junia Howell and Elizabeth Korver-Glenn were terrific supporters, allowing us to bounce ideas off of them and helping us improve our own work through their high quality, innovative ideas and research.

Emerson is incredibly grateful that his family agreed to move to a faraway land, knowing very little of what they were getting into. It was a gift to spend special time together in familial homelands.

Smiley is thankful for his parents, his brothers, and friends in Copenhagen, Houston, Tennessee, Kentucky, and beyond. A very special thanks to Sarita Panchang, whose support from this project's earliest kernels to its present form has been unwavering, and full of love.

METHODOLOGICAL APPENDIX

Data Sources

For the writing of this book, we used a diverse range of data sources. We describe them here in more detail. Whenever possible, we also provide websites for those interested in learning more information about our sources, or in accessing data.

Quantitative Data

Houston and Copenhagen Surveys

For comparative purposes, we conducted surveys in both Houston and Copenhagen. To increase our reliability, we conducted each city survey twice, in both 2014 and 2015. The Kinder Houston Area Survey has been conducted every year since 1982, so we piggybacked on that survey, adding additional questions specific to our project. The Copenhagen Area Survey was entirely new. Our goal was to keep it as comparable to the Houston survey as possible, again with the eye toward being able to make comparisons between the residents of each region. To do that, we worked with a Danish survey research firm—Epinion—to correctly translate not just the words but also the meaning of the questions, contextualized for the Copenhagen social environment. In particular, Epinion conducted focus groups on our behalf to ready the survey for the Danish context.

The Houston Area Survey is a random digit-dialing survey of landline and cell phones conducted in English and Spanish depending on the respondent's preference, surveying those aged eighteen and over. The survey tracks economic, social, and demographic trends in the Houston area and measures residents' attitudes and behaviors on a range of issues. In 2014, 1,353 respondents answered the survey, and the response rate was 33 percent (using AAPOR's RR3 formula).[1] In 2015, 1,611 respondents answered the survey, and the response rate was 21 percent. The data were weighted to correct for within-household selection, phone status, race/ethnicity, gender, age, education, home ownership, and population density, using the prior year's American Community Survey conducted by the U.S. Census Bureau. The 2014 survey was conducted from February 12 to March 12, and the 2015 survey was conducted from February 2 to March 4. More details about the Kinder Houston Area Surveys are located at kinder.rice.edu.

The Copenhagen Area Surveys employed matching sampling for a web survey of residents aged eighteen and older. The surveys were conducted in Danish. Similar to the Houston surveys, the Copenhagen Area Surveys tracked economic, social, and demographic trends in the Copenhagen area and measured residents' attitudes and behaviors on a range of issues. Samples using matching techniques purposively sampled potential respondents on the basis of known criteria about the same population from a large panel of potential respondents.[2] Using this known demographic and social information about the population, the goal was to create a sample that aligned with the greater population; this is the same overarching goal as in conventional random sampling.

Respondents were chosen for the matching sample from a panel maintained by Epinion that totals more than 240,000 panelists in Denmark. Panelists are continually recruited and can only stay in the panel for two years. Criteria used for the matching sample included the respondent's gender, age, education level, and whether the respondent lived in Copenhagen or Frederiksberg (the latter, though a different political entity, is circumscribed by and integrated into Copenhagen) or a suburb. The number of respondents for the 2014 and 2015 surveys were 1,093 and 1,058, respectively. The 2014 Copenhagen Area Survey was conducted in late March and April 2014, and the 2015 Copenhagen Area Survey was conducted from April 8 to May 7. Of those who opened the invitation e-mail to complete the survey, 77 percent answered the survey. More details about the Copenhagen Area Surveys can be found by visiting kinder.rice.edu and clicking on the reports under the Copenhagen Area Survey heading.

European Cities Survey Data

For our comparative analysis of European cities, we drew on the 2015 Flash Eurobarometer 419. This survey, conducted every three years, drew data from 40,798 Europeans living in seventy-nine different cities. It focuses on a variety of issues, especially quality of life measures. The survey includes all capital cities of the countries concerned, except for Switzerland, and samples about five hundred respondents in each city.

The surveys were conducted by TNS Political and Social Network between May 21 and June 9, 2015, on behalf of the European Commission, Directorate-General for Regional and Urban Policy. The interviews were conducted by telephone (landline and mobile phone) in each city's mother tongue. More information on this survey can be found by accessing the report at ec.europa.eu.

Qualitative Data

Interviews

We conducted several interviews from 2013 through 2017, of people in Copenhagen and Houston. Our interviews were always in person, conducted in English or Danish, and were recorded and later transcribed for analysis and use. Our interviews were conducted to learn information and gain depth we could not get from surveys, secondary sources, or online materials. Three people conducted the interviews: the two authors of this book and Julie Warner Markussen, a native Copenhagener who at the time of the interviews was a sociology graduate student at the University of Copenhagen.

Among those interviewed were five of the seven Copenhagen mayors, several area experts, a council person in Houston and a council person in Copenhagen, a business owner in each city, people who had lived in both cities, and current residents of each city.

Qualitative Classification of European Cities

As one measure of whether a city was a Market or People City—for use in chapter 7—we conducted a qualitative analysis of most cities sampled in the Eurobarometer survey (see above). Smiley and Kinder Institute staff member Kiara Douds, along with several students, conducted the work to create the classifications. All were instructed to classify cities on a five-point scale (Strong Market, Leans toward Market, In Between/ Mixed, Leans toward People, and Strong People Cities). For conducting the classifications, the researchers were instructed to examine the stated priorities of the city, as listed on the city government website, examine the two most recent city budgets, classifying what money is spent on, and draw on statements and speeches about the city from the mayor(s) and high-ranking local officials. They were also asked to study where, if at all, the respective cities showed up on world or European rankings of cities.

At least two researchers classified each city. If they agreed on their classification, the city received their classification. If they did not agree, a third person worked on classifying the city. If the third person classified the same as one or the other of the first two researchers, the classification with two votes was used. In a few cases, no agreement among the three researchers was reached. In such a case, a team meeting was held between Emerson, Smiley, and Douds to determine the most appropriate classification.

This effort was complex due to the many different languages of the cities represented. When we had researchers on the team who spoke the native tongue of the city, they were assigned those cities. But we had many instances where no one on the team could read or speak the language of the city under consideration. In such cases, Google Translate was used. This was not always perfect. At times, the translations did not seem right, or at least did not make clear sense. In such instances, we either found a native speaker to help us translate, used an alternative electronic translator, or sought additional documents to translate.

Secondary Sources

We drew from many secondary sources (see the bibliography). These included books, journal articles, historical documents, government reports, municipal websites, blogs, podcasts, videos, newspapers, maps, and other website locations. These were used purposively, to learn about the key topics explored in each of the book's chapters for each city, and for several other cities used for illustrative purposes.

Experiential

To get a deeper understanding and feeling for each city, both authors lived in both cities and visited them many more times. Emerson lived in Houston from 1999 to early 2013, and again from late 2014 to mid-2015. Smiley lived in Houston from 2012 to 2015. Each author also visited Houston on numerous occasions when not living there. Emerson lived and worked in Copenhagen from 2013 to 2014, and again for two months in 2015. He visited Copenhagen for extended visits and research in 2012, 2016, and 2017. Smiley lived in Copenhagen for five months in 2014, while attending the University of Copenhagen and conducting research for this book. He had an additional extended visit for research in 2016.

While in each city we lived largely as locals, complete with sending children to the local schools, learning the language (when needed), paying taxes, making friends, working, attending local events, meeting people, buying groceries, and renting places to live. The experience of fully living life in each locale was important for gaining a deeper understanding of the cultural ethos of each city and an intuitive feel of each place.

NOTES

INTRODUCTION

1 See Smiley and Emerson, 2017.
2 Katz and Bradley, 2013.
3 Sassen, 2006.
4 Glaeser, 2011.
5 Katz and Bradley, 2013.
6 We want to be clear on the distinction between city proper and metropolitan area. Often we refer in this book to the city proper, the political entity defined as the city. But because cities are also integrally woven into their larger metropolitan area (the core city plus the suburban areas surrounding the core cities), when it is more appropriate for our analysis we will draw on the metropolitan area.
7 Harvey, 1989; Logan and Molotch, 1987.

CHAPTER 1. BECOMING MARKET AND PEOPLE CITIES

1 Kotkin, 2005.
2 Much of our Copenhagen history is taken from an interview we conducted with Copenhagen historian Carsten Pape on June 15, 2015. He has authored a history of eighteenth-century Copenhagen, *Enevældens København: Historie og byvandringer*, and regularly teaches university courses on the history of the city.
3 Christensen and Mikkelsen, 2006.
4 Fabricius, 1999.
5 Barfod, 1993.
6 Ibid.
7 Christensen and Mikkelsen, 2006.
8 H. T. Andersen, 2008.
9 Copenhagenet, 2015; "kindergarten" is a German word meaning children's garden, coined by German educator Friedrich Fröbel in 1840.
10 H. T. Andersen, 2008.
11 See Lefebvre's 1968 book, *The Right to the City (Lefebvre 1996)*. This book argues, at its broadest level, for an alternate city vision to capitalism and neoliberalism. Influenced by Marxism, he argues that cities can be more democratic, socially just, and sustainable; that people must take the city back for themselves, rather than give it over to the whims of capitalist elites. As scholar David Harvey reflects, "it is the right to change ourselves by changing our city. It is, moreover, a common rather than an individual right" (Harvey, 2008, 23).

12 H. T. Andersen, 2008.

13 *Copenhagen Post*, 2012a.

14 Campbell, 2010; Gille, 1999; Texas Beyond History, 2009.

15 McComb, 1981.

16 Pratt, 2007.

17 McComb, 1981.

18 McComb, 1981, 94.

19 Barnett, 2007.

20 Feagin, 1988; Gorman, 2007.

21 Gorman, 2007.

22 Beeth and Wintz, 1992.

23 Boles, 2012.

24 Pruitt, 2013.

25 Beeth and Wintz, 1992.

26 De León, 2001.

27 McComb, 1981; Feagin, 1988.

28 McComb, 1981.

29 Feagin, 1988, 149.

30 Ibid.

31 Ibid.

32 Shelton, 2014b.

33 McKinney, 2007.

34 R. S. Thompson, 2007.

35 Bullard, 1987; Feagin, 1988; Fisher, 1992; McComb, 1981; Melosi and Pratt, 2007.

36 Beeth and Wintz, 1992; Bullard, 1987; Jensen, 1992.

37 Jensen, 1992.

38 Beeth and Wintz, 1992.

39 San Miguel, 2001.

40 Feagin, 1988, 74–75.

41 D. Thompson, 2013.

42 Greater Houston Partnership, 2014.

43 De León, 2001.

44 Statistics are from the U.S. Census's American Community Survey 2015 one-year estimates for the city of Houston.

45 Morris, 2014.

46 Gutherie, 2013; de Guzman, 2016; Gattis 2016.

47 Brennan, 2012.

CHAPTER 2. HOW GOVERNMENT AND LEADERS MAKE CITIES WORK

1 Miami, 2014.

2 Paris, 2014b.

3 Vancouver, 2015.

4 Kansas City, 2012a.

5 Nijman, 2011, viii

6 Kansas City, 2012b.

7 Paris, 2014b.

8 Paris, 2014a.

9 Vancouver, 2012.

10 City of Copenhagen, 2011b.

11 Ibid.

12 City of Houston, 2014b.

13 Parker, 2014.

14 Harris County Budget Management, 2013.

15 Malmö, 2014.

16 Miami, 2011.

17 Nijman, 2011.

18 Helft, 2010.

19 Velázquez, 2015.

20 Grimm et al., 2008; Elliott and Clement, 2014.

21 Participatory Budgeting Project, 2015.

22 Plesse, 2014.

23 Véron, 2015.

24 K. Thompson, 2015.

25 Morris, 2012.

26 Pinkerton, 2014.

27 Bayliss, 2007.

28 Gehl, 2010.

29 Leigh, 2014.

30 Hobby, 2014.

31 *Chronicle of Philanthropy*, 2015.

32 Trust for Public Land 2011.

33 Smiley et al., 2016.

34 Smiley, Rushing, and Scott, 2016b.

35 The Kinder Foundation is the lead funder of the Kinder Institute for Urban Research at Rice University, with which each of us is or has been affiliated.

36 Denmark, 2014; Ifversen, 2012.

CHAPTER 3. WHAT RESIDENTS THINK, BELIEVE, AND ACT UPON

1 Data for these statistics are from the 2015 Copenhagen Area Survey and the 2015 Houston Area Survey.

2 Data for these statistics are from the 2015 Copenhagen Area Survey and the 2015 Houston Area Survey.

3 Data for these statistics are from the 2015 Copenhagen Area Survey and the 2015 Houston Area Survey.

4 Data for these statistics are from the 2014 and 2015 Copenhagen Area Survey and the 2014 and 2015 Houston Area Survey.

5 Data for these statistics are from the 2014 Copenhagen Area Survey and the 2014 Houston Area Survey.

6 Chi-square tests for these income differences are statistically significant ($p < 0.05$) in both cities for (1) government is doing too many things, and (2) government should reduce inequalities. The relationship is not statistically significant for views on the causes of being poor in Houston, but it is in Copenhagen. There are no statistically significant relationships by income in either cities for (1) work hard and succeed or (2) faith in public authorities in both cities.

7 Wirth, 1938.

8 Harvey, 2013; Pickvance, 2003.

9 Smiley, Rushing, and Scott, 2016b.

10 Allyn, 2012; Carroll, 2012; Jaffe, 2014.

11 Dries, 2011.

12 Smiley, Rushing, and Scott, 2016a.

13 Clark, Lloyd, Wong, and Jain, 2002; Clark, 2011.

14 Bernelius and Kauppinen, 2011.

15 Bernelius and Vaattovaara, 2016.

16 Kosunen, 2014.

17 Organisation for Economic Co-operation and Development, 2015.

18 Rangvid, 2010.

19 *Copenhagen Post*, 2013.

20 There were eight main parties that contested elections between 2009 and 2014. In 2015, a new party, the Alternative, became a ninth main party.

21 Liberal Alliance, 2015.

22 Data for these statistics are from tables FVKOM, VALGK3, and EVKOM in the online tool StatBank from Statistics Denmark.

23 San Miguel, 2001.

24 Ibid.; De León, 2001.

25 Bobo, Kluegel, and Smith, 1997; Bonilla-Silva, 2009.

26 Binkovitz, 2016.

CHAPTER 4. GETTING THERE, BEING THERE

1 Kahneman et al., 2004.

2 Data for these statistics are from table AFSTB4 for 2014 in the online tool Stat-Bank from Statistics Denmark.

3 This distance figure uses an estimate from the U.S. Census. Because Denmark measures commuting in distance and the United States measures commuting in minutes, this creates a mismatch for the data. We convert the U.S. data to distance using the following formula. The average commute time in the U.S. is 26.1 minutes, and the average distance is 18.8 miles. We divide these two numbers: $18.8/26.1 = 0.72$. This figure denotes that the estimated distance traveled per minute of commute time in the United States is 0.72 miles. For all Houston statistics on commuting in this section, we multiplied the commute time by 0.72

to estimate the distance traveled. The source for the average commute time and average commute distance in the United States is from Rapino and Fields, 2012.

4   This statistic is calculated assuming a roundtrip commute for five days of work per week for 48 weeks in a year (240 total days). This distance is 5,328 miles. The distance for the roundtrip in a car from Washington, D.C., to Los Angeles, California, is 5,346 miles.

5   McKinney, 2007.

6   Data for these statistics are from the American Community Survey five-year pooled estimates for 2010–14. See https://www.census.gov/programs-surveys/acs.

7   Cathcart-Keays and Warin, 2016.

8   Lindholm, n.d.

9   Smiley, Rushing, and Scott, 2016a.

10 Florida, 2012.

11 Data for these statistics are from the 2014 and 2015 Copenhagen Area Survey.

12 Data for these statistics are from the 2014 and 2015 Copenhagen Area Survey.

13 Data for these statistics in Houston are from the 2015 one-year estimates from the American Community Survey.

14 Data for these statistics are from the 2015 Copenhagen Area Survey and the 2015 Houston Area Survey.

15 It might be noted here that while the surveys took place at similar times of the year in both places, one element of bias might emerge: warmer weather in Houston than in Copenhagen. Even so, Copenhagen had much higher rates of bicycle use in the previous thirty days. This means that some of our tests were a little conservative when it came to estimating these differences—we might speculate that had Copenhagen been as warm as Houston for the previous thirty days, the rates might be even higher.

16 We use the term "public transportation system" or "public transit," even though, in some cases, these are not truly "public" in terms of the ownership of the particular train or bus. But we use the terms "mass transit" and "public transportation" interchangeably because of their popular use that way, and because there is a public nature to taking a form of transportation—like a bus or train—in which space is shared.

17 Data for these statistics are from the 2015 Copenhagen Area Survey and the 2015 Houston Area Survey.

18 A chi-square test for the cross-tabulation is statistically significant ($p < 0.05$).

19 A chi-square test for the cross-tabulation is statistically significant ($p < 0.05$).

20 A chi-square test for the cross-tabulation is statistically significant ($p < 0.05$).

21 A chi-square test for the cross-tabulation is statistically significant ($p < 0.05$).

22 Data for these statistics are from American Community Survey five-year pooled estimates for 2010–14.

23 Data for these statistics are from table BOL1 in the online tool StatBank from Statistics Denmark, which can be found at https://www.statbank.dk/statbank5a/default.asp?w=1366.

24 Glaeser, 2011, 192.
25 Greater Houston Partnership, 2016.
26 Kotkin, 2014.
27 Logan and Molotch, 1987.
28 Kotkin and Gattis, 2014.
29 Juul-Sandberg and Norberg, 2014.
30 Hammar, 2013.
31 Feser, 2016; Alexander, 2013.
32 City of Copenhagen, 2016a.
33 Hammar, 2013; Bloze and Skak, 2009.
34 Data for these statistics are from table BOL1for 2014 in the online tool StatBank from Statistics Denmark. Data for these statistics in Houston are from the 2009–14 five-year pooled estimates from the American Community Survey.
35 Juul-Sandberg and Norberg, 2014.
36 Houston Association of Realtors, 2016; Frohlich, 2014.
37 Data for these statistics are from table BM010 for 2014 in the online tool from the Association of Danish Mortgage Banks.
38 This is for detached dwellings in Copenhagen. No median is given for the Copenhagen region (it is in categories), but we calculated the midpoint between the categories given the distribution of the values.
39 Data for these statistics are from table BM010 for 2015 in the online tool from the Association of Danish Mortgage Banks. Inflation is accounted for using the consumer price index available through Statistics Denmark.
40 Data for these statistics are from American Community Survey one-year pooled estimates for the municipality of Houston in 2015.
41 O'Sullivan, 2016b.
42 City of Copenhagen, 2016b.
43 Jacobs, 1961.
44 Mumford, 1961/1989.
45 Data for these statistics are from the 2014 Copenhagen Area Survey and the 2014 Houston Area Survey.
46 A chi-square test for the cross-tabulation is statistically significant ($p < 0.05$).
47 A chi-square test for the cross-tabulation is statistically significant ($p < 0.05$).
48 Data for these statistics are from the 2015 Copenhagen Area Survey and the 2015 Houston Area Survey.
49 A chi-square test for the cross-tabulation for Copenhagen is statistically significant ($p < 0.05$). The association is not statistically significant in Houston ($p = 0.768$).
50 Danish Nature Agency, 2015.
51 City of Houston, 2016.
52 Holeywell, 2015.
53 *The Onion*, 2014.
54 Bureau of Transportation Statistics, 2016; Collier, 2013.

55 Bureau of Transportation Statistics, 2016.
56 Texas Parks and Wildlife, 2016.

CHAPTER 5. ENVIRONMENT/ECONOMY

1 Betsill and Bulkeley, 2007.
2 Grimm et al., 2008.
3 Glaeser, 2011; Bettencourt and West, 2010.
4 C40 Cities, 2015.
5 McComb, 1981.
6 Kever, 2013.
7 Energistyrelsen, 2016.
8 Roberts, 2016.
9 Ibid.
10 City of Copenhagen, 2012.
11 Data for the statistics are from the 2015 Copenhagen Area Survey and the 2015 Houston Area Survey.
12 A chi-square test for the cross-tabulation is statistically significant ($p < 0.05$).
13 Data for the statistics are from the 2015 Copenhagen Area Survey and the 2015 Houston Area Survey.
14 Data for the statistics are from the 2015 Copenhagen Area Survey and the 2015 Houston Area Survey.
15 Smiley, 2017.
16 Hamilton and Saito, 2015; McCright and Dunlap, 2011.
17 Foster, Clark, and York, 2010.
18 Inglehart, 1981; Mol and Spaargaren, 2000; Foster, Clark, and York, 2010.
19 Biesbroeck et al., 2010; Bauer, Feichtinger, and Steurer, 2012.
20 European Commission, 2014.
21 City of Copenhagen, 2012.
22 Ibid.
23 Ibid.
24 London School of Economics and Political Science, 2014.
25 Gerdes, 2013; Billing, 2015; Hoare, 2016.
26 This includes concerns about the ecological footprint of an array of products created elsewhere on the planet but used by Copenhagen.
27 U.S. Green Building Council, 2013.
28 Feser, 2015.
29 City of Houston, 2014a.
30 City of Houston, 2008.
31 We chose 120,000 metric tons because this is the lowest amount of emissions from a Copenhagen area facility in 2013. More facilities reported levels below that in Houston, but we do not have comparable data in Denmark.
32 The capital region is Hovedstaden.
33 Tally and Gardner, 2008.

34 Environmental Protection Agency, 2016.
35 Melosi, 2005.
36 Hoornweg, Bhada-Tata, and Kennedy, 2013.
37 Bullard, 1990; Pellow, 2002.
38 Kjær, 2013.
39 Amager Resource Center, 2016.
40 Michler, 2011.
41 B&W Vølund, 2016.
42 Zero Waste Europe, 2014; *Copenhagen Post*, 2012b.
43 Slavin, 2016.
44 Ellick, 2008; Satija, 2014.
45 Sass, 2015.
46 Martin, 2016; City of Houston, 2015b.
47 Bullard, 1990.
48 Satija, 2014.
49 Texas Campaign for the Environment Fund and Zero Waste Houston Coalition, 2014.
50 Martin, 2016.
51 City of Houston, 2015b.
52 Morris, 2016b.
53 *Houston Chronicle*, 2016.
54 Morris, 2016a.
55 Morris, 2016b.
56 Ng, 2015.
57 *Houston Chronicle*, 2016; Scruggs, 2016.
58 Chu, 2012.
59 Goldschalk, 2003.
60 Dansk Meteorologisk Selskab, 2011.
61 Ibid.
62 Beredshabs Styrelsen, 2012.
63 Seeberg, 2011.
64 Berlingske, 2011.
65 Andersen, 2016.
66 Kilhof, 2014.
67 Gerdes, 2012.
68 City of Copenhagen, 2011a.
69 Ibid.
70 McComb, 1981.
71 Berg, 2009.
72 Texas Division of Emergency Management, 2008.
73 Roth, 2010.
74 Berg, 2009.
75 Satija et al., 2016.

76 Ibid.
77 Ibid.
78 Ibid.
79 Morss and Hayden, 2010.
80 Banerjee, Song and Hasemyer, 2015; Jennings, Grandoni, and Rust, 2015.

CHAPTER 6. LIFE TOGETHER AND APART

1 Data for the statistics are from the 2014 Copenhagen Area Survey and the 2014 Houston Area Survey.
2 Social life is complex. We are not saying a Market City directly causes mistrust between its residents and a People City directly causes trust between residents. Far from it. For one, we do not know the causal order. Does higher generalized trust lead to more people-leaning cities, or do more people-leaning cities lead to higher generalized trust? Second, as we will see later in this chapter, People and Market Cities are made up of a constellation of factors, most of which impact one another—social diversity, crime levels, inequality, trustworthiness of institutions, to name a few—and all intersect and impact generalized trust. It is this dynamic nexus of interactions between these factors that we believe leads to higher trust in People Cities compared to Market Cities. We unpack this in more detail as the chapter unfolds.
3 Svendsen, 2014, 30.
4 Booth, 2014, 44–45. We witnessed similar results. One busy Christmas season in Copenhagen, Emerson dropped a one hundred Kroner bill (about fifteen U.S. dollars) on the floor of a store. It was not until twenty minutes later, when he went to make a purchase, that he noticed the hundred Kroner bill was missing. He had an idea of where he may have dropped it—at the opposite end of the store from the cash register—and went back looking for it. Sure enough, there it lay on the floor, people purposively walking around it so as not to disturb it. And in 2017, Emerson was bound on a train from Copenhagen Central Station to what he thought was the airport. It turned out he was heading in the exact opposite direction of the airport, so he rushed off the train to get on a return train in an attempt to catch his flight. What he failed to notice until fifteen minutes later was that he had left his backpack on the train, a backpack that contained his passport, cash, debit and credit cards, his smart phone, and his PC with his only electronic copy of this book on it. He went back to Copenhagen Central Station and told the Lost and Found division of the lost backpack. After asking a few questions, the clerk promptly called the conductor of the train. Though nearly two hours had passed since Emerson had disembarked and left his backpack on board the train, sitting in plain sight, and despite several train stops during that time with people getting on and off, the backpack was found exactly where it had been left. When the train returned to Copenhagen Central Station an additional two hours later, the clerk went onboard the train and delivered to Emerson the backpack, with everything—cash and all—still in the backpack.

5 Edmondson and Reynolds, 2016.
6 Glaeser and Sacerdote, 1996.
7 Morris, 2013.
8 Hassan and Pinkerton, 2014.
9 Gattis, 2016.
10 Brooks, 2016.
11 We should note that such provisions don't just happen. They often are the result of citizen request, protest, or much political debate. So while we are describing differences between Market Cities and People Cities, these differences always are the result of negotiations and power struggles.
12 Data for these statistics are from table IFOR41 for 2014 in the online tool StatBank from Statistics Denmark.
13 YouGov Civic Dashboards, 2017.
14 According to an *Urban Affairs Review* article, in the United States there is quite a range of views of inequality among city mayors. When asked to name their top two policy priorities, 18 percent of U.S. mayors in the sample named some version of reducing inequality (25 percent of Democratic mayors, 9 percent of Republican mayors). When asked directly if cities should try to reduce income inequality, even if doing so comes at the expense of business or wealthy residents, 30 percent of U.S. mayors agreed (about half of Democratic mayors, and 6 percent of Republican mayors). When asked if it is good for a neighborhood to experience rising property values, even it means displacement of current residents, 30 percent disagreed, and there was no difference along party lines. The researchers also found that 20 percent of mayors in their sample have actually implemented programs to reduce inequality. See Einstein and Glick, 2016.
15 The tradition of philanthropy, of endowing foundations to give money to causes is strong in Houston, as it is in many Market Cities, especially Market Cities in the United States. Many advantages ensue from such practices, not the least of which is that such philanthropic foundations are the lifeblood of nonprofit work in the Houston region. Funding Houston's non-economic activities in this way has many advantages: people take pride in their community through these connections, through seeing each other support the development of the city, through extensive volunteering, through taking ownership, and much more. And funding non-economic activity in this way has very real risks: what causes foundations fund are typically based on the wealthy founder's special concerns or the interests of a local elite serving on the boards of the foundations. As a result, important causes can be overlooked. Also, as we have witnessed, to receive money from these foundations one must speak the language of the elite, know their rules, and have connections to them to raise awareness of the importance of one's nonprofit endeavor. Some people and some communities are better at this than others and have many more connections to the elite to get noticed and funded. Unfortunately, this differential success rate is often divided along color and class lines, regenerating already existing inequalities.

16 Wilkinson and Pickett, 2011; Stiglitz, 2013.

17 Massey and Denton, 1993; Sampson, 2012; Sharkey, 2013; Wilson, 1987/2012. The literature addressing these issues is vast, so we can cite only some of it.

18 City of Copenhagen, 2011b, 18.

19 Christian, 2015.

20 Data for these statistics are from the 2015 Houston Area Survey.

21 Lewis, Emerson, and Klineberg, 2011.

22 City of Houston, 2017a.

23 City of Houston Fire Department, n.d.

24 City of Houston, n.d.

25 City of Houston, 2017b.

26 Rahman, 2016.

27 Emerson et al., 2012.

28 City of Houston, 2015a.

29 Andersen, Blach, and Nielson, 2014, 12.

30 Ibid., 19.

31 Ibid., 14.

32 Ibid., 11.

33 Ibid.

34 For an analysis of these questions that takes into account political views and perceptions of crime in Copenhagen, see Smiley, Emerson, and Markussen, 2017.

35 Data for these statistics are from the 2015 Copenhagen Area Survey and the 2015 Houston Area Survey. A chi-square test for the cross-tabulation is statistically significant ($p < 0.05$).

36 Data for these statistics are from the 2014 and 2015 Copenhagen Area Survey and the 2014 and 2015 Houston Area Survey. A chi-square test for the cross-tabulation is statistically significant ($p < 0.05$).

37 We analyzed all immigrants, regardless of ancestry or national origin.

38 European Union, 2016. The three cities with rates of satisfaction less than 75 percent were Palermo (67 percent), Athens (67 percent), and Istanbul (65 percent).

CHAPTER 7. ACROSS CITIES

1 Kneese, DeMers, and Ashby, 2015.

2 Stroganov, 2015.

3 European Union, 2016.

4 The capital of Switzerland is not included because it does not have one. The de facto capital, Bern, was not surveyed.

5 Also integral are the sociodemographic characteristics of individuals. For instance, more highly educated respondents disagree or are less satisfied with their city's climate change politics, transit system, streets and buildings, green spaces, and are more in agreement that their neighborhood and cities are safe. Compared to respondents who have had no trouble paying their bills, those who have had trouble from time to time or most of the time are less likely to agree or be satis-

fied on each of the measures except for the climate change question. Less robust individual-level relationships across the independent variables, including gender, age, being a parent, and tenure in the city are sometimes linked with the dependent variable under examination and sometimes are not.

6 For the statistically trained and curious, a factor analysis was conducted. These variables all loaded strongly onto a single factor and thus are used together. Specifically, only one factor variable was predicted with an eigenvalue greater than 1; the value is 3.57. Each variable plays a major role in the creation of the new factor variable.

7 Empirically, cities were classified as Strong People Cities if we qualitatively ranked them as People Cities, they had at least a 0.10 lower standard deviation than the mean standard deviation, and scored 0.3 or higher on the factor score.

8 Empirically, cities were classified as Strong Market Cities if we qualitatively ranked them as Market Cities, they had a standard deviation at least 0.07 higher than the mean standard deviation, and scored −0.3 or lower on the factor score.

9 Ackroyd, 2000; A. T. Kearney, 2015; Shorto, 2013.

10 Fainstein, 2010.

11 Shorto, 2013.

12 Ackroyd, 2000, 714.

13 Fainstein, 2010, 164.

14 Ackroyd, 2000, 749.

15 Fainstein, 2010, 164.

16 Delmendo, 2016.

17 Global Property Guide, 2016.

18 Monaghan, 2016.

19 Ruhe, 2016.

20 Mayor of London, 2015; I Am Amsterdam, 2016.

21 Pruijt, 2003; Van Gent, 2013.

22 Butler, 2007; Hamnett, 2003.

23 O'Sullivan, 2016c.

24 Shorto, 2016.

25 O'Sullivan, 2016a.

26 Boland, 2017.

27 O'Sullivan, 2016a.

28 *Economist*, 2016.

CHAPTER 8. TO BE OR NOT TO BE

1 Glaeser, 2011, 184.

2 Cohen, 2013.

3 O'Sullivan, 2016a.

4 Secret Copenhagen, 2017.

5 Moyer, 1987.

6 Kostadinova, 2014.

AFTERWORD
1 Boburg and Reinhard, 2017.
2 Belkin and Mahtani, 2017.

METHODOLOGICAL APPENDIX
1 American Association for Public Opinion Research, 2016.See page 62 of the AAPOR Standard Definitions report for the formula and explanation of RR3, found at http://www.aapor.org/AAPOR_Main/media/publications/Standard-Definitions20169theditionfinal.pdf.
2 Ansolabehere and Schaffner 2014.

BIBLIOGRAPHY

A. T. Kearney. 2015. *Global Cities 2015: The Race Accelerates*. Chicago: A. T. Kearney.

Ackroyd, Peter. 2000. *London: The Biography*. New York: Nan A. Talese.

Alexander, Heather. 2013, December 10. "Houston Renters Getting Hit with Some of the Highest Increases in Nation." *Houston Chronicle*. Retrieved January 21, 2017. www.houstonchronicle.com.

Allyn, Bobby. 2012, December 9. "Sprawling Memphis Aims to Be a Friendlier Place for Cyclists." *New York Times*. www.nytimes.com.

Amager Resource Center. 2016. "ARC og Amager Bakke." Retrieved February 12, 2015. www.a-r-c.dk.

American Association for Public Opinion Research. 2016. *Standard Definitions: Final Dispositions of Case Codes and Outcome Rates for Surveys*. Oakbrook Terrace, IL: American Association for Public Opinion Research.

Andersen, Hans Thor. 2008. "Copenhagen, Denmark: Urban Regeneration at Economic and Social Sustainability." In *Sustainable City Regions: Space, Place, and Governance*, ed. T. Kidokro, N. Harata, L. P. Subanu, L. Jessen, A. Motte, and E. P. Seltzer, 203–26. Tokyo: Springer Japan.

Andersen, Hans Thor, Vigdis Blach, Anne Winther Beckman, and Rikke Skovgaard Nielson. 2014. *Assessment of Urban Policies on Diversity in Copenhagen*. Copenhagen: Danish Building Research Institute, Aalborg University.

Andersen, Kare. 2016, March 24. "10 Ways Citizens Can Make Their Cities Even Better." Retrieved March 4, 2017. www.sayitbetter.com.

Andersen, Ulrik. 2016, March 27. "Skybrud affødte bølge af projekter." *Ingeniøren*. Retrieved June 13, 2016. ing.dk.

Ansolabehere, Stephen, and Brian F. Schaffner. 2014. "Does Survey Mode Still Matter? Findings from a 2010 Multi-Mode Comparison." *Political Analysis* 22(3): 285–303.

B&W Vølund. 2016. "ARC, Copenhill / Amager Bakke, Copenhagen, Denmark." Retrieved February 13, 2015. www.volund.dk.

Banerjee, Neela, Lisa Song, and David Hasemyer. 2015, September 16. "Exxon the Road Not Taken: Exxon's Own Research Confirmed Fossil Fuels' Role in Global Warming Decades Ago." *Inside Climate News*. Retrieved September 17, 2015. insideclimatenews.org.

Barfod, Jørgen H. 1993. "Copenhagen as a Naval Base." In *Garrison Towns and Society in Early Modern Europe*, ed. T. Riis, 79–91. Odense: University of Southern Denmark Studies in History and Social Sciences.

Barnett, William C. 2007. "A Tale of Two Texas Cities: Houston, the Industrial Metropolis, and Galveston, the Island Getaway." In *Energy Metropolis: An Environmental History of Houston and the Gulf Coast*, ed. M. V. Melosi and J. A. Pratt, 185–206. Pittsburgh: University of Pittsburgh Press.

Bauer, Anja, Judith Feichtinger, and Reinhard Steurer. 2012. "The Governance of Climate Change Adaptation in Ten OECD Countries: Challenges and Approaches." *Journal of Environmental Policy and Planning* 14(3): 279–304.

Bayliss, Darrin. 2007. "The Rise of the Creative Class: Culture and Creativity in Copenhagen." *European Planning Studies* 15(7): 889–903.

Beeth, Howard, and Cary D. Wintz, eds. 1992. *Black Dixie: Afro-Texan History and Culture in Houston*. College Station: Texas A&M University Press.

Belkin, Douglas, and Shibani Mahtani. 2017, September 11. "In Harvey's Wake, Houston Rethinks Real Estate Development." *Wall Street Journal*. Retrieved September 12, 2017. www.wsj.com.

Beredshabs Styrelsen. 2012, July 2. "Redegørelse vedrørende skybruddet i Storkøbenhavn lørdag den 2. juli 2011." Retrieved June 13, 2016. brs.dk.

Berg, Robbie. 2009, January 23. "Tropical Cyclone Report: Hurricane Ike." *National Hurricane Center Tropical Cyclone Reports*. Retrieved May 29, 2016. www.nhc.noaa.gov.

Berlingske. 2011, July 21. "Sådan genkender du den farlige rottesygdom." *Berlingske*. Retrieved June 13, 2016. www.b.dk.

Bernelius, Venla, and Timo M. Kauppinen. 2011. "School Outcomes and Neighborhood Effects: A New Approach Using Data from Finland." In *Neighborhood Effects Research*, ed. M. van Ham, D. Manley, N. Bailey, L. Simpson, and D. Maclennan. Houten, Netherlands: Springer Netherlands.

Bernelius, Venla, and Mari Vaattovaara. 2016. "Choice and Segregation in the 'Most Egalitarian' Schools: Cumulative Decline in Urban Schools and Neighbourhoods of Helsinki, Finland." *Urban Studies* 53(15): 3155–71.

Betsill, Michele, and Harriet Bulkeley. 2007. "Looking Back and Thinking Ahead: A Decade of Cities and Climate Change Research." *Local Environment* 12(5): 447–56.

Bettencourt, Luis, and Geoffrey West. 2010. "A Unified Theory of Urban Living." *Nature* 467:912–13.

Biesbroeck, G., Rob J. Swart, Timothy R. Carter, Caroline Cowan, Thomas Henrichs, Hanna Mela, Michael D. Morecroft, and Daniela Ray. 2010. "Europe Adapts to Climate Change: Comparing National Adaptation Strategies." *Global Environmental Change* 20:440–50.

Billing, Sören. 2015, July 16. "Copenhagen on Bumpy Road to Carbon Neutrality." *Local DK*. Retrieved May 31, 2016. www.thelocal.dk.

Binkovitz, Leah. 2016, August 30. "The Most Economically Segregated School District Boundaries in the Country." *Urban Edge*. Retrieved January 17, 2017. urbanedge.blogs.rice.edu.

Bloze, Gintautas, and Morten Skak. 2009. "Rent Control and Misallocation." *Discussion Papers on Business and Economics* 7:1–25.

Bobo, Lawrence, James R. Kluegel, and Ryan A. Smith. 1997. "Laissez-Faire Racism: The Crystallization of a Kinder, Gentler, Antiblack Ideology." In *Racial Attitudes in the 1990s: Continuity and Change*, ed. Steven A. Tuch and Jack K. Martin, 15–42. Westport, CT: Praeger.

Boburg, Shawn, and Beth Reinhard. 2017, August 29. "Houston's 'Wild West' Growth." *Washington Post*. Retrieved September 12, 2017. www.washingtonpost.com.

Boland, Vincent. 2017, January 24. "Dublin Jockeys for Brexit Spoils." *Financial Times*. Retrieved February 13, 2017. www.ft.com.

Boles, John B. 2012. *A University So Conceived: A Brief History of Rice University*. Houston: Rice University.

Bonilla-Silva, Eduardo. 2009. *Racism without Racists: Color-Blind Racism and the Persistence of Racial Inequality in America*. Lanham, MD: Rowman and Littlefield.

Booth, Michael. 2014. *The Almost Nearly Perfect People: The Truth about the Nordic Miracle*. London: Jonathan Cape.

Brennan, Morgan. 2012, July 26. "Houston Tops Our List of America's Coolest Cities." *Forbes*. Retrieved February 27, 2017. www.forbes.com.

Brooks, David. 2016, June 3. "Where America Is Working." *New York Times*. Retrieved March 4, 2017. www.nytimes.com.

Bullard, Robert D. 1987. *Invisible Houston: The Black Experience in Boom and Bust*. College Station: Texas A&M University Press.

———. 1990. *Dumping in Dixie: Race, Class, and Environmental Quality*. Boulder, CO: Westview Press.

Bureau of Transportation Statistics. 2016. "Table 1–57: Tonnage of Top 50 U.S. Water Ports, Ranking by Total Tons." Retrieved May 30, 2016. www.rita.dot.gov.

Butler, Tim. 2007. "Re-urbanizing London Docklands: Gentrification, Suburbanization, or New Urbanism?" *International Journal of Urban and Regional Research* 31(4): 759–81.

C40 Cities. 2015. "*Climate Action in Megacities 3.0*." Retrieved May 27, 2016. www.cam3.c40.org.

Campbell, Thomas N. 2010. "Akokisa Indians." *Handbook of Texas Online*. Texas State Historical Association. Retrieved October 30, 2014. www.tshaonline.org.

Carroll, Scott. 2012, August 10. "Magazine Names Memphis 'Most Improved City.'" *Commercial Appeal*. www.commercialappeal.com.

Cathcart-Keays, Athlyn, and Tim Warin. 2016, May 5. "Story of Cities #36: How Copenhagen Rejected 1960s Modernist 'Utopia.'" *Guardian*. Retrieved May 30, 2016. www.theguardian.com.

Christensen, Søren Bitsch, and Jørgen Mikkelsen. 2006. "The Danish Urban System Pre-1800: A Survey of Recent Research Results." *Urban History* 33(3): 484–510.

Christian, W. 2015, May 8. "Marginalised Youth in Copenhagen Committing Less Crime." *Copenhagen Post*. Retrieved March 3, 2017. cphpost.dk.

Chronicle of Philanthropy. 2015. "Houston-Sugarland-Baytown 2012 Giving Profile." Retrieved May 12, 2015. philanthropy.com.

Chu, Jennifer. 2012, March 13. "'Storm of the Century?' Try 'Storm of the Decade.'" *MIT News*. Retrieved June 8, 2016. news.mit.edu.

Copenhagen. 2011a. *Copenhagen Climate Adaptation Plan*. Retrieved May 31, 2016. en.klimatilpasning.dk.

———. 2011b. "Municipal Plan 2011." Retrieved May 10, 2015. www.kk.dk.

———. 2012. *CPH 2025 Climate Plan: A Green, Smart, and Carbon Neutral City*. Accessed October 11, 2014. www.kk.dk.

———. 2016a. "Huslejenævnene—introduktion." Retrieved May 22, 2016. www.kk.dk.

———. 2016b, February 11. "Mere af den oprindelige Papirø skal bevares." Retrieved May 23, 2016. kabell.kk.dk.

Clark, Terry Nichols, ed. 2011. *The City as an Entertainment Machine*. Lanham, MD: Lexington Books.

Clark, Terry Nichols, Richard Lloyd, Kenneth K. Wong, and Pushpam Jain. 2002. "Amenities Drive Urban Growth." *Journal of Urban Affairs* 24(5): 493–515.

Cohen, Craig. 2013, July 24. "10 Things I Love About Houston So Far." *Houston Public Media*. Retrieved March 5, 2017. www.houstonmatters.org.

Collier, Kiah. 2013, May 13. "Houston Has the Busiest Seaport in the U.S." *Houston Chronicle*. Retrieved May 30, 2016. www.houstonchronicle.com.

Copenhagenet. 2015. "Brief History about Copenhagen." Retrieved July 9, 2015. www.copenhagenet.dk.

Copenhagen Post. 2012a, April 1. "Copenhagen Is the Best City at Being a Best City." *Copenhagen Post*. Retrieved February 22, 2017. cphpost.dk.

———. 2012b, July 8. "Incinerators: Better than Landfills, but a Recycling Loser." *Copenhagen Post*. Retrieved February 13, 2016. cphpost.dk.

———. 2013, November 9. "Party Profile: Liberal Alliance." *Copenhagen Post*. Retrieved April 21, 2015. cphpost.dk.

Danish Nature Agency. 2015. "The Finger Plan: A Strategy for the Development of the Greater Copenhagen Area." Retrieved May 29, 2016. danishbusinessauthority.dk.

Dansk Meteorologisk Selskab. 2011. "Vejret: tidsskrift for vejr og kilma [entire issue]." *Vejret: tidsskrift for vejr og kilma* 3(33): 1–50.

de Guzman, Dianne. 2016, July 6. "California City Ranked on List of Rudest Places." *San Francisco Chronicle*. Retrieved February 24, 2017. www.sfgate.com.

De León, Arnoldo. 2001. *Ethnicity in the Sunbelt: Mexican Americans in Houston*. College Station: Texas A&M Press.

Delmendo, Lalaine C. 2016, August 16. "Dutch Housing Prices Rise Sharply." *Global Property Guide*. Retrieved February 15, 2017. www.globalpropertyguide.com.

Denmark. 2014. "Superkilen Celebrates Diversity in Copenhagen." Retrieved September 5, 2015. denmark.dk.

Dries, Bill. 2011, June 6. "To Bike or Not to Bike." *Memphis Daily News*. Retrieved October 11, 2011. www.memphisdailynews.com.

Economist. 2016, July 2. "From Folly to Fragmentation." *Economist*. Retrieved February 14, 2017. www.economist.com.

Edmondson, Amy C., and Susan Salter Reynolds. 2016, June 12. "Smart Cities? It Takes More than a Village." *LinkedIn Pulse*. Retrieved March 5, 2017. www.linkedin.com.

Einstein, Katherine Levine, and David M. Glick. Forthcoming. "Mayors, Partisanship, and Redistribution: Evidence Directly from U.S. Mayors." *Urban Affairs Review*.

Ellick, Adam B. 2008, July 29. "Houston Resists Recycling, and Independent Streak Is Cited." *New York Times*. Retrieved June 3, 2016. www.nytimes.com.

Elliott, James R., and Matthew Thomas Clement. 2014. "Urbanization and Carbon Emissions: A Nationwide Study of Local Countervailing Effects in the United States." *Social Science Quarterly* 95(3): 795–816.

Emerson, Michael O., Jenifer Bratter, Junia Howell, P. Wilner Jeanty, and Mike Cline. 2012. *Houston Region Grows More Racially/Ethnically Diverse, with Small Declines in Segregation. A Joint Report Analyzing Census Data from 1990, 2000, and 2010.* Houston: Kinder Institute for Urban Research.

Energistyrelsen. 2016. "Ny Energi." Retrieved May 31, 2016. nyenergi.nu.

Environmental Protection Agency. 2016. "Greenhouse Gas Equivalencies Calculator." Retrieved June 3, 2016. www.epa.gov.

European Commission. 2014. "Copenhagen Application: Local Contribution to Global Climate Change." Retrieved May 27, 2016 ec.europa.eu.

European Union. 2016. *Flash EuroBarometer 419: Quality of Life in European Cities.* Retrieved May 23, 2016. ec.europa.eu.

Fabricius, Hanne. 1999. "Development of Town and Harbor in Medieval Copenhagen." In *Maritime Topography and the Medieval Town*, ed. J. Bill and B. L. Clausen, 221–35. Copenhagen: National Museum of Denmark.

Fainstein, Susan S. 2010. *The Just City*. Ithaca, NY: Cornell University Press.

Feagin, Joe R. 1988. *Free Enterprise City: Houston in Political and Economic Perspective.* New Brunswick, NJ: Rutgers University Press.

Feser, Katherine. 2015, June 14. "Greenest of the Green: Houston's LEED Platinum Projects." *Chron*. Retrieved June 1, 2016. blog.chron.com.

———. 2016, September 22. "Houston Apartment Rents Are Down, but Not for Everyone." *Houston Chronicle*. Retrieved January 21, 2017. www.houstonchronicle.com.

Fisher, Robert. 1992. "Organizing in the Private City: The Case of Houston, Texas." In *Black Dixie: Afro-Texan History and Culture in Houston*, ed. H. Beeth and C. D. Wintz, 253–77. College Station: Texas A&M University Press.

Florida, Richard. 2012. *The Rise of the Creative Class, Revisited*. New York: Basic Books.

Foster, Bellamy, Brett Clark, and Richard York. 2010. *The Ecological Rift: Capitalism's War on Earth*. New York: Monthly Review.

Frohlich, Thomas C. 2014, December 20. "The Cities with the Largest Homes." *24/7 Wall Street*. Retrieved May 28, 2016. 247wallst.com.

Gattis, Tory. 2016, July 18. "Elements of an Opportunity City." *Houston Strategies Blog*. Retrieved February 27, 2017. houstonstrategies.blogspot.com.

Gehl, Jan. 2010. *Cities for People*. New York: Island Press.

Gerdes, Justin. 2012, October 31. "What Copenhagen Can Teach Cities about Adapting to Climate Change." *Forbes*. Retrieved May 31, 2016. www.forbes.com.

———. 2013, April 12. "Copenhagen's Ambitious Push to Be Carbon Neutral by 2025." *Guardian*. Retrieved May 31, 2016. www.theguardian.com.

Gille, Frank H., ed. 1999. *Encyclopedia of Texas Indians*. St. Clair Shores, MI: Somerset.

Glaeser, Edward. 2011. *Triumph of the City: How Our Greatest Invention Makes Us Richer, Smarter, Greener, Healthier, and Happier*. New York: Penguin Books.

Glaeser, Edward, and Bruce Sacerdote. 1996. "Why Is There More Crime in Cities?" NBER Working Paper Series. Working Paper 5430. Cambridge, MA: National Bureau of Economic Research.

Global Property Guide. 2016, June 2. "Dramatic Surge in UK's Housing Market Caused by Stamp Duty Increase—but Central London May Be at a Tipping Point." *Global Property Guide*. Retrieved February 15, 2017. www.globalpropertyguide.com.

Goldschalk, David R. 2003. "Urban Hazard Mitigation: Creating Resilient Cities." *Natural Hazards Review* 4(3): 136–43.

Gorman, Hugh S. 2007. "The Houston Ship Channel and the Changing Landscape of Pollution." In *Energy Metropolis: An Environmental History of Houston and the Gulf Coast*, ed. M. V. Melosi and J. A. Pratt, 52–68. Pittsburgh: University of Pittsburgh Press.

Greater Houston Partnership. 2014. "Houston Facts." Retrieved October 31, 2014. www.houston.org.

———. 2016. "Housing Cost Comparison." Data from 2015 Cost of Living Index by Council for Community and Economic Research. Retrieved May 23, 2016. www.houston.org.

Grimm, Nancy B., Stanley H. Faeth, Nance E. Golubiewski, Charles L. Redman, Jianguo Wu, Xuemei Bai, and John M. Briggs. 2008. "Global Change and the Ecology of Cities." *Science* 319:756–60.

Gutherie, Dan. 2013, December 2. "Best and Worst of Houston 2013." *Houston Chronicle*. Retrieved March 6, 2017. www.houstonchronicle.com.

Hamilton, Lawrence C., and Kei Saito. 2015. "A Four-Party View of US Environmental Concern." *Environmental Politics* 24(2): 212–27.

Hammar, Magnus. 2013. "Indebted Owners and Self-Governed Tenants." *Global Tenant* 8–9. Retrieved May 20, 2016. www.iut.nu.

Hamnett, Chris. 2003. "Gentrification and the Middle-Class Remaking of Inner London, 1961–2001." *Urban Studies* 40(12): 2401–26.

Harris County Budget Management. 2013. "Population Study." Retrieved May 11, 2015. www.harriscountytx.gov.

Harvey, David. 1989. "From Managerialism to Entrepreneurialism: The Transformation in Urban Governance in Late Capitalism." *Geografiska Annaler* 71 B(1): 3–17.

———. 2008. "The Right to the City." *New Left Review* 53:23–40.

———. 2013. *Rebel Cities: From the Right to the City to the Urban Revolution*. London: Verso.

Hassan, Anita, and James Pinkerton. 2014, June 7. "Lack of Houston Police Follow-Up on Less Severe Crimes Worries Residents." *Houston Chronicle*. Retrieved March 4, 2017. www.houstonchronicle.com.

Helft, Miguel. 2010, March 26. "Cities Rush to Woo Broadband before Friday Deadline." *New York Times*. Retrieved May 11, 2015. www.newyorktimes.com.

Hoare, Steve. 2016, March 5. "Which City Will Be the First to Carbon Neutrality?" *Cities Today*. Retrieved May 31, 2016. cities-today.com.

Hobby, Paul. 2014. "Paul Hobby Remarks." Greater Houston Partnership, 2014 annual meeting. Retrieved March 10, 2017. www.houston.org.

Holeywell, Ryan. 2015, September 8. "Forget What You've Heard, Houston Really Does Have Zoning (Sort Of)." *Urban Edge Blog*. Retrieved May 29, 2016. urbanedge. blogs.rice.edu.

Hoornweg, Daniel, Perinaz Bhada-Tata, and Chris Kennedy. 2013. "Environment: Waste Production Must Peak this Century." *Nature* 502:615–17.

Houston. 2008. "Emissions Reduction Plan." Retrieved March 10, 2017. www.greenhoustontx.gov.

———. 2014a. "Mayor's Biography." Retrieved April 14, 2014. houstontx.gov.

———. 2014b, February 18. "Developer Lauded for Saving Trees." Press release from mayor's house. Retrieved February 22, 2014. www.houstontx.gov.

———. 2015a. "Houston's General Plan: Quality of Life Committee." Retrieved March 8, 2017. www.houstontx.gov.

———. 2015b. "One Bin for All: Recycling Reimagined in Houston." Report from mayor's office. Retrieved June 3, 2016. www.houstontx.gov.

———. 2016. "Parking Requirements." Retrieved May 29, 2016. www.houstontx.gov.

———. 2017a. "Office of Business Opportunity." Retrieved March 8, 2017. www.houstontx.gov.

———. 2017b. "Office of New Americans and Immigrant Communities." Retrieved March 8, 2017. ww.houstontx.gov.

———. N.d. "Cavazos: A Local Advertising Representatives for the Houston Airport System." Retrieved March 8, 2017. www.houstontx.gov.

Houston Association of Realtors. 2016. "The Houston Real Estate Market Maintains a Healthy Balance in April." Retrieved May 28, 2016. www.har.com.

Houston Chronicle. 2016. "Editorial: Cutting Trash." *Houston Chronicle*. Retrieved June 4, 2016. www.houstonchronicle.com.

Houston Fire Department. N.d. "Study Guide." Retrieved March 8, 2017. www.houstontx.gov.

I Am Amsterdam. 2016. "City Policy: Housing in Amsterdam." Retrieved February 15, 2017. www.iamsterdam.com.

Ifversen, Karsten R. S. 2012, June 22. "Nørrebros nye byrum er et stød i kuglerne på den gode smag." *Politken*. Retrieved September 15, 2015. politiken.dk.

Inglehart, Ronald. 1981. "Post-Materialism in an Environment of Security." *American Political Science Review* 75(4): 880–900.

Jacobs, Jane. 1961. *The Death and Life of Great American Cities*. New York: Random House.

Jaffe, Eric. 2014. "How Memphis Became a Great Bicycling City." *CityLab*. Retrieved November 2, 2014. www.citylab.com.

Jennings, Katie, Dino Grandoni, and Susanne Rust. 2015, October 23. "How Exxon Went from Leader to Skeptic on Climate Change Research." *Los Angeles Times*. Retrieved November 2, 2015. graphics.latimes.com.

Jensen, F. Kenneth. 1992. "The Houston Sit-In Movement of 1960–61." In *Black Dixie: Afro-Texan History and Culture in Houston*, ed. H. Beeth and C. D. Wintz, 211–22. College Station: Texas A&M University Press.

Juul-Sandberg, Jakob, and Per Norberg. 2014. "National Report for Denmark." *TEN-LAW: Tenancy Law and Housing Policy in Multi-Level Europe*. Retrieved May 24, 2016. www.tenlaw.uni-bremen.de.

Kahneman, Daniel, Alan B. Krueger, David A. Schkade, Norbert Schwarz, and Arthur A. Stone. 2004. "A Survey for Characterizing Daily Life Experience: The Day Re-construction Method." *Science* 306(5702): 1776–80.

Kansas City. 2012a. "Phase 1: Competitive Snapshot." Retrieved May 11, 2014. kcmo.gov.

———. 2012b. "Strategic Plan." Retrieved May 11, 2014. kcmo.gov.

Katz, Bruce, and Jennifer Bradley. 2013. *The Metropolitan Revolution: How Cities and Metros Are Fixing Our Broken Politics and Fragile Economy*. Washington, DC: Brookings Institution Press.

Kever, Jeannie, 2013, May 3. Houston's Economy—Diversified but Still All about En-ergy. *Houston Chronicle*. Retrieved March 13, 2015. www.houstonchronicle.com.

Kilhof, Sandra. 2014, October 3. "Copenhagen Weather Change Prompts Audacious Flood Plan." *New Economy*. Retrieved June 13, 2016. www.theneweconomy.com.

Kjær, Birgitte. 2013, March 6. "Nu bygger Amager sin skibakke—i 80 meters højde." *Politiken*. Retrieved February 13, 2015. politiken.dk.

Kneese, Carolyn, John DeMers, and Lynn Ashby. 2015. *Bragging Rights: The Dallas-Houston Rivalry*. Houston: Bright Sky Press.

Kostadinova, Gloria. 2014, April 11. "How to Form a Successful Social Movement." *The Borgen Project*. Retrieved February 23, 2017. borgenproject.org.

Kosunen, Sonja. 2014. "Reputation and Parental Logics of Action in Local School Choice Space in Finland." *Journal of Education Policy* 29(4): 443–66.

Kotkin, Joel. 2005. *The City: A Global History*. New York: Random House.

———. 2014. *Opportunity Urbanism: Creating Cities for Upward Mobility*. Retrieved May 24, 2016. www.houston.org.

Kotkin, Joel, and Tory Gattis. 2014. "America's Opportunity City." *City Journal*. www.city-journal.org.

Lefebvre, Henri. 1968/1996. *Writings on Cities*. Trans. and ed. Eleonore Kofman and Elizabeth Lebas. Cambridge, MA: Blackwell, Leigh, Gabriel, 2014. "Most Livable City: Copenhagen." Retrieved September 15, 2015. https://monocle.com/film/affairs/most-liveable-city-copenhagen.

Lewis, Valerie A., Michael O. Emerson, and Stephen L. Klineberg. 2011. "Who We'll Live With: Neighborhood Racial Composition Preferences of Whites, Blacks, and Latinos." *Social Forces* 89(4): 1385–1407.

Liberal Alliance. 2015. "Liberal Alliances 2025-plan. Valgvideo fra folketingsvalget 2015." Retrieved June 1, 2015. www.youtube.com/watch?v=029dPGCy64E.

Lindholm, Lasse. N.d. "Cycling in Copenhagen—the Easy Way." Retrieved May 30, 2016. denmark.dk.

Logan, John, and Harvey Molotch. 1987. *Urban Fortunes: The Political Economy of Place*. Berkeley: University of California Press.

London School of Economics and Political Science. 2014. *"Copenhagen: Green Economy Leader Report."* London: London School of Economics and Political Science.

Malmö. 2014. "Comprehensive Plan for Malmö." Retrieved September 5, 2015. malmo. se.

Martin, Florian. 2016, January 18. "What Happened to Houston's 'One Bin for All' Program?" *Houston Public Media*. www.houstonpublicmedia.org.

Massey, Douglas S., and Nancy A. Denton. 1993. *American Apartheid: Segregation and the Making of the Underclass*. Cambridge, MA: Harvard University Press.

Mayor of London. 2015. *Housing in London in 2015*. Retrieved on February 15, 2017. www.london.gov.uk.

McComb, David G. 1981. *Houston: A History*. Austin: University of Texas Press.

McCright, Aaron M., and Riley E. Dunlap. 2011. "The Politicization of Climate Change and Polarization in the American Public's Views of Global Warming 2001–2010." *Sociological Quarterly* 52:155–94.

McKinney, Tom Watson. 2007. "Superhighway Deluxe: Houston's Gulf Freeway." In *Energy Metropolis: An Environmental History of Houston and the Gulf Coast*, ed. M. V. Melosi and J. A. Pratt, 148–72. Pittsburgh: University of Pittsburgh Press.

Melosi, Martin. 2005. *Garbage in the Cities: Refuse, Reform, and the Environment*. Pittsburgh: University of Pittsburgh Press.

Melosi, Martin V., and Joseph A. Pratt. 2007. *Energy Metropolis: An Environmental History of Houston and the Gulf Coast*. Pittsburgh: University of Pittsburgh Press.

Miami. 2011. "City of Miami Strategic Plan." Retrieved May 10, 2014 www.miamigov. com.

———. 2014. "Mayor's International Council." Retrieved May 10, 2014. www.miamigov. com.

Michler, Andrew. 2011, January 27. "BIG Unveils a Ski Slope Waste Incinerator for Copenhagen." *Inhabitat*. Retrieved February 10, 2015. inhabitat.com.

Mol, Arthur P. J., and Gert Spaargaren. 2000. "Ecological Modernisation Theory in Debate: A Review." *Environmental Politics* 9(1): 17–49.

Monaghan, Angela. 2016, December 29. "London Housing Prices Rise Less Than the UK Average for First Time since 2008." *Guardian*. Retrieved February 15, 2017. www.theguardian.com.

Morris, Mike. 2012, December 15. "City Looking to Expand Its Urban Development Rules beyond Loop." *Houston Chronicle*. Retrieved May 8, 2015. www.houston-chronicle.com.

———. 2013, January 24. "Crime Dips, but Not Everyone Feels Safe." *Houston Chronicle*. Retrieved March 4, 2017. www.houstonchroniclecom.

———. 2014, April 27. "Skeptical Parker Gives Go-Ahead for a 'General Plan.'" *Houston Chronicle*. Retrieved October 13, 2014. www.houstonchronicle.com.

———. 2016a, March 22. "City's Free Ride to Recycling Success about to End." *Houston Chronicle*. Retrieved June 4, 2016. www.houstonchronicle.com.

———. 2016b, February 23. "Council Votes Wednesday on Recycling Contract That's Pricier than Other Texas Cities." *Houston Chronicle*. Retrieved June 4, 2016. www.houstonchronicle.com.

Morss, Rebecca E., and Mary H. Hayden. 2010. "Storm Surge and 'Certain Death': Interviews with Texas Coastal Residents Following Hurricane Ike." *Weather, Climate, and Society* 2 (July 2010): 174–89.

Moyer, Bill. 1987. "History Is a Weapon." Retrieved March 4, 2017. historyisaweapon.com.

Mumford, Lewis. 1961/1989. *The City in History*. New York: Harcourt.

Ng, Serena. 2015, April 22. "High Costs Put Cracks in Glass-Recycling Programs." *Wall Street Journal*. Retrieved June 4, 2016. www.wsj.com.

Nijman, Jan. 2011. *Miami: Mistress of the Americas*. Philadelphia: University of Pennsylvania Press.

The Onion. 2014, September 2. "Mayor Hits on Crazy Idea of Developing City's Waterfront, Green Spaces." *Onion*. Retrieved May 30, 2016. www.theonion.com.

Organisation for Economic Co-operation and Development. 2015. "Finland." Retrieved January 18, 2017. www.compareyourcountry.org.

O'Sullivan, Feargus. 2016a. Even Copenhagen Makes Mistakes. Retrieved March 10, 2017. nextcity.org.

———. 2016b, February 16. "How Copenhagen Paused Its Waterfront Development." *CityLab*. Retrieved February 17, 2016. www.citylab.com.

———. 2016c, July 6. "Which European Cities Will Grab London's Post-Brexit Business?" *CityLab*. Retrieved February 13, 2017. www.citylab.com.

Pape, Carsten. 2014. *Enevældens København: Historie og byvandringer*. Aarhus: Systime.

Paris. 2014a. "Île de France 2030 Regional Plan." Retrieved January 27, 2015. www.iledefrance.fr.

———. 2014b. "Revivez l'élection d'Anne Hidalgo." Retrieved January 27, 2015. www.paris.fr.

Parker, Annise. 2014. "2014 State of the City Address." Retrieved April 14, 2014. www.houstontx.gov.

Participatory Budgeting Project. 2015. "What Is PB?" Retrieved May 12, 2015. www.participatorybudgeting.org.

Pellow, David Naguib. 2002. *Garbage Wars: The Struggle for Environmental Justice in Chicago*. Cambridge, MA: MIT Press.

Pickvance, Chris. 2003. "From Urban Social Movements to Urban Movements: A Review and Introduction to a Symposium on Urban Movements." *International Journal of Urban and Regional Research* 27(1): 102–9.

Pinkerton, James. 2014, October 28. "Crashes Double at Houston Intersections after Red Light Cameras Pulled." *Houston Chronicle*. Retrieved May 14, 2015. www.houstonchronicle.com.

Plesse, Richelle Harrison. 2014, October 8. "Parisians Have Their Say on City's First €20m 'Participatory Budget.'" *Guardian*. Retrieved May 12, 2015. www.theguardian.com.

Pratt, Joseph A. 2007. "A Mixed Blessing: Energy, Economic Growth, and Houston's Environment." In *Energy Metropolis: An Environmental History of Houston and the Gulf Coast*, ed. M. V. Melosi and J. A. Pratt, 20–51. Pittsburgh: University of Pittsburgh Press.

Pruijt, Hans. 2003. "Is the Institutionalization of Urban Movements Inevitable? A Comparison of the Opportunities for Sustained Squatting in New York City and Amsterdam." *International Journal of Urban and Regional Research* 27(1): 133–57.

Pruitt, Bernadette. 2013. *The Other Great Migration: The Movement of Rural African Americans to Houston, 1900–1941*. College Station: Texas A&M University Press.

Rahman, Fauzeya. 2016, September 23. "Sylvester Turner Calls Houston Nation's Most Diverse City." *PolitiFact Texas*. Retrieved March 8, 2017. www.politifact.com.

Rangvid, Beatrice Schindler. 2010. "School Choice, Universal Vouchers and Native Flight from Local Schools." *European Sociological Review* 26(3): 319–35.

Rapino, Melanie A., and Alison K. Fields. 2012. "Mega-Commuting in the U.S." Presentation at Association for Public Policy Analysis and Management, Baltimore. Retrieved June 3, 2016. www.census.gov.

Roberts, Dave. 2016, March 12. "Got Denmark Envy? Wait until You Hear about Its Energy Policies." *Vox*. Retrieved May 31, 2016. www.vox.com.

Roth, David. 2010. *Texas Hurricane History*. Retrieved May 31, 2016. www.wpc.ncep.noaa.gov.

Ruhe, Corina. 2016, June 21. "In Amsterdam, the Housing Markets Are Showing Signs of Over-Heating." *Bloomberg News*. Retrieved February 15, 2017. www.bloomberg.com.

Sampson, Robert J. 2012. *Great American City: Chicago and the Enduring Neighborhood Effect*. Chicago: University of Chicago Press.

San Miguel, Guadalupe, Jr. 2001. *Brown, Not White: School Integration and the Chicano Movement in Houston*. College Station: Texas A&M University Press.

Sass, Ronald L. 2015. "One Bin or Not One Bin: Is That the Question?" Baker Institute for Public Policy Paper Series. *Retrieved September 5, 2015*. bakerinstitute.org.

Sassen, Saskia. 2006. *Cities in a World Economy*. Thousand Oaks, CA: Pine Forge Press.

Satija, Neena. 2014, March 20. "To Promote Recycling, a City Wants to Eliminate Spending." *New York Times*. Retrieved June 3, 2016. www.nytimes.com.

Satija, Neena, Kiah Collier, Al Shaw, and Jeff Larson. 2016, March 3. "Hell and High Water." *ProPublica* and *Texas Tribune*. Retrieved March 3, 2016. projects.propublica.org.

Scruggs, Melanie. 2016, March 23. "Recycling Will Stay—Zero Waste Should Be Next." *Texas Campaign for the Environment News and Announcements*. Retrieved June 2, 2016. www.texasenvironment.org.

Secret Copenhagen. 2017. "Talks." Retrieved March 5, 2017. heartbeats.dk.

Seeberg, Kenan. 2011, July 3. "København flyder med døde rotter og affald." *BT*. Retrieved June 12, 2016. www.bt.dk.

Sharkey, Patrick. 2013. *Stuck in Place: Urban Neighborhoods and the End of Progress toward Racial Equality*. Chicago: University of Chicago Press.

Shelton, Kyle. 2014a. "Houston (Un)limited: Path-Dependent Annexation and Highway Practices in an American Metropolis." *Transfers* 7(3): 97–115.

———. 2014b. *Power Moves: Houston, Texas and the Politics of Mobility, 1950–1985*. PhD diss., University of Texas at Austin.

Shorto, Russell. 2013. *Amsterdam: A History of the World's Most Liberal Cities*. New York: Vintage Books.

———. 2016, August 30. "Amsterdam, Revisited." *New York Times Magazine*. Retrieved February 13, 2017. www.nytimes.com.

Slavin, Terry. 2016, October 26. "An Incinerator with a View: Copenhagen Waste Plant Gets a Ski Slope and Picnic Area." *Guardian*. Retrieved January 23, 2017. www.theguardian.com.

Smiley, Kevin T. 2017. "Climate Change Denial, Political Beliefs, and Cities: Evidence from Copenhagen and Houston." *Environmental Sociology* 3(1): 76–86.

Smiley, Kevin T., and Michael Oluf Emerson. 2017. "Market Cities, People Cities, and a Spirit of Urban Capitalism: The Cases of Copenhagen and Houston." *SocArXiv*. Retrieved from osf.io/preprints/socarxiv/uexh9.

Smiley, Kevin T., Michael Oluf Emerson, and Julie Werner Markussen. 2017. "Immigration Attitudes before and after Tragedy in Copenhagen: The Importance of Political Affiliation and Safety Concerns." *Sociological Forum* 32(2): 321–38.

Smiley, Kevin T., Wanda Rushing, and Michele Scott. 2016a. "Behind a Bicycling Boom: Governance, Cultural Change and Place Character in Memphis, Tennessee." *Urban Studies* 53(1): 193–209.

Smiley, Kevin T., Wanda Rushing, and Michele Scott. 2016b. "Massive Investments in Bike Infrastructure Have Got More People Moving in Memphis, but They Have Also Affected Social Inequality." *London School of Economics' American Politics and Policy Blog*. Retrieved May 1, 2016. blogs.lse.ac.uk.

Smiley, Kevin T., Tanvi Sharma, Alan Steinberg, Sally Hodges-Copple, Emily Jacobson, and Lucy Matveeva. 2016. "More Inclusive Parks Planning: Park Quality and Preferences for Park Access and Amenities." *Environmental Justice* 9(1): 1–7.

Stiglitz, Joseph E. 2013. *The Price of Inequality: How Today's Divided Society Endangers our Future*. New York: W. W. Norton.

Stroganov, Vassili. 2015, February 17. "Aarhus vs. Copenhagen." *Jutland Station*. Retrieved February 15, 2017. www.jutlandstation.dk.

Svendsen, Gert Tinggaard. 2014. *Trust: Reflections*. Aarhus, Denmark: Aarhus University Press.

Tally, Steve, and Elizabeth Gardner. 2008. "Top CO2 Emitting Counties in the United States Identified." Retrieved November 12, 2014. www.purdue.edu.

Texas Beyond History. 2009. "Mitchell Ridge: Ethnohistory." *Texas beyond History*. University of Texas at Austin. Retrieved October 30, 2014. www.texasbeyondhistory.net.

Texas Campaign for the Environment Fund and Zero Waste Houston Coalition. 2014. "It's Smarter to Separate: How Houston's Trash Proposal Would Waste Our

Resources, Pollute Our Air, and Harm Our Community's Health." Retrieved June 3, 2016. www.texasenvironment.org.

Texas Division of Emergency Management. 2008, December 8. "Hurricane Ike: Impact Report." Retrieved May 29, 2016. www.fema.gov.

Texas Parks and Wildlife. 2016. "Fish Consumption Bans and Advisories." Retrieved May 30, 2016. tpwd.texas.gov.

Thompson, Derek. 2013, May 28. "Houston Is Unstoppable: Why Texas' Juggernaut Is America's #1 Job Creator." *Atlantic*. Retrieved October 31, 2014. www.theatlantic. com.

Thompson, Krissah. 2015, March 17. "Houston's Annise Parker, a Gay Mayor in a Red State, Ponders Political Future." *Washington Post*. Retrieved May 14, 2015. www. washingtonpost.com.

Thompson, Robert S. 2007. "'The Air Conditioning Capital of the World': Houston and Climate Control." In *Energy Metropolis: An Environmental History of Houston and the Gulf Coast*, ed. M. V. Melosi and J. A. Pratt, 88–104. Pittsburgh: University of Pittsburgh Press.

Trust for Public Land. 2011. "City Park Facts." Retrieved April 24, 2015. www.tpl.org.

U.S. Green Building Council. 2013. "Texas 2013 Green Building Market Activity." Retrieved June 1, 2016. usgbc-centraltexas.org.

Vancouver. 2012. "Greenest City: 2020 Action Plan." Retrieved May 8, 2015. vancouver.ca.
———. 2015. "Mission and Values." Retrieved May 8, 2015. vancouver.ca.

Van Gent, W. P. C. 2013. "Neoliberalization, Housing Institutions, and Variegated Gentrification: How the 'Third Wave' Broke in Amsterdam." *International Journal of Urban and Regional Research* 37(2): 503–22.

Velázquez, Daniela. 2015, February 6. "Lessons from Google's First Fiber Rollout." *Fast Company*. Retrieved May 12, 2015. www.fastcompany.com.

Wilkinson, Richard, and Kate Pickett. 2011. *The Spirit Level: Why Greater Equality Makes Societies Stronger*. London: Bloomsbury Press.

Wilson, William Julius. 1987/2012. *The Truly Disadvantaged: The Inner City, the Underclass, and Public Policy*. Chicago: University of Chicago Press.

Wirth, Louis. 1938. "Urbanism as a Way of Life." *American Journal of Sociology* 44(1): 1–24.

World Bank. 2016. "Urban Population: Percent of Total." Retrieved February 15, 2017. data.worldbank.org.

YouGov Civic Dashboards. 2017. "Gini Index for Houston, TX." Retrieved March 6, 2017. www.civicdashboards.com.

Zero Waste Europe. 2014, January 27. "(The Story of) Denmark's Transition from Incineration to Zero Waste." Retrieved February 15, 2016. www.zerowasteeurope.eu.

INDEX

ABOUT THE AUTHORS

Michael Oluf Emerson, Ph.D., is Provost and Professor of Urban Studies at North Park University in Chicago, and a Kinder Fellow at Rice University's Kinder Institute for Urban Research. He was formerly a professor at Rice University and the University of Notre Dame. He has authored or co-authored fifteen books and over sixty journal articles and reports.

Kevin T. Smiley is Assistant Professor of Sociology at the University at Buffalo. He is an environmental and urban sociologist. His research investigates the roots of environmental inequality, particularly disparities across cities.